Language and Identity in the Balkans

Language and Identity in the Balkans

Serbo-Croatian and its Disintegration

ROBERT D. GREENBERG

OXFORD
UNIVERSITY PRESS

OXFORD

UNIVERSITY PRESS

Great Clarendon Street, Oxford OX2 6DP

Oxford University Press is a department of the University of Oxford.
It furthers the University's objective of excellence in research, scholarship,
and education by publishing worldwide in

Oxford New York

Auckland Bangkok Buenos Aires Cape Town Chennai
Dar es Salaam Delhi Hong Kong Istanbul Karachi Kolkata
Kuala Lumpur Madrid Melbourne Mexico City Mumbai Nairobi
São Paulo Shanghai Singapore Taipei Tokyo Toronto

Oxford is a registered trade mark of Oxford University Press
in the UK and in certain other countries

Published in the United States
by Oxford University Press Inc., New York

© Robert D. Greenberg 2004

The moral rights of the authors have been asserted
Database right Oxford University Press (maker)

First published 2004
First Published in paperback 2008

British Library Cataloguing in Publication Data

(Data available)

Library of Congress Cataloging in Publication Data

(Data available)

Typeset by SPI Publisher Services, Pondicherry, India
Printed in Great Britain
on acid-free paper by
Biddles Ltd, King's Lynn, Norfolk

ISBN 978-0-19-925815-4 (Hbk.)
978-0-19-920875-3 (Pbk.)

1 3 5 7 9 10 8 6 4 2

Contents

Acknowledgements

I began work on this project in 1997, when I was on a research leave from the University of North Carolina at Chapel Hill. An extended visit to the former Yugoslavia, a month of research in Washington, DC, and a semester as a fellow at the University of North Carolina's Institute for the Arts and Humanities allowed for the completion of the first two articles on language, identity, and ethnic politics in ex-Yugoslavia (cf. Greenberg 1998 and 1999). Subsequent visits to the Balkans provided me with additional opportunities to gather materials, interview individuals, and consult with colleagues. In addition, while working as a fellow at the Woodrow Wilson International Center for Scholars in 1999, I gathered materials at the Library of Congress for a third article (Greenberg 2000). The final stages of the project were made possible while on research leave in Fall 2002, when I became a visiting scholar at Columbia University's Harriman Institute.

I am deeply grateful for the advice, assistance, and patience of many individuals. My colleague Prvoslav Radić has provided me with countless words of encouragement and guidance, not to mention obscure works published in Serbia, which he made available despite the economic sanctions imposed on the Federal Republic of Yugoslavia. I would also like to acknowledge the assistance I received from Sofija Miloradović, Miodrag Jovanović, Dalibor Brozović, Slobodan Remetić, Grace Fielder, Josip Raos, and Zuzana Topolińska. Special thanks are due to Katharine Nepomnyashchy and Gordon Bardos for facilitating my affiliation with the Harriman Institute, to Martin Sletzinger at the Woodrow Wilson International Center for Scholars, and to Grant Harris at the Library of Congress.

Research for the various stages of this project was supported by grants from the Woodrow Wilson International Center for Scholars (1997 and 1999); the International Research and Exchanges Board, with funds provided by the U.S. Department of State (Title VIII), and the National Endowment for the Humanities (1996 and 1998); the Fulbright program, administered through the Council for the International Exchange of Scholars (2001); and the University Research Council (1997), Institute for the Arts and Humanities (1998), and the Partners grant (2001) from the University of North Carolina-Chapel Hill. None of these organizations are responsible for the views expressed in the manuscript.

I am also indebted to my various research assistants and students who never failed to amaze me, especially Curtis Ford, Geoffrey Anisman, Jeffrey Upchurch, and William Hein; and the native readers who suffered my presence: Mirjana Dedaić, Beka Nanić, and Katerina Vasileska. Special thanks to Mirjana Dedaic for her patience and diligence in correcting the proofs, and to Ronelle Alexander for pointing out the various errata and inaccuracies from the first edition. I am deeply grateful to Orna Weinroth who edited the final manuscript, assisted with the maps, and has provided essential feedback for this project. I have tried my best to avoid errors, although these inevitably slip into any manuscript. It has perhaps been even more challenging to write about this topic without offending one side or another. Still I felt that this scholarly approach might enhance the tenor of the debate and will shed light on the problems and thus contribute to a future solution.

September 2003   Robert D. Greenberg
New Haven, Connecticut

1

Introduction

To this very day ethnicity strikes many Westerners as being peculiarly related to "all those crazy little people and languages out there", to the unwashed (and unwanted) of the world, to phenomena that are really not fully civilized and that are more trouble than they are worth.

(Fishman 1989: 14–15)

1.0 Overview

It must have been only my third day in Yugoslavia, when my Croat friends took me to Zagreb's Mirogoj Cemetery. I had arrived in Yugoslavia to complete dissertation research. My topic was in theoretical Slavic linguistics on Serbo-Croatian appellative forms, which essentially included forms of address, commands, and prohibitions. I came armed with my charts of verb classes, imperative endings in dozens of dialects, and the rough draft of a questionnaire. I planned to travel to each republic, and was going to seek out dusty hand-written records of dialect forms. However, on that day in September 1989, I was still the tourist taking in the sights. I was amazed when my friends asked me if I wanted to see the grave of Ljudevit Gaj. I felt the kind of excitement the wide-eyed student might experience when going on a field trip to a place they had only read about. When we reached the grave, my friends knelt down, genuinely moved. With visible emotion, they explained that Gaj, who had sought the unity of all Southern Slavs in the nineteenth century, embodied for them a lost dream of ethnic harmony, and of pan-Slavic cooperation. In retrospect, their feeling of loss preceded the events that were to occur only a few years later: as if they knew that Yugoslavism no longer had a chance. In that conversation, they told me that Serb–Croat relations would never recover from the upsurge of nationalism in the late 1980s. I had studied about Gaj primarily for his role in bringing about the unity of the Serbo-Croatian language. Was I to understand my friends' mournful comments as an indication that Serbo-Croatian was also no longer possible?

Six months later I was back in Zagreb at the Institute for Language to disseminate my questionnaire on Croatian appellative forms. I had painstakingly produced two versions of the questionnaire—one in the Eastern (Belgrade) variant of Serbo-Croatian, and one in the Western (Zagreb) variant. I did my best to adjust my speech from Belgrade to Zagreb mode. However, in a slip of the tongue, I innocently mentioned something about my plans for July. Much to my embarrassment, my interlocutors chastised me for using the Serbian form *jul* 'July', rather than the Croatian form *srpanj*. To add insult to injury, one of the Institute's staff then took me aside and made me repeat after her all the proper Croatian forms for all twelve months. I knew that language was a sensitive issue, but did not realize the emotional and ideological baggage each word carried. Most Croats had simply praised my excellent "Croatian," even though I could have sworn that I had been speaking with a Belgrade accent. When I received the questionnaires from the various Croatian linguists, who graciously agreed to provide data from their native dialects, I was pleased at the level of cooperation. Only one or two questionnaires were returned blank, with a terse note to the effect that they could not answer my questions, since I was primarily interested in phenomena occurring only in Serbian.

Later that month, I attended a reception at the Belgian Embassy in Belgrade. One distinguished guest, having discovered that I am a budding linguist, came up to me, and asked if I would answer a question which had long troubled him. I braced myself for yet another potentially embarrassing moment, but was relieved to hear that he simply wanted to know if I thought that Serbo-Croatian was one language or two. It was 1990, and the answer seemed obvious to me—officially the language was still united, and mutual intelligibility among its speakers was still possible. It was true that two literary languages had the potential to emerge, but it was too early to determine if this split had really occurred. This answer could not have made my questioner happier; having listened intently to my explanations, he became animated, and thanked me profusely for bringing closure to an issue that had been tormenting him for years. My theory about the basic unity of the language had been confirmed some weeks earlier, when I joined dialectologists from all over Yugoslavia at a weekend working session in the Serbian town of Arandjelovac. Perhaps I was naïve, but it seemed that the Croat dialectologists had cordial relations with their Serb counterparts, and that they were all cooperating on the joint project of producing the Common Slavic Linguistic Atlas.

When I returned to the region after the cataclysmic events of the wars in Croatia and Bosnia-Herzegovina, the language situation had changed radically. Having landed at Sarajevo Airport in June 1998, I struck up a conversation with one of the airport's land crew. Her first comment was that she was impressed with my skills in the Bosnian language. Frankly, I had had no idea that I was even capable of speaking Bosnian, since during my previous visit to Sarajevo in 1990, I had openly admitted to speaking Serbo-Croatian. Relaxing at a café the next day, I was told by a Bosnian Croat colleague from Sarajevo University that he felt that the officials at the university were forcing the Bosnian language on everyone. He felt uncomfortable speaking it. The friends I stayed with were a Serb and Bosniac couple. She was not afraid to tell me that even though she speaks the Bosnian language, she completely rejects the initiatives of the Bosniac language planners, who in her view are insisting that everyone unnaturally adopt the speech characteristics of her grandmother from a small village. The next morning I crossed the inter-entity boundary in order to catch the bus to Belgrade. In Bosnian Serb territory, I spoke the same language I had used the day before, only now I was treated as a Serb. When the Yugoslav border guards singled me out for extra questioning upon my entry to Serbia, the bus driver told them to let me through, because he considered me to be one of theirs. While it still seemed as though Bosnian and Serbian were variants of one language, it was not at all clear how many years were needed before a foreigner would truly encounter difficulties in switching from one language to the other.

When I visited Montenegro that same summer, I gingerly asked my linguist colleagues whether or not they took seriously the moves to split off a Montenegrin language from the Republic's prevailing Serbian language in its ijekavian pronunciation. They retorted that supporters of a separate Montenegrin language were extremist Montenegrin nationalists, and that nobody in the community of linguists took them seriously. One colleague, a dialectologist, went so far as to say that it is impossible to identify a single linguistic form that would identify all Montenegrins. "If there were such forms," he chuckled, "they could be counted on one or two fingers." Since then, however, the advocates for a Montenegrin language have remained vocal, and with Montenegro's secession from the joint Serbian-Montenegrin state in 2006, a separate Montenegrin language gained official acceptance within an independent Montenegro in 2007.

In recent years the nightmarish events surrounding the collapse of the Socialist Federal Republic of Yugoslavia have attracted much attention. Scholars have attempted to come to grips with such questions as the causes of ethnic conflict, the role of the international community, the nature of nationalism at the end of the twentieth century in Europe, and the painful process of recovery and healing of the former Yugoslav republics. The many monographs which resulted from studies of Yugoslavia's demise and the resulting armed conflicts in the 1990s were approached by scholars of military, historical, economic, anthropological, and political science disciplines. Scholars appealing to English-speaking audiences have largely neglected the significance of the disintegration of the Serbo-Croatian language in 1991. This work fills an important gap in Balkan studies, as it constitutes the first comprehensive study devoted to the intersection of language, nationalism, and identity politics in the former Yugoslavia. It provides an analysis of the linguistic processes that took place between 1800 and the present. The language rifts in ex-Yugoslavia have long been both a symptom of ethnic animosity, and a cause for perpetuating and further inflaming ethnic tensions. This study addresses specific controversies surrounding the codifications of the four successor languages to Serbo-Croatian: Serbian, Montenegrin, Croatian, and Bosnian. It also shows the close link between the national image, personal and group identity, and the spoken word.

1.1 Goals and methodology

Since the break-up of the Serbo-Croatian language in 1991, several monographs on this subject have appeared in the successor states of the former Yugoslavia. Often these works, given the ethnic affiliations of their authors, are subjective and at times lack the scholarly rigor required in the study of linguistics. Thus, Brborić (2001) presents a collection of newspaper columns and documents with a distinctly Serbo-centric point of view regarding the proliferation of new languages in ex-Yugoslavia, while Kačić (1997) attempts to correct all historical delusions and distortions purportedly employed to explain the relationship between Croatian and Serbian. Bugarski (1995 and 1997) has focused much of his attention on language developments affecting the new Serbian standard in the context of the wars in ex-Yugoslavia and the social crisis in the Federal Republic of Yugoslavia. Writing in German, Okuka, in a 1998 monograph, *One Language, Many Heirs*,[1] provides much valuable information on the nineteenth-century language politics, but focuses primarily on the language situation in Bosnia-Herzegovina. Experts from outside the former Yugoslavia have largely treated individual successor languages, with few attempts to incorporate data from the entire Serbo-Croatian speech territory. Thus, Langston (1999) has treated recent developments in Croatian, Greenberg (2000) focused on Serbian, and both Ford (2001) and Magner and Marić (2002) have written on Bosnian.

Many of the leading scholars on the language issue in the former Yugoslavia participated in two conferences organized by Celia Hawkesworth and Ranko Bugarski at the School of Slavonic and East European Studies at the University of London. The first conference took place in 1989 on the eve of Yugoslavia's demise, and the papers appeared in Hawkesworth and Bugarski (1992). This volume includes papers given by some of the key linguists from ex-Yugoslavia, including Pavle Ivić, Dubravko Škiljan, Radoslav Katičić, and Damir Kalogjera. These individuals were joined by leading non-Yugoslav scholars on this subject, including Kenneth Naylor and George Thomas. Their contributions are valuable in that they represent the final comprehensive view on the state of the joint Serbo-Croatian language. Within a few years of the conference, Ivić and Katičić became major actors in the dismantling of the unified language. The second conference in London took place in September 2000, and included papers on Serbian, Croatian, Bosnian, and Montenegrin language planning, presented by specialists from the United States, Europe, and the former Yugoslavia. Most of the presenters discussing language policy and language planning at the conference focused on a specific successor language; the volume with this second conference's papers (see Hawkesworth and Bugarski 2004) is a useful companion to the current monograph."

---

[1] The translation of the title is my own. Unless otherwise noted, all translations in this work are my own.

The current contribution provides a comprehensive analysis of the history of the joint literary language (Chapter 2), followed by detailed discussions of each of the four successor languages to Serbo-Croatian: Serbian (Chapter 3), Montenegrin (Chapter 4), Croatian (Chapter 5), and Bosnian (Chapter 6). The concluding chapter demonstrates that language planners for each of the four successor languages have faced similar obstacles in the race to standardize new languages without social upheavals. It further establishes that many of the language controversies from the past continue to destabilize the language standardization processes.

The analysis in this monograph is based on close readings of the recently published works on each of the successor languages. The types of works consulted can be divided into the following categories: (1) instruments of codification; (2) articles and monographs by linguists from Bosnia-Herzegovina, Croatia, Montenegro, and Serbia discussing specific linguistic concerns; (3) blueprints for the new successor languages, or reinterpreting the years of the unified language; and (4) articles from the popular press on language issues.

The instruments of codification include the many dictionaries, orthographic manuals, grammars, and handbooks of the new successor languages published since 1991. Each publication of an instrument of codification has political, rather than linguistic, significance. As Chapter 2 demonstrates, Vuk Karadžić's 1818 Serbian dictionary caused heated debates among members of the Serbian elites, and the effort to codify a new Serbian standard was described in epic terms, as one man's valiant war to bring literacy to his people.[2] Several grammars, orthographic manuals, and dictionaries were so politically explosive that they were destroyed upon printing (cf. Moskovljević 1966, Babić et al. 1972, and Težak and Babić 1996). The controversial nature of language handbooks (grammars, orthographic manuals, dictionaries, and language pedagogy materials) continued in the 1990s for all the Yugoslav successor states. Competing orthographic manuals appeared in 1993–4 in Serbia (cf. 3.3), and in 2000–1 in Croatia (cf. 5.3). Nikčević's 1997 orthographic manual (1997b) reads more like a treatise on the rights of the Montenegrins to a language and an identity, rather than a manual to teach correct spelling.

The articles and monographs consulted in the discussions below admittedly represent only a fraction of the vast literature published on the language issue. My approach has been thematic; rather than attempt to cover all facets of language change and the differentiation of the successor languages, I have sought articles that inform readers about the main controversies surrounding the new successor languages. In particular, I have focused on orthographic controversies, debates on literary dialects, disagreements on vocabulary, and issues related to the constitutional status of the successor languages. Many of the source materials are still largely unavailable in Western libraries, including the Montenegrin

---

[2] Cf. Daničić (1847), Belić (1949), and Butler (1970).

journals *Riječ, SPONE, Vaspitanje i obrazovanje,* and the Croatian Serb journal *Znamen.*[3] The number of conferences and congresses held in the Yugoslav successor states since 1991 has been staggering, and the articles consulted include conference papers delivered at such venues as the First Croatian Slavic Congress in Pula (1995), the Symposium on the Bosnian Language in Bihać (1998), a conference on the status of the Serbian language in Croatia held in Petrinja just months before it fell to Croat forces in Operation Storm (1995), and a conference on the two official pronunciations of Serbian held in Montenegro (1994).

Finally, the popular press in the Yugoslav successor states has provided many valuable sources for gauging the wider implications of specific developments in the emergence of the four successor languages. Many publications have regular columns on correct language usage, or on contemporary linguistic debates. Some of the Croatian language columns have been reprinted in collections by Matica hrvatska (cf. Kuljiš 1994), while others are available on the Internet from *Vjesnik, Globus,* and *Slobodna Dalmacija.* Similarly, the Internet has been a valuable tool for uncovering articles from the Bosnian daily *Dani,* Radio Free Europe/Radio Liberty broadcasts to the Western Balkans, the Institute for War and Peace Reporting, and the Montenegrin weekly *Monitor.* The clippings from Serbian newspapers were taken between 1991 and 1996 from *Politika* and *Naša borba.*[4]

Through a synthesis of these primary source materials, I highlight the main trends in the processes of language birth and re-birth within the former Serbo-Croatian speech territory. I address the means by which language planners attempt to differentiate among the various languages, and suggest that their decisions have at times been undermined by some of their own ethnic kin, who have objected when overly prescriptive norms were proposed. My goal is to document the political motivations and social forces that have brought about the unprecedented linguistic transformations in the former Yugoslavia. How have these transformations affected nearly twenty million citizens, who once spoke a unified language? These sociolinguistic issues are best understood in the context of the broader scholarship on the relationship between language and ethnicity (1.2) language and nationalism (1.3).

1.2   Language as a marker of ethnic identity

When describing the disintegration of Yugoslavia, scholars frequently define matters in terms of ethnicity and ethnic conflict. The wars in ex-Yugoslavia were

---

[3] I was able to acquire many of these works in research trips to ex-Yugoslavia in 1997, 1998, and 2001.

[4] I wish to thank Milan Petrović, who greatly assisted me in the gathering of some 20 clippings from the Belgrade press during those years.

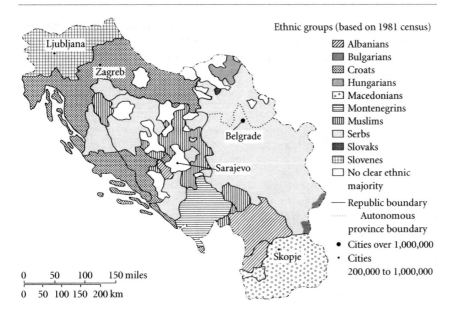

MAP 1. Geography and ethnicity in the Central South Slavic area
From *Encyclopaedia Britannica*, vol. 29 (1990), p. 1090.

linked to the breakdown of ethnic relations, and international organizations have been toiling to diminish ethnic tensions, and bring about ethnic reconciliation. As Fishman (1989: 9) suggested, "many discussions of ethnicity begin with the struggle to define 'it'." He proceeded to include in ethnicity

[b]oth the sense and the expression of "collective, intergenerational cultural continuity," i.e. the sensing and expressing of links to "one's own kind (one's own people)," to collectivities that not only purportedly have historical depth but, more crucially, share putative ancestral origins and, therefore, the gifts and responsibilities, rights and obligations deriving therefrom.

This linkage between "ethnic group" and "one's own people" is crucial for an understanding of the peoples of the former Yugoslavia. As Map 1 reveals, the republican or administrative boundaries have never corresponded with the ethnic ones. Moreover, the ethnic terms have been fluid. In this 1992 map, adapted from the CIA's website, the Bosniacs were still defined as "Muslims." Not only have members of a given group switched their ethnic allegiances over time (e.g., Serbs becoming Croats or vice versa), but the preferred ethnic labels also have changed. For instance, a Slav of the Muslim faith born in the Serbian Sandžak around 1930 would have almost certainly switched his ethnic identity three times in the course of his life. In his youth, he probably would have self-identified as a Serb, in Tito's Yugoslavia as a Muslim, and after 1992 as a Bosniac.

Edwards (1985: 6) suggests that a definition of ethnicity must take into consideration both subjective and objective considerations. In his view, the objective aspect includes "immutable" factors such as language, race, geography, religion, and ancestry. The subjective aspect implies that ethnic belonging is voluntary, mutable, and a reflection of belief, rather than based on tangible facts.[5] His overall definition of ethnicity joins these objective and subjective considerations with other factors to create the following comprehensive definition of ethnic identity:

Allegiance to a group—large or small, socially dominant or subordinate—with which one has ancestral links. There is no necessity for a continuation, over generations, of the same socialisation or cultural patterns, but some sense of a group boundary must persist. This can be sustained by shared objective characteristics (language, religion, etc.), or by more subjective contributions to a sense of "groupness", or by some combination of both. Symbolic or subjective attachments must relate, at however distant a remove, to an observably real past.[6]

The two flaws in this definition in relation to ethnic identity in the former Yugoslavia are that (1) language has proven to be neither an objective factor, nor an immutable one, and (2) religion and ancestry have been insufficient in determining group identity. While the Croats are overwhelmingly Catholic, the Serbs and Montenegrins predominantly Orthodox Christians, and the Bosniacs exclusively Muslim, large majorities of each ethnic group speak mutually intelligible dialects, blurring their religious and ancestry marking. In Naylor's terminology (1992: 83), language in the Balkans has functioned as a "flag," with which each people has asserted its independence and sovereignty. Thus, one of the first tangible manifestations of a Macedonian identity was the decision to establish a literary Macedonian language at the second meeting of the Anti-Fascist Council for the National Liberation of Macedonia in 1944.[7] In a parallel fashion, the first instruments for the codification of a new Bosnian language (Isaković 1995 and Halilović 1996) were written while war was raging in Bosnia-Herzegovina, and the future of the Bosnian state was still unclear. At approximately the same time, the Bosnian Serb leadership attempted to force its subjects to abandon their native dialect in favor of the Serbian spoken in Belgrade. In this manner, they hoped to achieve a "Greater Serbia" linguistically, even as their project to create a "Greater Serbia" politically was unrealized.

These examples reveal that the language component of ethnic identity in ex-Yugoslavia cannot be interpreted in terms of an "objective attachment." As shown below, the former Yugoslavia's rival ethnic groups have rarely been able to agree what to name their language(s). Such a problem does not exist for the Welsh speakers in Wales, or the Russian speakers in Latvia. Rather, the Bosniacs, Croats,

---

[5] The subjective approach is reminiscent of the notion of the "imagined community" put forth by Anderson (1983).

[6] Edwards (1985: 10).

[7] This decision pre-dated by 23 years the establishment of a separate Macedonian Orthodox Church, and by 47 years the creation of an independent Macedonian state.

Montenegrins, and Serbs have long disagreed on fundamentals: do they speak a single language or multiple languages, which dialects should be official, and which alphabets and writing systems best suit their needs? In the 1990s, members of the four ethnic groups had to choose which successor languages they felt an allegiance to. Some former and current citizens of the former Yugoslavia still subscribe to the notion that they are speakers of Serbo-Croatian, while Serbs who lived through the siege of Sarajevo may reject their own "ethnic" Serbian language and claim they speak Bosnian. In Montenegro, those individuals supporting an independent Montenegro assert that they speak Montenegrin, while pro-Serbian, self-identified Montenegrins say they speak Serbian. These language choices are subjective and politically motivated, and have little relation to whether or not the four ethnic groups truly have four separate languages or varieties of a single language. The purpose of this monograph is to make some sense from this chaotic multilingual and multi-dialectal situation.

1.3 Language in the context of Balkan nationalism

Having endured centuries under foreign domination, the Balkan peoples began embarking on their respective national revivals in the nineteenth and early twentieth centuries. As Edwards (1985: 24ff.) suggested, the linguistic nationalism espoused by Herder toward the end of the eighteenth century was "enthusiastically received" in Eastern Europe. At the root of this brand of nationalism was the Herderian belief that a nation's existence was inconceivable without its own language. Hence, in the Austro-Hungarian Empire the Slovenes, Croats, and Serbs became wholeheartedly engaged in establishing literary languages in the context of other national and linguistic revivals. This principle that a "people" ("narod") needs its own language and literature is underscored in the very opening of the Literary Agreement signed by Serb and Croat intellectuals in 1850 that established a joint literary language:

We the undersigned—well aware that one people must have one literature, and seeing with sadness how our literature is splintered, not only in its writing system, but also in its spelling, have met to discuss how it might be possible to understand each other and to unite in our literature.[8]

The signatories of this Agreement shared the conviction that the Central Southern Slavs of the Catholic, Orthodox, and Islamic faiths were at that time "one people" worthy of a single language. Later, however, in the two unified Yugoslav states

---

[8] See Appendix A for the entire Serbo-Croatian text of the Literary Agreement and its translation into English.

MAP 2.   The Former Yugoslavia

(1918–41 and 1945–91), these same Central Southern Slavs were recognized as two, three, or four separate peoples who still were supposed to speak a single language.[9] These states violated a basic rule that seemed to pervade the psyche of Slavic peoples, whereby any group with national pretensions was somehow incomplete without its own language. This principle was applied with a vengeance in the post-1991 formation of the Yugoslav successor states, the boundaries of which had been set in 1945 by the communist authorities, as shown in Map 2.

---

[9] Serbs and Croats were recognized as peoples forming the Kingdom of Serbs, Croats, and Slovenes in 1918. Serbs, Croats, and Montenegrins were proclaimed three of the five constituent peoples/nations forming Tito's Yugoslavia, while the Muslim Slavs were recognized as an additional Yugoslav constituent people/nation by 1971.

Under Tito's Socialist regime, all forms of nationalism, including linguistic nationalism, were suppressed. While the Macedonians and Slovenes were given the rights to their own republics and their own languages, the other constituent peoples/nations used the Serbo-Croatian language, which also served as the language of wider communication among the diverse ethnic groups within Yugoslavia's borders.[10] Thus, Serbo-Croatian was the language of the Yugoslav People's Army (JNA), and of Yugoslav diplomatic missions in foreign countries. However, Socialist Yugoslavia had violated a fundamental rule; it had denied the right of each people to its own language. This denial sparked linguistic nationalism initially in Croatia (1967), and later in Serbia (1986). A poignant example can be seen in the stance of the Serbian Academy of Sciences and Arts as expressed in the 1986 "Memorandum":

Over the past two decades, the principle of unity has become weakened and over-shadowed by the principle of national autonomy, which in practice has turned into the sovereignty of the federal units (the republics, which as a rule are not ethnically homo-geneous). The flaws which from the very beginning were present in this model have become increasingly evident. Not all the national groups were equal: the Serbian nation, for instance, was not given the right to have its own state. The large sections of the Serbian people who live in other republics, unlike the national minorities, do not have the right to use their own language and script; they do not have the right to set up their own political or cultural organizations or to foster the common cultural traditions of their nation together with their co-nationals. The unremitting persecution and expulsion of Serbs from Kosovo is a drastic example showing that those principles which protect the autonomy of a minority (the ethnic Albanians) are not applied to a minority within a minority (the Serbs, Montenegrins, Turks, and Roms in Kosovo).[11]

The authors of this document believed that the largest of the ethnic groups in Yugoslavia, the Serbs, were deprived of their language and script outside the borders of Serbia proper and Vojvodina, i.e., Croatia, Bosnia-Herzegovina, and Kosovo. They felt threatened in Croatia because the Croats had openly called the language "Croatian" since the 1960s, and "Serbian" was not taught in schools. The authorities in Bosnia-Herzegovina enforced a variant of the unified language which Serbs did not feel was their own. It is possible that this Serbian complaint was about the supremacy of the Latin alphabet over the Cyrillic one. If so, then Belgraders themselves were contributing to the marginalization of the Cyrillic script in Serbia, since they used both alphabets interchangeably. The nationalist overtones of the statement in the

---

[10] The English terms "people" and "nation" are both rendered as *narod* in the former Serbo-Croatian language. This term permeated political discourse in Tito's Yugoslavia, where references would repeatedly be made to the "nations and nationalities" of the country. In this work I will use "people/nation" in this context.

[11] The Memorandum was published in 1995 together with a long section addressing "answers to criticisms." This 142-page text is available in English at http://members.aol.com/sipany/memorandum.html.

"Memorandum" are clear: by "denying" the Serbs the right to their language and script, the other Yugoslav ethnic groups (Muslim Slavs, Croats, Albanians) were trying either to assimilate or to discriminate against their Serb minorities. The Memorandum represented a rallying call for all Serbs to come to the protection of their threatened ethnic kin. In Fishman's terms, language was being used by the elites as a convenient means for mobilizing the population. In this logic, not only were the other peoples chipping away at Serb identity through the denial of inalienable language rights, but they were also solidifying their own languages or dialects in the process. Thus, later, the authors of the Memorandum alleged that pan-Albanian language planning was a part of the Kosovo Albanian strategy to create a greater Albanian state, whereby:

> At a suitable moment the autonomous region [of Kosovo] acquired the status of an autonomous province, and then the status of a "constituent part of the Federation," with greater prerogatives than the remaining sections of the Republic, to which it only de jure belongs. Thus the preparations for the next step, in the form of the Albanianization of Kosovo and Metohija, were carried out in full legality. Similarly, unification of the literary language, the national name, flag, and school textbooks, following instructions from Tirana, was carried out quite openly, and the frontier between the two state territories was completely open.

The unification of the literary language refers to the 1968 decision of the Kosovo Albanians to abandon their native Gheg dialect in favor of the Tosk standard used in Albania.[12] The Serbs considered the moves to unify the Albanian language as a manifestation of the ultimate goal of the Kosovo Albanians: secession and a design for a greater Albanian state.[13]

When nationalist rhetoric gave way to ethnic strife after 1991, language continued to constitute a litmus test measuring a given group's faithfulness to its nation and ethnic identity. Thus,

> [i]n the 1990s Croats, whose variant of Serbo-Croatian had been quite similar to the Serbian variant save for the alphabets (Latin letters for the Croats, Cyrillic and Latin letters for the Serbs) and slight differences in vocabulary and syntax, initiated a campaign of language purification, purging forms deemed to be "Serbian" and replacing them with old Croatian forms or crafting new ones from "pure" Croatian roots.[14]

Simultaneously, the Serbs in Croatia, who had voted to secede from Croatia and in 1991–2 captured nearly one-third of Croatian territory, insisted upon the use of the Cyrillic alphabet in their enclaves. Glenny observed that,

> According to moderate Knin Serbs I met in 1990, only about 5 percent of the local Serbs used the Cyrillic script, the rest not only spoke the Croatian variant, they used the Latin

---

[12] The unity of the Albanian language was officially declared at a Congress in Tirana in 1972.

[13] Cf. also 7.1 for a parallel development in Macedonia during 2001.

[14] Magner and Marić (2002: 56).

script. Eighteen months later, on my return, I witnessed the extraordinary spectacle of a Knin Serb attempting to write the address of his relations in Belgrade in Cyrillic—he could not do it. Half-way through the address, he gave up and wrote it in Latin.[15]

In such an atmosphere, linguistic nationalism impinges upon one of the basic functions of language, i.e., language as a means of inter-personal communication. Furthermore, language planners are charged with the task of setting up new barriers to communication, rather than to the facilitation of mutual intelligibility.

The emergence of four successor languages to Serbo-Croatian since 1991 suggests that language birth in the Balkans came as a direct result of the explosive nationalist policies in Croatia, Bosnia-Herzegovina, Serbia, and Montenegro. However, prior to the surge of the overt and often extreme nationalist ideologies, the unity of the Serbo-Croatian language had been threatened. Balkan nationalism alone did not cause its eventual demise; as seen in the next section, the process of "language death" of the unified language had begun much earlier. Such processes are well documented in the sociolinguistic literature.

1.4   Serbo-Croatian: A dying tongue?

The demise of the Serbo-Croatian language does not seem to fall within the conventional definitions of language death put forth in the linguistic literature. This language has not disappeared due to the death of its final speaker, nor has it been overwhelmed by a stronger neighboring language through a process known as "language shift." Universities in some countries still offer "Serbo-Croat" or "Serbo-Croatian" language courses, or have renamed these courses "Serbian/ Croatian/Bosnian," and many ex-Yugoslavs living outside the Balkans still refer to their native language as "Serbo-Croat." Perhaps the Serbo-Croatian language is still in the throes of language death, and at some time in the twenty-first century it will be relegated to the realm of other extinct languages such as Cornish. Or, perhaps it really never existed as a living language, since it always had such a variety of urban and rural dialects.

The process leading to the demise of the unified Serbo-Croatian language can be understood in terms of what Kloss (1978) called the distinction between languages developing through either *Abstand* or *Ausbau* processes. The former refers to languages, such as English and German, that drifted apart "naturally," while the latter encompasses languages, such as Hindi and Urdu, which separated through the active intervention of language planners, linguists, and policy makers. Such intensive language interventions are frequently a result of a national consciousness awakening. The late eighteenth and much of the nineteenth centuries were characterized by national revivals within multi-ethnic

---

[15] Cf. Glenny (1996: 11).

states, such as the Austro-Hungarian and Ottoman empires. The use of the Czech vernacular had declined precipitously before Joseph Dobrovský helped resuscitate the Czech language in the 1810s and 1820s. Similarly, in Ljubljana and Zagreb the Slavic vernaculars gave way to the Empire's more powerful languages—German and Hungarian. As Auty (1958) has demonstrated, individuals played a crucial role in the linguistic revivals among the Slavs of the Austro-Hungarian Empire, especially for the Slovaks, Slovenes, and Croats. It is at this time that Czech and Slovene re-emerge, and the Slovak literary language took shape for the first time as distinct from Czech. Similarly, in the territories of the Ottoman Empire, two standard languages formed in the Eastern South Slavic dialect area: Bulgarian and Macedonian. While the dialects in these regions drifted apart through the *Abstand* process, the rival literary norms are examples of *Ausbau* relationships.

Another example of the *Ausbau* phenomenon is that of the Scandinavian languages, which are mutually intelligible, but were separated after the establishment of independent modern nation-states in the region.[16] Relying on this Scandinavian model, the Linguistics Society of America agreed with the Oakland Unified School District's decision to recognize African American Vernacular English (Ebonics) as a language separate from standard English. The Society's 1997 Resolution on this matter concluded that

[t]he distinction between "languages" and "dialects" is usually made more on social and political grounds than on purely linguistic ones. For example, different varieties of Chinese are popularly regarded as "dialects," though their speakers cannot understand each other, but speakers of Swedish and Norwegian, which are regarded as separate "languages," generally understand each other.

In a similar vein, the category of "mutual intelligibility" has had no bearing on the debate regarding the status of Serbo-Croatian as a single language or as three or four languages. What is clear is that as of 1991–2 Serbo-Croatian officially ceased to exist in the Yugoslav successor states. All sides agreed that the unified language was to be jettisoned and probably never again to be resurrected. The successor languages—Croatian, Serbian, Bosnian, and Montenegrin—had been in various kinds of *Ausbau* relationships during Tito's Yugoslavia, but ultimately the demise of the territorial borders contributed to "nominal language death," which Kloss (1984) defined as a phenomenon caused by the splitting of a language or the intentional downgrading of a standard language to the status of a dialect.[17]

---

[16] Cf. Haugen (1982).

[17] Kloss defined two other types of language death: (1) language death without language shift, i.e., the last speaker of a language dies, and the language becomes extinct; and (2) language death through language shift, whereby speakers of a language abandon their original tongue in favor of a second language.

In the territory of the former Yugoslavia, however, no such splitting could be achieved in a precise manner, since the splitting occurred along ethnic lines, rather than geographic or political boundaries. Moreover, the split has not taken place in either an orderly or a planned manner. The Serbs and the Croats still do not accept the new name of the Bosnian language, while the Serbs and some Montenegrins categorically deny the existence of a separate Montenegrin language. Even a two-way split of Serbo-Croatian into its two constituent parts—Serbian and Croatian—would not have been an easy task, since many of the Serbs living in Croatia, whose dialect is similar to that on which the standard Croatian is based, have rejected all of the post-1991 Croatian language reforms intended to maximally differentiate Croatian from Serbian. Simultaneously, the Bosniacs could accept neither Croatian nor Serbian since such an acceptance would have signaled the Bosniac assimilation into either the Croatian or Serbian ethnic spheres.

The following advertisement for an instructor of Bosnian illustrates the degree of confusion the demise of Serbo-Croatian has caused outside observers:

We are seeking to identify a "Bosniac" Instructor for an interesting assignment with a federal government agency (in this context, "Bosniac" refers to the heavily colloquialized form of Serbo-Croatian used by residents of Bosnia and Herzegovina. It has been described as "Serbian with more than the usual amount of Turkish words and expressions thrown in") . . . . The instructor will preferably be a native-speaker of Bosnian from the villages or surrounding areas, who has spent considerable time in-country recently and is very familiar with current usage and the current cultural/political climate, educated and able to impart his/her knowledge and experience to a class of adult language students.[18]

Such an announcement reinforces perceptions outside ex-Yugoslavia that while the emergence of Serbian and Croatian may be legitimate, the Bosnian language is truly a montage consisting of disparate colloquial elements, village speech, and Turkish loanwords. Is it a variant of Serbo-Croatian or of Serbian? Do all residents of Bosnia-Herzegovina use this "heavily colloquialized" form of the language?

While this job vacancy announcement raises questions which will be answered in the following chapters, it also reflects the desire of the employer to train its students in a politically correct manner. It is unlikely that so much care would be given to find a teacher of Swiss German for the student planning to conduct business in Switzerland. Thus, while the American company has little understanding of the language situation in Bosnia-Herzegovina, it does comprehend to what degree language is politicized in the former Yugoslavia. Indeed, as shown in this study, the very discipline of linguistics had been highly politicized in the Balkans, well before the break-up of Yugoslavia. Furthermore, while in the West the linguist is often tucked away in the academic ivory tower, in ex-Yugoslavia linguists have been major actors on the political stage. It is no wonder, then, that language politics has been such a prolific pastime in that region.

---

[18] I received the announcement by e-mail on 31 March 2003 from MultiLingual Solutions, Inc.

2

Serbo-Croatian: United or not we fall

> In 1967 ... it was suggested that a Croatian translation was needed of the Serbian language as used for official proceedings in Serbia, and vice versa. This proposal would have involved making Croats foreigners in Serbia and Serbs in Croatia, and there was strong Governmental reaction to such a shaking of the foundations of "brotherhood and unity."
>
> (Wilson 1986: 313)

2.0 Introduction: The precarious language union

One of the most striking facets of the Yugoslav experiment under Tito was the state's commitment to a joint literary language for Serbs, Croats, and Montenegrins. This joint language came into being in the mid-nineteenth century, but endured a turbulent history. In the first unified South Slavic state (1918–41), language controversies contributed to an atmosphere of ethnic animosity between the state's Serb and Croat communities. Subsequently, in 1941 the Croat Nazi puppet state, the Independent State of Croatia (NDH) broke with a nearly 100-year old tradition of the joint literary language for Serbs and Croats, and proclaimed its brand of a pure Croatian language, cleansed of any Serbian influence. In Socialist Yugoslavia, any damage done to the unified language was to be forgotten and forgiven, and unity was re-created replete with the assurances of the equality of all nations, nationalities, and national minorities in the State.

If Yugoslavia were truly to be a state in which the principle of "brotherhood and unity" was to prevail, then language unity would be one of the foundations for maintaining ethnic unity throughout Yugoslavia.

The motivations for restoring the unified language in 1945 were not purely political, but had scholarly linguistic merit. Writing on the eve of the break-up of Yugoslavia, Jahić (1990: 54) argued that the Croat, Serb, Bosnian Muslim, and

Montenegrin "traditions joined together in one, albeit in truth, elastic idiom," not because of social forces, but rather because the language of these four groups is so similar and originating from the same linguistic stock.[1] As Friedman (1999) and others have noted, centripetal and centrifugal forces have long been at play in the Balkans. In the case of Serbo-Croatian, the language union endured the simultaneous and contradictory influences of both kinds of forces. The centripetal forces were on the level of the Yugoslav federation, and were reinforced by the objective linguistic facts; by contrast, the centrifugal forces operated on the level of the individual Yugoslav republics seeking greater autonomy within the Federation, and working towards the sharpening of ethnic divisions. In the 1970s and 1980s these contradictory pressures had greatly weakened the unity of the language, which by then had four standard or semi-standard variants. Despite this weakened unity, most foreign scholars considered the language to be unified, and university curricula in the United States and Western Europe continued to offer language instruction in "Serbo-Croat/Serbo-Croatian," and library catalogues maintained exclusively the category "Serbo-Croatian" rather than "Serbian" and "Croatian." This state of affairs prompted Bugarski (1997) to claim that the unified language had a "strong" external identity, but a "weak internal identity."[2] Such an analysis suggests that the attitude of those living outside Yugoslavia did not correspond with that of those living within the borders of the country. The external identity was strong, because most non-Yugoslavs never questioned the unity of the language; by contrast, Croats, Montenegrins, and Bosnian Muslims began asserting their local varieties, and were keen on splintering the internal language unity, thereby greatly weakening the internal identity.[3] This weak identity eventually collapsed, once competing nationalist agendas tore Yugoslavia apart in 1991.

The history of the unified language reveals that the strength of the external identity did not have significant influence on the internal identity. The internal Serbo-Croatian language unity was precarious at best and never truly embraced by its speakers from the rival ethnic groups (cf. Greenberg 2001*a*: 18). When political leaders endeavored forcibly to fortify the internal language identity, their efforts consistently failed. Thus, King Alexander's attempt in 1929 to impose a

---

[1] "Četiri nacionalne tradicije uklopile su se u jedan, stoga, istina, elastičan idiom, ne zbog toga što je to bila težnja društvenih snaga koje su na taj jezik uticale već prije svega zbog toga što je to istorija sklopila i što je baš takav idiom njeno genetsko ishodište."

[2] Bugarski attempts to explain the reasons for the disintegration of the Serbo-Croatian language by defining these notions of an "external identity," i.e., how the language is viewed by outsiders, and "internal identity," i.e., the attitudes of the speakers of the language living within Socialist Yugoslavia's borders.

[3] Serbs tended to maintain that the unified language had a strong internal identity until the break-up of Yugoslavia in 1991. For them, the term Serbo-Croatian was commonly employed, and the belief in the unity of this language was pervasive.

super-ethnic Yugoslav identity reinforced by a more strongly united language only heightened Croat fears that the Serbs were bent on completely destroying the Croatian culture and language. Similarly, after Tito's break with Stalin in 1948, efforts of the Yugoslav Communist Party to promote a Yugoslav identity anchored in a unified Serbo-Croatian language caused resentment among some Croats, who considered this policy a reversal of the decision of the Anti-Fascist Council for the National Liberation of Yugoslavia (AVNOJ) to recognize four Yugoslav languages—Croatian, Macedonian, Serbian, and Slovene.[4] However, as seen below, these efforts did not magically eliminate the entrenched ethnic identities among the population. Just as the peoples of Yugoslavia would not unify under the guise of a non-ethnic Yugoslav identity, they refused to strengthen their linguistic unity, or to transform the Serbo-Croatian language into a unitary Yugoslav language with clear norms that would apply equally to Croats, Serbs, Muslims, and Montenegrins.

The purpose of this chapter is to provide an analysis of the heated language controversies that have flared in the Serbo-Croatian speech territory since the nineteenth century. These debates have triggered events that have either fostered or weakened the Serbo-Croatian language union. I first place this discussion within a theoretical framework of what I define as three models of language unity, and describe how each of these models had been used to maintain a Serb/ Croat linguistic union (2.1). I then treat the two primary written accords, which formalized the language union, highlighting the debates and controversies they evoked (2.2). I next suggest that the inability of all the ethnic groups to consistently promote and advance a single dialect proved to be the most significant impediment to language unity (2.3). This failure affected every facet of the debate, from the symbolic functions of competing alphabets and orthographic systems (2.4) to the role of vocabulary as a marker of distinct cultural identities for the various ethnic groups (2.5). As I demonstrate, true unity was finally undermined by compromises that never seemed to satisfy all language planners in the Central South Slavic speech territory.

2.1   Models for unified languages

As Bugarski has posited, the unified Serbo-Croatian language had a "weak internal identity," whereby language planners representing the perspectives of the rival Yugoslav peoples/nations contested the norms, dialect base, and sociolinguistic structure of the language. The phenomenon of competing standard norms of a given language is not unique to the former Yugoslavia; in other societies and cultures competing standard languages have evolved. Scholars have called such a

---

[4] This issue was brought up in Pavletić (1969). Cf. also 5.1.2.

development "pluricentricity" (Kloss 1978: 66–7 and elaborated in Clyne 1992). Pluricentric languages include Norwegian, Chinese, English, Hindi/Urdu, Dutch/ Flemish, and Armenian. English boasts several standards and despite the differences between American and British English, there has been no pressure to split English into separate languages, nor has there been an effort to unify all the standards. By contrast, German admits a single standard pronunciation (High German), while many of its regional variants, such as Swiss German, Bavarian German, or Austrian German remain vibrant but still subservient to the unified standard. How have some languages maintained their unity, while others have been split? What is the role of the state in preserving or destroying language unity? How do languages maintain unity across political boundaries, and how do languages create new borders?

The state or ruling elites can manipulate the symbolic power of language as a unifying force or a means of excluding segments of the population. When Bosnia-Herzegovina was recognized as an independent state by the European Community in 1992, the authorities in Sarajevo changed the official name of their language from the Serbo-Croatian language to the Bosnian language. This action served to underscore their political aims of creating a unitary Bosnian state, alienating the Bosnian Serb and Bosnian Croat populations, who preferred to adopt Croatian and Serbian, respectively, as their official languages. These developments represented the culmination of a process begun in the 1960s, when the Yugoslav state was becoming increasingly decentralized, and when the six republics with their six constituent peoples/nations were seeking greater autonomy. In language matters, these political processes sparked a period of what Fishman (1972: 58) would have called "contrastive self-identification." This behavior was characterized by the desire of the Croats to underscore unique Croatian linguistic features in order to differentiate themselves from the Serbs. Simultaneously, the Serbs sought to prove that fellow Serbs living in Croatia had a different dialect from their Croat neighbors with whom they had lived in ethnically mixed towns and villages for several centuries. Hence, the Yugoslav peoples/nations hoped to stress their individuality and distinct cultural-religious identity by asserting the separateness of "their" language or dialect. As long as the unified state continued, the unified Serbo-Croatian language could retain its symbolic unifying function, despite the increase in pluricentricity of the language, but once the political structure fractured, the same language acquired new names and definitions.

In order to comprehend the history of the unified Serbo-Croatian language in the context of other standard languages, I posit the following three kinds of language planning paradigms, which I call "language unity models":[5]

(1) centrally monitored unity;
(2) government-imposed unity;
(3) pluricentric unity.

---

[5] Cf. also Greenberg (1999) for a discussion of these three models.

2.1.1   Centrally monitored unity

The centrally monitored model of preserving language unity is typically found in societies in which a language academy, state-sponsored institute, or even a government ministry bears primary responsibility for language planning, for upholding the purity and unity of a standard language, and for fostering the dignity and norms of the state language.[6] In such societies, a central language academy or board functions as the arbiter with regard to the admittance of new forms or expressions into the standard. These institutions also produce many of the "official" grammars, dictionaries, and school textbooks. Frequently, these grammars and textbooks are prescriptive in nature, since it is the role of the academy to have the final word on spellings, grammatical usage, or definitions of words as standard, sub-standard, or merely a dialectal form. Thus, in recent years the Academie Française has spoken out against the infiltration of English words into the French language, seeking to maintain the purity of the French standard based on the Paris dialect.

The first language institute in the Central South Slavic speech territory was founded in Zagreb at the Yugoslav Academy of Sciences and Arts in 1867. Both the founder of the Academy, Bishop Josip Juraj Strossmayer (1815–1905), and the Academy's first president, Franjo Rački (1828–94), were promoters of the Yugoslav idea, and they sought to "unite the Yugoslav peoples by means of one language, one book, and in this manner to create unity in the Slavic South." The Yugoslav Academy was established 17 years after the signing of the 1850 Vienna Literary Agreement, which marked the inception of a joint literary language for Serbs and Croats (cf. 2.2.1). By 1901, Serb and Croat linguists at the Academy had produced an authoritative grammar (Maretić 1899), several volumes of a comprehensive dictionary (*Rječnik* 1882–1975), a more concise two-volume dictionary (Broz and Iveković 1901), and an orthographic manual (Broz 1892). All these works served as the instruments of codification, assuring the supremacy of the Southern dialect, which had been designated as the standard dialect in the Literary Agreement.[7] Furthermore, these instruments of codification consolidated the position of the Yugoslav Academy as the main institution implementing the centrally monitored approach for ensuring the acceptance and indivisibility of the newly declared unified language.

---

[6] In Europe, the French were one of the first to establish a language academy in 1635. The Academie Française still takes on the leading role in preserving and promoting the French language (cf. Edwards 1985: 27–8).

[7] As seen below (2.6), this dialect, known as the Neo-Štokavian ijekavian dialect is the one dialect shared by all of the currently designated ethnic groups in the Central South Slavic speech territory, i.e., Serbs, Croats, Bosniacs, and Montenegrins.

Having gained complete independence in 1878, the Serbian state, through the Serbian Royal Academy of Sciences and Arts founded in 1886, sanctioned the elevation of the Belgrade-Novi Sad dialect, as opposed to the one put forth by the Yugoslav Academy in Zagreb. Thus, the competition between Zagreb and Belgrade/Novi Sad regarding language matters began well before the establishment of the first joint state of Serbs and Croats. The centrally monitored model for nurturing the language union was successful as long as Serbia remained weak and divided. However, once Serbia gained independence, pluricentrism was on the rise, as the Serbian Royal Academy came into direct competition with the Yugoslav Academy in Zagreb.

2.1.2 Government-imposed unity

Government-imposed language unity is characteristic of totalitarian systems, where often the head of state or a state ministry assumes direct control over language policy. For instance, in 1939 in the Soviet Union, Stalin required the Soviet Union's Central Asian Republics to adopt the Cyrillic script. This measure had the symbolic effect of squarely placing these republics within the Russian-Soviet sphere of influence. It also had the effect of creating temporary illiteracy among the citizens of the Uzbek Soviet Socialist Republic or the Turkmen Soviet Socialist Republic. In such a manner, Stalin could institute a kind of language terror in the mostly Muslim republics of his domain, forcing citizens to adopt a foreign writing system. Another dictator, General Franco in Spain, considered the use of any of the minority languages as "anti-patriotic," insisting on Castilian Spanish as the single norm (cf. Mar-Molinero 2000: 97). This enforced language policy was particularly intolerant of the Basque language and any notions of the Basque people's autonomy.

From its inception, the Kingdom of Serbs, Croats, and Slovenes (1918–29) was weakened by strained inter-ethnic relations between Serbs and Croats. Begun as a constitutional monarchy, the Kingdom's political system seemed to limp from crisis to crisis. In an attempt to maintain the stability of the state, King Alexander assumed absolute control in 1929 and renamed the country the Kingdom of Yugoslavia. With this new name, King Alexander hoped to usher in an era of absolutist Yugoslavism, whereby the traditional ethnic identifications were to be scrubbed in favor of an over-arching, unifying Yugoslav identity. The term "Yugoslav" had originated in the Croat lands among the founders and supporters of the Yugoslav Academy in Zagreb during the previous century. The Serbian monarch presiding over the joint state had appropriated the name "Yugoslavia," much to the dismay of the Croats. For them at that point in history, this action represented the aspirations of Serbs to absorb the Croats and deny them their distinct cultural and linguistic identity. Thereafter, they would view Yugoslavism suspiciously, and understand it to be a Serb agenda to dominate all other groups living in their midst.[8]

During the 1930s, one of the ways in which the Kingdom of Yugoslavia sought to impose a Yugoslav identity was through language. Within a year of the declaration of absolute rule, Aleksandar Belić (1876–1963) published a new orthographic manual as decreed by the Kingdom's Ministry of Education (cf. Belić 1930). This orthographic manual was the first step towards the imposition of a single norm of the unified language on members of all ethnic groups within the country's borders. Some school textbooks of the period brazenly affirm the linguistic and cultural unity of all Serbs, Croats, and Slovenes in the Yugoslav Kingdom. "It will become especially clear that Serbs, Croats and Slovenes are a single, unified people, of one blood and one language" (Poljanec 1940: 6).[9] After the assassination of King Alexander, and as war became increasingly likely across Europe, the strict government control over language matters relaxed. Permission was granted for Boranić's alternative Croatian orthographic manual, which was first published in 1921, to appear in its fourth edition, a decade after it had been banned by King Alexander's government (cf. Boranić 1940). This manual reaffirmed some traditional orthographic conventions, which had been developing around Zagreb during the latter half of the nineteenth century.

According to Bašić (2001a: 45), the Croats continued to endure government-imposed language policies well after the fall of the Yugoslav Kingdom in 1941. She contended that language policies were imposed in both the Fascist Independent State of Croatia (1941–5), and Tito's Yugoslavia. In the latter, she argued that language policy was governed through "programmed, agreed-upon linguistics" ("programiranim i dogovornim jezikoslovljem"). This assertion is consistent with Bašić's view of Tito's regime as "Bolshevik," and that such "bolshevism" imposed language policy on the entire country. Imposed or not, Tito's Yugoslavia adopted a pluricentric model of language unity, one which allowed for the development of two full-fledged variants of a single language.

---

[8] With the signing of the Belgrade Agreement on 13 March 2002, the Federal Republic of Yugoslavia was to be renamed Serbia and Montenegro, thereby relegating the name Yugoslavia to the history books. This agreement was ratified by the Serbian, Montenegrin, and federal parliaments in February 2003. In 1992, the Serbian and Montenegrin authorities had agreed to preserve the name Yugoslavia, and the anti-secessionist bloc campaigning in the 2000 Montenegrin republican elections was known as "Together for Yugoslavia" ("Zajedno za Jugoslaviju"). According to Croatian Radio (15 March 2002), Croatian government officials were pleased to see the name "Yugoslavia" dropped, since in their view Yugoslavia represented the interests of "Greater Serbia" and this ideology had been responsible for the "aggression against Croatia" in the 1990s.

[9] "Naročito će postati jasna činjenica da su Srbi, Hrvati i Slovenci jedan jedinstven narod, jedne krvi i jednog jezika."

2.1.3   Pluricentric unity

Pluricentric unity is typical of states with more than one cultural ι
that could boast a vibrant vernacular literature, or a competing lanξ
In Norway, for instance, both Dano-Norwegian and New Norw
official status; both languages are considered to be equally "l
although Dano-Norwegian is more widely spoken, and likely to be the language
taught to foreigners. In other states, tolerance of local varieties may become
imperative in order to preserve the balance among regions. In Spain, for
instance, the Spanish Constitution guarantees the rights of the speakers of the
Spanish languages, including speakers of Castilian, Galician, Andalusian, and
other local varieties. Similarly, the Federal Republic of Germany is tolerant
towards regional varieties of German, including Bavarian, Alsatian, and German
standards across the borders in Switzerland and Austria. Perhaps the quintes-
sential model of a pluricentric language unity is that of Chinese, with its
many, often not mutually intelligible regional varieties, such as Mandarin and
Cantonese.

The case of Serbo-Croatian is unique in that the initial standardization
reversed several centuries of natural *Abstand* developments for the languages of
Orthodox Southern Slavs and Catholic Southern Slavs.[10] Unlike the codifiers of
the modern Scandinavian languages or the founders of modern Hindi and Urdu,
the linguists and literary figures who embraced the unified Serbian/Croatian
language in 1850 hoped to use language as a unifying force for the peoples of the
speech territory. When the single dialect proposition failed by the end of
the nineteenth century, and the stages of imposed unity failed in the 1930s, the
postwar regime sought to formalize linguistic "brotherhood and unity" through
the Novi Sad Agreement of 1954 (cf. 2.2.2).

Serb and Croat linguists agreed that their language was unified, but that this
unity was achieved through compromise and tolerance of local language varieties, which enjoyed the same level of prestige throughout the country. This
tolerance was extended through the 1974 Federal Constitution, allowing local
varieties of the language to gain official status in the constituent republics. The
Constitution allowed for further subdivisions of the Serbo-Croatian language
and the establishment of "standard linguistic idioms" in Croatia, Bosnia-
Herzegovina, and Montenegro. Therefore, from the mid-1970s until 1991, four
regional variants were tolerated: (1) Croatian, known as the "Western variant" of
the unified language; (2) Serbian, known as the "Eastern variant" of the unified
language; (3) Bosnia-Herzegovinian, known as the republic's "standard linguistic
idiom"; and (4) Montenegrin, known as the republic's "standard linguistic
idiom."

---

[10] For a discussion of *Abstand* and *Ausbau* relationships among languages, cf. 1.4.

The models of language unity expounded upon here present a useful framework for discussing the history of the language policies which have since 1850 affected the development of the Serbo-Croatian unified language. In the following sections I turn to some of the main obstacles to unity, and demonstrate that every step towards a unified language seemed to arouse controversy, ethnic rivalry, and competitions over linguistic issues, which became symbolic markers for ethnic identity.

2.2 Controversies connected with Serb/Croat language accords

In a volume he edited on first language conferences, Fishman (1993) discussed the implications of the "first language conference phenomenon" for language planning. Such a conference has had far-reaching effects on both status planning, i.e., selection of the norm and its functional implementation, and corpus planning, i.e., the codification of the norm and its elaboration in society. In the case of Serbo-Croatian, two significant language conferences have been held. The conference in Vienna led to the signing of the Literary Agreement on 28 March 1850.[11] This meeting was dedicated largely to status planning.[11] It affirmed the principle that the language should be a unified standard for Serbs and Croats, even though there had hitherto been no normative works supporting the notion of such a literary language union. The second conference, which brought together leading Serb and Croat linguists, was held in Novi Sad in 1954, and involved a revision of the language status decisions of the Literary Agreement, and considered many corpus planning issues, from painstaking debates on synchronizing grammatical terminology to compromises on the spellings of foreign words.[12] Both meetings were controversial, and attitudes towards both meetings have hardened since the official break-up of the Serbo-Croatian language in 1991. The controversies surrounding both agreements gave birth to new interpretations, and the re-writing of the language history (cf. 4.1.2, 5.1.1, and 5.1.2).

2.2.1 The Literary Agreement (1850)

Ostensibly, the signing of the Vienna Literary Agreement was a surprise, since the literary languages of both the Serbs and Croats had been following diverging

[11] The only substantive corpus planning issues agreed upon in Vienna involved the spelling of vocalic *r*, the spelling of the genitive plural without a final *h*, and the velar fricative *h*, which is lost in many Štokavian dialects. Cf. Appendix A.

[12] For instance, the Serbs had used the terms *zapeta* 'comma', and *tačka* 'period' while the Croats used *zarez* and *točka*, respectively. The two sides compromised in Novi Sad, agreeing to use *zarez* and *tačka*.

courses of development over the centuries. Prior to 1850, Croatian literature was written in several regional centers, where disparate dialects were elevated to the status of regional literary varieties. Thus, one could find literary works in the Stokavian dialect of the Dubrovnik area, the Čakavian dialects of Dalmatia and the Adriatic islands, the Štokavian dialects of Slavonia, and the Kajkavian dialects of the Zagreb area.[13]

By contrast, prior to 1850 the Serbs had a tradition of writing in an artificial Slaveno-Serbian language, which bore no resemblance to a single living Serbian dialect. This language included many Russian and archaic Church Slavonic elements incomprehensible to ordinary people. Albin (1970: 484) described this language as the literary language of the Vojvodina Serbs, and suggested that the Slaveno-Serbian language was of utmost importance for the Vojvodinian elites. He considered the eighteenth century in Vojvodina as a period of enlightenment, during which the Serbian people, supported by the members of the Orthodox Church, were constantly striving to establish their own schools, print their own Cyrillic books, and thus achieve a certain educational standard. However, the artificial literary norm was an impediment for broader literacy, and this Slaveno-Serbian language bore little resemblance to living dialects.

With such disparate traditions, the Literary Agreement can best be comprehended as a historical coincidence, as the agendas of two distinct language reformers—the Croat Ljudevit Gaj (1809–72) and the Serb Vuk Stefanović Karadžić (1787–1864)—overlapped.

Gaj played a crucial role in forming a modern Croatian national identity. In the 1830s he led the Illyrian Movement, which Despalatović defined as:

The framework for the Croatian national renaissance in which the vernacular was made into a modern literary language; it was a political movement which sought to preserve the traditional rights of the Croatian kingdom within a militantly nationalist Hungary; it was an attempt to lay the basis for future Croatian territorial and ethnic unity; and it was a movement to establish cultural unity among all of the Southern Slavs. Although its impact extended far beyond the borders of the small Croatian kingdom, the Illyrian Movement rose directly out of the particular cultural and political needs of the Croats in the first half of the nineteenth century and its goal was to establish a modern national identity for the Croats.[14]

Gaj had accepted the notions of pan-Slavism, which had been spreading among the Slavs of the Austro-Hungarian Empire at that time under the influence of romanticism. For Gaj, four main Slavic languages existed: Russian, Polish, Czecho-Slovak, and Illyrian (South Slavic). He conceived of the Croats as belonging to the Illyrian nation, which was primarily defined by its language, since, as Gaj himself wrote in 1835, "A nation has nothing holier nor dearer than

---

[13] For an explanation of the dialectal division of the Central South Slavic speech territory, cf. 2.3.

[14] Cf. Despalatović (1975: 75).

its natural language, for it is only through language that a nation, as a particular society, continues or vanishes."[15] Gaj sought to unify the Croatian Latin orthography, and to elevate the Dubrovnik brand of the Štokavian dialect to literary status. Given his pan-Slavic ideology and preference for this South-western dialect, Gaj could find a natural ally in Vuk Karadžić—often referred to by his first name Vuk—who had independently proposed a reform of the Ser-bian language based on essentially the same Southwestern dialect.

Vuk had begun his literary and linguistic activities in 1814 when he published a collection of Serbian folk songs, and a short Serbian grammar. His first major work was his *Srpski rječnik* ("Serbian Dictionary") of 1818, in which he intro-duced a new Serbian standard built upon his native Eastern Herzegovina-type dialect. A believer in the principle that the Serbian language should be based entirely on the vernacular, he introduced a new and simplified writing system which diverged markedly from the cumbersome and artificial written norms of the Slaveno-Serbian literary language.

The Literary Agreement was signed by Vuk Karadžić and Djura Daničić for the Serbs, and Ivan Kuljević, Ivan Mažuranić, Dimitrije Demeter, Vinko Pacel, and Stjepan Pejković for the Croats.[16] The Agreement contained only the following five main points:

(1)　It is better to elevate a popular dialect to literary status, rather than create an artificial super-dialectal standard.
(2)　The Southern dialect is designated as literary.
(3)　The velar-fricative *h* will always be written in the literary language.
(4)　The velar-fricative *h* will not be written in the genitive plural of nouns.
(5)　The syllabic *r* will be written simply as *-r-*, as in *prst* 'finger' (rather than **perst*).

Points (1), (2), (4), and (5) were agreed upon unanimously. However, on the issue of the writing of the grapheme |x| (Cyrillic) |h| (Latin), Vuk comprom-ised with the Illyrians. Vuk had omitted this grapheme from his 1818 Dictionary, since the phoneme |h| had been widely lost among the Orthodox population, and for this reason Vuk felt it had no place in his phonological writing system. On this point, the text of the Literary Agreement made no references to the unanimity of this decision, and stated instead that:

We found it to be good and necessary that the writers of the Eastern faith should write *x*, wherever it is etymologically appropriate, just as those [writers] of the Western faith write *h*, and as our people of both faiths in many places in our southern region speak.[17]

---

[15] Cf. Despalatović (1975: 74).

[16] In Štambuk (1972: 40), the Croat signatories are described as "Illyrian literary figures" ("ilirski književnici").

[17] For the text in the original, cf. Appendix A.

The Literary Agreement was not a binding document; intellectuals from both sides signed it without the overt blessing of any official organizations, state organs, or councils. Gaj was not a signatory to the Agreement, and was cautious in his reactions to the accord. In his introduction to the text of the Agreement published in *Narodne novine,* he wrote:

Time will soon show whether this proposal is practical, and whether it will lead in today's situation to the expected agreement and equality, or will it, on the contrary, lead to even greater separateness and literary discord.[18]

Despite this lukewarm assessment, Vuk had succeeded in influencing the work of Serb and Croat linguists, who over the course of the following decades worked towards the realization of the joint literary language at the Yugoslav Academy of Sciences and Arts in Zagreb. These linguists, frequently referred to as "Vuko-vites" (*vukovci*), included Djura Daničić, and his Croat collaborators Tomislav Maretić, Ivan Broz, and Petar Budmani. Their success was evident in the sheer volume of new language handbooks written between 1850 and 1901.[19] Still, compromise had eluded the signatories of the Literary Agreement on one important issue: what should the new language be called? The name of the new joint literary language was nowhere to be found in the text of the 1850 Agreement. In 1861 the Croatian Sabor (Assembly) tried to remedy the situation by voting to name the unified language the "Yugoslav"—i.e., "South Slav"—language.[20] However, the authorities in Vienna overturned the Sabor's decision, and promulgated the terms "Serbian-Illyrian (Cyrillic)" and "Serbian-Illyrian (Latin)" for this new South Slavic literary language.[21]

Until the official abandonment of the joint language in 1991, Serbs and Croats could not agree on a single common name for the language. Thus, the Croat Vukovites used the name "Croatian or Serbian," while Vuk, and to some extent Daničić, used the term "Serbian." Thus, reacting to Croat proposals that the language be called "Illyrian," Vuk vowed that "we would be crazy if we agreed to abandon our famous name and adopt another one which is dead and has no meaning in itself."[22]

---

[18] Štambuk (1972: 40): "Vrijeme će na skoro pokazati da li je ovaj prijedlog praktičan i vodi li u današnjem našem položaju k ožuđenoj slozi i jednakosti, ili pak naprotiv još k većemu cijepanju i književnom razdoru."

[19] See 2.1.1 for the list of materials published at that time.

[20] Cf. Okuka (1998: 19–20) for further details on the Sabor's decision.

[21] These complex terms were flawed since they include the ethnic affiliation of one group (the Serbs), and the political, rather than ethnic, affiliation of the other group (the Croats).

[22] Cf. Wilson (1986: 301). Both the 1818 and 1852 editions of Vuk's dictionary are called *Srpski rječnik* 'Serbian Dictionary'; similarly, Daničić published some works with only the term "Serbian" in the title, cf. Daničić 1864, reprinted in 1983.

While the disputes over the name of the language pointed to some fundamental disagreements among the signatories of the Literary Agreement, the more
threatening challenges to this accord came from the Vojvodina Serbs and Croat
nationalists. The Vojvodina Serbs had bitterly opposed Vuk since the publication
of his 1818 Dictionary. They looked down upon Vuk's choice of the Eastern
Herzegovina-type dialect, which they considered to be alien and inferior to their
own dialect. They also resisted his phonological writing system until the 1860s
(cf. 2.4.1), when it was accepted by the Society of Serbian Literacy ("Društvo
srpske slovesnosti," 1841–64). This Society, which evolved into the Serbian
Scholarly Society ("Srpsko učeno društvo," 1864–86), was formed in order to
cultivate the Serbian language and to encourage the production of scholarly
works written in the Serbian language (cf. Krleža 1955: 32ff.). While accepting
Vuk's reformed orthography and principles of basing the standard language on
the vernacular, the Society rejected the brand of the literary language emerging
in Zagreb under Daničić and the Croat Vukovites. Rather, it supported the
Belgrade-Novi Sad dialect for the written language, instead of the Eastern
Herzegovina-type dialect adopted in the 1850 Literary Agreement.

The Croat nationalists, led by Ante Starčević, considered cooperation with
Serbs such as Vuk and Daničić to be equivalent to a surrender of Croatian
national identity, and that Vuk's language, based on the popular vernacular,
was undignified and merely the language of "ploughmen and cow herdsmen."
Less vociferous was the opposition of linguists in Croatian regional centers,
who opposed the choice of the Southern dialect, including members of the
Zagreb, Rijeka, and Zadar schools. The Zadar linguists believed that the
Štokavian ikavian dialect was the ideal basis for a new Croatian standard. They
argued that this dialect was predominantly spoken by Croats in Western
Bosnia, Western Herzegovina, Slavonia, Posavina, and Central Dalmatia.[23]
Linguists in Rijeka and Zagreb advocated a Croatian standard language based
not on a single existing dialect, but on an artificial dialect created from an
amalgamation of dialectal and artificial features. The members of the Rijeka
school supported a pan-Slavic philosophy broader than the one exhibited
by the members of the Illyrian movement. They endeavored to bring Croatian
in line with other Slavic languages, especially the North Slavic ones. Therefore,
they insisted upon an etymological orthography, and the introduction of a
set of morphological endings in the system of dative, instrumental, and
locative plural nominal declension paradigms. These endings, such as (locative
plural) –*ah*, are typical of languages such as Russian, Czech, Slovene,
and Polish; moreover, they are found in the Croat Kajkavian and Čakavian

---

[23] Ikavian is also spoken by some Bosniacs; Greenberg (1996: 401) classifies the Serbs as
non-ikavian speakers. C.f. also 2.3 below for details on the Štokavian sub-dialects and
where and by whom they are spoken.

dialects.[24] Through such language planning, the Croatian language would have significantly diverged from the Vukovian norm based on Štokavian and a phonetic orthography. The Zagreb linguistic school objected to the jettisoning of the Croat Kajkavian and Čakavian dialects, and advanced the notion of a super-dialect to be created for literary Croatian. This approach resembled that taken by the Slovenes, who combined elements from the two central Slovene dialects (Upper and Lower Carniola) to form Contemporary Standard Slovene.

Despite the opposition of these groups, the Croatian Sabor declared in 1867 that "Every citizen is allowed to use the Croatian or Serbian language as the official language and they can choose freely the Latin or Cyrillic script" (Okuka 1998: 20). The Literary Agreement that had seemed to be a kind of non-binding gentlemen's agreement at the time of its signing now received official endorsement as the unified language for the citizens of the regions under the Sabor's jurisdiction. No other credible literary language was taking hold in the region, and by the end of the nineteenth century the notion of a unified language had been widely accepted outside the region among French, English, and German scholars (Okuka 1998: 27).

2.2.2   *The Novi Sad Agreement (1954)*

As seen above (2.1.1), the centrally monitored model for maintaining the unity of the Serbo-Croatian language became increasingly difficult after the rise of the independent Serbian state in 1878, and the subsequent establishment of the Serbian Royal Academy of Sciences and Arts. The Serbian Academy did not initially take an active role in producing instruments of codification for the joint language. However, works written in Serbia at that time did not conform to the norms emanating from the Yugoslav Academy in Zagreb. Rather, the Serbs accepted Vuk's reforms but adapted them to their main urban dialects of Belgrade and Novi Sad, the so-called Eastern dialect of the joint language. By the early 1900s, Aleksandar Belić had emerged as a leading Serb linguist, who later played a central role in the language politics of the first (Royalist) Yugoslav state. Belić was a firm believer in the unity of the Serbo-Croatian language, and sought control over language unity monitoring, wresting this privilege away from the Yugoslav Academy in Zagreb. Therefore, once Belić became ensconced at the Serbian Royal Academy, the attempts at maintaining a single institution to monitor the language unity finally collapsed. Nonetheless, embracing the principle of unity, the Serbs embarked on promulgating their Eastern standard and increasingly there were calls to come to a new compromise between Zagreb and Belgrade. One of the most noteworthy of these appeals was that of Jovan Skerlić

---

[24] In the Štokavian dialects, the original distinctive endings in the dative, locative, and instrumental plural have been lost. In these three cases, the endings *–ima/-ama* have been generalized in a Štokavian innovation.

(1877–1914) who in 1913 called for a single joint standard taking elements from the Zagreb and Belgrade codifications. According to his proposal, the Serbs would switch completely to the Latin script, and the Croats would adopt the Eastern, rather than the Southern dialect. Such a unification was never attempted; rather, a much more ambiguous compromise was agreed upon through the 1954 Novi Sad Agreement.

The Novi Sad Agreement resulted from a meeting of Serb and Croat linguists (8–10 December 1954), initiated by the editorial board of the journal *Letopis Matice srpske* to discuss matters of status and corpus planning for the unified language, with the immediate aim of normalizing the orthographic conventions. As a result of their deliberations, the delegates agreed on the following ten "conclusions" (*zaključci*):

(1) Serbs, Croats, and Montenegrins share a single language with two equal variants that have developed around Zagreb (Western) and Belgrade (Eastern).

(2) Officially, the name of the language must include reference to its two constituent parts (i.e., both "Serb" and "Croat").

(3) The Latin and Cyrillic alphabets have equal status, and Serbs and Croats are expected to learn both alphabets in school.

(4) The two pronunciations—ijekavian and ekavian—have equal status in all respects.[25]

(5) The Matica srpska will cooperate with the Matica hrvatska in the production of a new dictionary of the joint language.[26]

(6) Work will proceed on the establishment of common terminology for all spheres of economic, scholarly, and cultural life.

(7) Both sides will cooperate in the compiling of a joint orthographic manual (*Pravopis*).

(8) Care must be given to the natural development of Croato-Serbian, and no longer should texts be altered from one variant to the other.

(9) The composition of a Commission for the *Pravopis* and terminology will be decided by universities in Zagreb, Belgrade, and Sarajevo, the Academies in Zagreb and Belgrade, Matica hrvatska, and Matica srpska.

---

[25] Cf. 2.5 for an explanation of the relationship between the two pronunciations and the two variants.

[26] The Matica srpska was founded in Pest in 1826 as a Serbian cultural-scholarly institution. It moved to Novi Sad in 1864. Since 1945, the Matica srpska has primarily been a society promoting scholarly research and scholarly publications in the areas of Serbian language, literature, and culture. The Matica hrvatska was founded in 1842, and has served as a primary Croatian cultural and publishing society. In 2002, the Matica hrvatska celebrated its one hundred and sixtieth anniversary. As seen below, the two cultural societies have played important roles in the language controversies in the former Yugoslavia.

(10)   The conclusions will be made available by M
       Executive Council (i.e., the federal Yugoslav
       ments of Serbia, Croatia, Bosnia-Herzegovina,
       the universities, the Matica hrvatska in Zagreb,
       journals.

The Novi Sad Agreement seemed finally to resolve the co:
of the joint language. It was to be called *srpskohrvatski* '!
Eastern variant, and *hrvatskosrpski* 'Croato-Serbian' for
These terms were always to be written without a hyph
politically correct and official names of the joint language.

As a direct outcome of the Novi Sad Agreement, two equal and official
versions of the joint *Pravopis* for the Serbo-Croatian/Croato-Serbian language
appeared in 1960 in both Zagreb and Novi Sad. In Zagreb the manual was
printed in the Latin script and in the Western variant, while in Novi Sad the
manual appeared in the Cyrillic script and the Eastern variant (cf. *Pravopis* 1960).
Thereafter, work began on a joint dictionary which was to have six volumes and
two parallel versions—one for each variant. The Dictionary's first volume
appeared in 1967 (cf. Stevanović and Jonke 1967). By that time, however, Serb/
Croat tensions had surfaced with the publication in 1966 of a highly controversial rival one-volume dictionary in Serbia, followed in 1967 by the adoption of the "Declaration on the Name and Position of the Croatian Literary
Language" ("Deklaracija o nazivu i položaju hrvatskoga književnog jezika") in
Croatia. After the publication of the one-volume dictionary of the joint language
by the Serb Miloš Moskovljević, Magner wrote:

Seventy-six copies were sold before the publishers, *Nolit* and *Tehnička knjiga*, were
informed that the nature of some entries made their handsome book a veritable package
of dynamite. By court order all the remaining issues of the original printing of 5,000 were
delivered to the nearest furnace while the responsible publishers were punished. What had
Dr. Moskovljević, an elderly Serb, wrought with his 1,000-page dictionary? For one thing
he had no entry for *Hrvat*, "Croat", while *Srbin*, "Serb", and related words...were well
represented....Next to his omission of *Hrvat*, Moskovljević's greatest error in the eyes of
the authorities lay in his definition of *četnik* and *partizan*. A *četnik* was defined as an
irregular soldier who fought "a) during the Balkan war for freedom from the Turks, b)
during the Second World War against the Partisans", a definition which puts the Turks
and the Partisans in a parallel classification and which ignores the official mythology
about the Partisan. A *partizan* was defined as "(1) a participant in a guerilla struggle, (2) a
person who blindly follows the interests of his political party". Such clear hints of Serb
nationalism were not tolerated by the Tito regime.[27]

The "Declaration," put forth by prominent members of the Zagreb linguistic
circle, asserted that Croats have the right to their own literary language.

---

[27] Cf. Magner (1967: 340).

Novi Sad-inspired name, "Croato-Serbian," they argued that the people had the right to choose their own name for their literary language, and that the most appropriate name of the language was the "Croatian literary language." The "Declaration" was perceived as a threat to ethnic relations. Tito intervened only in 1971 when the Croatian Spring Movement (see below) threatened the unity and stability of the state. Between 1967 and 1971 the joint Serb-Croat dictionary project fell apart, and its remaining four volumes were published unilaterally by Matica srpska (cf. Stevanović 1969–76). Therefore, in 1971, it was the turn of several Croatian language books advocating a separate Croatian literary language to be sent to the furnace, and the perpetrators of the Croatian Spring were branded "counter-revolutionaries," and many of them were imprisoned.

The unraveling of the Novi Sad Agreement was symptomatic of other transformations occurring within the Yugoslav Federation. The federal government in the 1960s began transferring authority to the republics. The Croat "Declaration" ushered in a period of political unrest in Croatia, culminating in the Croatian Spring movement (1971), when the Croats sought greater independence from Belgrade. At the same time, the Yugoslav authorities elevated the Muslim Slav population to the status of a constituent people/nation of Yugoslavia. Through this action the Yugoslav authorities equated religious and ethnic identity, and created the forerunner to the post-1992 Bosniac people. By the late 1960s, it was anomalous for a Serb to self-identify as a Catholic or Muslim, just as it was most unlikely for a Croat to self-identify as Orthodox or Muslim. This policy isolated those citizens whose parents belonged to different communities. These citizens usually self-identified as "Yugoslavs," but none of them could call their language by this non-ethnic term.

Taken in a broader context, however, the Novi Sad Agreement failed because few of the recurring controversial issues surrounding standardization of the joint language were ever truly and satisfactorily resolved. The most salient of these issues included the key status planning matter concerning the appropriate "standard dialect" (2.3), corpus planning debates surrounding alphabets and writing systems (2.4), and decisions on vocabulary (2.5).

2.3   The power of competing dialects

The types of dialects spoken in the Central South Slavic speech territory are numerous and diverse, and the task of finding a single dialect to satisfy the demands of the competing ethno-religious groups has proven to be problematical since the times of the 1850 Literary Agreement. The territory has traditionally been divided into three main dialects, whose names originate in the divergent forms of the interrogative pronoun 'what', which is rendered by *kaj* in

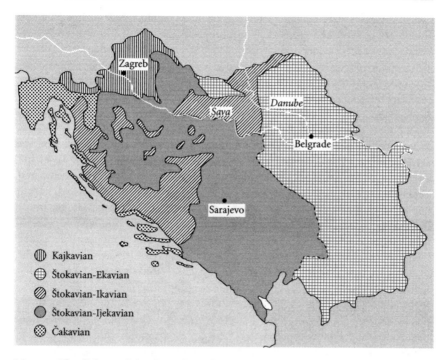

MAP 3. The dialects of the Central South Slavic speech territory
Note: This map was adapted from the dialect map printed at the end of the first volume of the journal *Hrvatski dijalektološki zbornik* (1956), published by the Yugoslav Academy of Sciences and Arts in Zagreb.

Kajkavian, *ča* in Čakavian, and *što/šta* in Štokavian. Over the past few hundred years, the Štokavian dialects have expanded at the expense of both Čakavian and Kajkavian, and currently are spoken over the largest geographic area, and boast the vast majority of speakers (see Map 3). Moreover, these dialects are mutually intelligible, and spoken by members of the four peoples/nations in Tito's Yugoslavia: Croats, Montenegrins, Muslim Slavs, and Serbs.[28] Thus, the difference between the two main Štokavian dialects (Southern or Western vs. Eastern), on which the two standard variants of the Novi Sad Agreement were based, has been likened to the differences between American and British English (cf. Magner 1967: 342). The subdivisions of Štokavian are based on types of accentual systems (old Štokavian vs. Neo-Štokavian), and on three different realizations of a vowel inherited from a presumed late Common Slavic language that broke apart in approximately the tenth century AD. It is assumed that this vowel, known as *jat'* (transcribed as *ě*), was originally pronounced like a low front

---

[28] By contrast, the Kajkavian and Čakavian dialects are spoken exclusively by Croats.

vowel, similar to the *a* in English 'bag'. The three Štokavian sub-dialects derive their names from the modern realizations of *jat*, i.e., *e* for ekavian, *ije* for ijekavian,[29] and *i* for ikavian.

Language planners have championed several of these dialects and sub-dialects since the inception of the joint literary language for Serbs and Croats in 1850, resulting in several heated controversies. These controversies have been both inter-ethnic and intra-ethnic. They have involved: (1) the status of the Štokavian/ ijekavian dialects, which are spoken by most Muslim Slavs (Bosniacs), Montenegrins, Serbs living west of the Drina River, and most Croats (2.3.2); and (2) debates surrounding "standard variants," "standard pronunciations," and "standard linguistic idioms" in Tito's Yugoslavia (2.3.3).

Before analyzing these controversies, I will discuss the degree to which a given Štokavian sub-dialect may be associated with the four ethnic groups in the Central South Slavic speech territory.

2.3.1   The Štokavian dialects and ethnicity: An overview

It is generally assumed that the division of the Štokavian dialect into its three sub-dialects—ekavian, ijekavian, and ikavian—had fully developed by the time of the Ottoman invasions in the fourteenth and fifteenth centuries. At that time, the geographic distribution of these sub-dialects was as follows: ikavian was spoken to the West, ijekavian to the South, and ekavian to the East.[30] Historically, the ekavian dialects have been spoken by the Serbs' ancestors, and have remained predominantly Serbian. By contrast, the ikavian dialects spoken in parts of Slavonia, Western Bosnia, Western Herzegovina, and Central Dalmatia were originally spoken by Catholic Southern Slavs (Croats), some of whom converted to Islam under Ottoman rule. The speakers of the ijekavian dialect had originally adopted Christianity from both Rome (Croats) and Byzantium (Serbs and Montenegrins), and during Ottoman times many ijekavian speakers converted to Islam (Bosniacs).

---

[29] In the Štokavian/ijekavian dialects, the *ije* reflexes of 'jat' occurred in syllables where 'jat' was a long vowel in early South Slavic; in original short syllables it is rendered by *je, e,* or *i* depending on the phonetic environment.

[30] This interpretation differs from that posited by Banac (1984: 206ff.), who suggested that the original division of Štokavian was between "Western" and "Eastern." His scheme assumes that the Western dialects were spoken by Croats and the Eastern ones by Serbs. However, according to his map (p. 208), the ijekavian dialects are split with most of them falling under Eastern Štokavian. Linguistically, such a classification fails to account for the archaic ijekavian dialects found in Montenegro and the Sandžak.

The dialectological history of Štokavian is complicated by the mass migrations of populations resulting from the spread of the Ottoman Empire. These migrations took place after the fifteenth century, when the Štokavian/ijekavian dialects had already adopted a system of tonal accents and stress known by the term Neo-Štokavian. Many Neo-Štokavian/ijekavian speakers of the Orthodox faith migrated from their ancestral homeland in Eastern Herzegovina and Montenegro to Eastern Bosnia, Western Serbia, the Bosnian military borderlands located south of the Sava River, the Croatian military borderlands north of the Sava, and to portions of Slavonia, Western Srem, and Southern Baranja. In addition, some Catholic ijekavian speakers also participated in these migrations,[31] although the majority of the descendants of the migrant families currently self-identify as Serbs. The descendants of these migrants have retained many of the basic characteristics of the Neo-Štokavian ijekavian dialect type, including the *ije/je* renditions of *jat'*, and the Neo-Štokavian accentual patterns. Hence, in the regions where the speakers of the ijekavian dialect constitute the autochthonous population, this Štokavian sub-dialect is not marked for ethnicity—it is identifiable as the dialect of Croats in Southern Dalmatia, or the dialect of Serbs in Eastern Herzegovina, and the dialect of Montenegrins and Serbs in Northwestern Montenegro. However, in the regions settled by these speakers, this dialect is often associated with the Serbian population, especially in the military borderlands of Lika, Banija, and Kordun, and northwestern Bosnia, where the Orthodox Serbs settled among a non-Serb ikavian-speaking population. Similarly, in Eastern Bosnia the Serbs display an Eastern Herzegovina-type ijekavian dialect, while the autochthonous (mostly Bosniac) population in that region exhibit a more archaic Eastern Bosnian-type ijekavian dialect (cf. 6.3.1 below). The mostly Serb population of migrants helped spread the Neo-Štokavian accentuation throughout the Central South Slavic region, influencing the ikavian and ekavian dialects as well.

By the time the Literary Agreement and Novi Sad Agreements were signed, the link between ethnic/religious identity and dialect types had become blurred, since the populations had mixed, many urban dwellers in Bosnia-Herzegovina had converted to Islam, and the Štokavian dialects had expanded in all directions.

2.3.2 Dilemmas of dialects: Ownership and citizenship?

The inter-ethnic dialect controversy has mostly focused on the status of the so-called Southern dialect, which was upgraded to the status of the literary language through the 1850 Literary Agreement. This dialect has traditionally been

---

[31] For instance, some ijekavian-speaking Croats fled from the Ottoman Empire to the Austro-Hungarian territories in the seventeenth century; cf. Greenberg (1998: 714).

classified linguistically as Neo-Štokavian/ijekavian, geographically as the Eastern Herzegovina-type dialect or simply the "Southern" dialect, and culturally as the dialect of Dubrovnik's medieval literature and Serbia's epic poetry. Four periods have been critical regarding the status of this dialect and its appropriateness as the literary standard, including: (1) 1836–99, when Neo-Štokavian/ijekavian was implemented as the standard in Western and Southern Štokavian areas; (2) 1913–39, when the proponents of the Eastern, Štokavian-ekavian (Serbian) dialects championed their own dialect at the expense of the Southern Štokavian/ijekavian dialect; (3) 1954–74, when the Southern dialect became synonmous with the Western variant (Croato-Serbian) of the joint language, and the boundaries between "Eastern" and "Western" variants were hotly disputed; and (4) 1991–present, when the four successor languages to Serbo-Croatian have all claimed ownership of the Southern Neo-Štokavian/ijekavian dialect.

The initial controversies over the Southern dialect were sparked by Gaj's decision in 1836 to abandon his native Kajkavian in favor of the Dubrovnik-based Štokavian/ijekavian dialect. By doing so, he rejected the native dialect of the citizens of Zagreb, and thereafter the local Zagreb dialect would have limited influence on the development of a Croatian standard. As Banac (1984: 220) suggested, Gaj and the leaders of the Illyrian Movement attempted

to reconcile several incompatible goals. They tried to promote the widest South Slavic linguistic unity and at the same time to assuage regional sensitivity which stood in the way of unity; in addition, they wanted to make sure that their solutions did not widen the gap between the South Slavs and the Czechs and Poles, and they wanted to remain faithful in some measure to the normative character of the Croat literary tradition, especially that of Štokavian spoken in Dubrovnik, Dalmatia, and Slavonia.

Gaj was attempting to please all sides; he hoped to appease his fellow Croats by incorporating elements of their dialects into his newly found Štokavian standard. Simultaneously, he was reaching out to Vuk Karadžić, who at the time was locked in a battle over his new orthography and choice of the Southern dialect with his ethnic kin—the Vojvodina Serbs. The success in implementing this Southern dialect as the literary norm hinged upon Serb-Croat collaboration, which aroused much suspicion on both sides.

Some Croats felt threatened by Vuk's pronouncements that all Štokavian speakers were actually Serbs of different faiths—Catholic Serbs, Muslim Serbs, and Orthodox Serbs. To counterbalance Serbian influence, Gaj was keen on infusing elements from the Croat literary vernaculars of Slavonia, the Kajkavian, and Čakavian areas, and even advocated the introduction of neologisms borrowed from the Czech lands as part of the Czech national revival. However, in implementing the Literary Agreement, Vuk's followers, led by Daničić, reversed many of Gaj's proposals. They excluded Kajkavian dialect materials from the dictionary published by the Yugoslav Academy of Sciences and Arts beginning in 1880. According to the "Postscript" ("Pogovor") to the final twenty-third volume of this dictionary, Daničić was criticized for this exclusion of Croat dialectal material for the volumes he oversaw (cf. *Rječnik* 1880–1975 v.23: 64ff.).[32]

Since Daničić was a Serb, who had been teaching at the Velika škola in Belgrade before Rački and Strossmayer invited him to Zagreb, many Serbs have contended that the Croats were indebted to the Serbs for their standard language. Furthermore, some Serbs have even alleged that for the Croats the Literary Agreement

is not only about the adoption of Vuk's ijekavian pronunciation, but also about the acceptance of his orthography, orthoepic practices, lexicon, morphology, word formation, phraseology, syntax, and style. Hence, it is not at all strange...that it has been said that the Croats in fact adopted the Serbian language, accepted the Serbian standard, called it Croatian, although it was difficult for them to bear the uncomfortable consequences this action had for their own national identity.[33]

The second period, between 1913 and 1939, marked an escalation in ethnic conflict and a growing of contentiousness regarding the status of the Southern dialect. The Štokavian/ijekavian dialect became a marker of Croat linguistic identity, while the Štokavian/ekavian dialect marked Serb linguistic identity. The year 1913 is given as a starting point, since it is when Jovan Skerlić proposed a Serb-Croat language compromise, whereby the Croats would give up their ijekavian pronunciation, and adopt the Štokavian-ekavian dialect of Belgrade, while the Serbs would in turn switch from their Cyrillic to the Latin alphabet. Although this proposal was never seriously considered, Belić (1930) attempted to implement the provisions about the dialects by insisting on the supremacy of the Belgrade pronunciation in the Kingdom of Yugoslavia (cf. 2.1.2). The Serbian pro-ekavian bias was threatening not only to Croats, but to ijekavian-speaking Serbs, Muslim Slavs, and Montenegrins. In the first Yugoslavia, the Montenegrins and Muslim Slavs were not recognized as constituent ethnic groups; therefore, only the Croats had the political clout to defend the threatened ijekavian standard. The more the Serbs expressed their desire to abandon the ijekavian standard, the more the Croats seemed to come to its defense.

In the third period the Serbs and Croats agreed that both the ijekavian and ekavian standards would become official variants of the unified language through the 1954 Novi Sad Agreement. With this decision, the ijekavian dialect metamorphosed into the Western variant, while the ekavian dialect became

---

[32] For an expanded discussion on Croat attitudes towards Daničić and his Croat followers, cf. 5.1.1 below.

[33] Cf. Brborić (1996: 18): "I nije tu reč samo o preuzimanju karadžićevskog ijekavskog izgovora nego i o prihvatanju karadžićevske ortografije, ortoepije, leksike, morfologije, tvorbe reči, frazeologije, sintakse i stila. Stoga nije nikakvo čudo što se...znalo govoriti o tome da su Hrvati zapravo preuzeli srpski jezik, prihvatili srpski jezički standard, nazvali ga hrvatskim jezikom, ali su teško podneli neugodne posledice tog preuzimanja po svoj nacionalni identitet."

identified with the Eastern variant. Point 1 of the Novi Sad Agreement explicitly stated that the Western variant was based on the standard that had developed around Zagreb, whereas the Eastern variant was the standard that had evolved around Belgrade. This formula was flawed; whereas the ekavian dialect was contained mostly within the boundaries of the Socialist Republic of Serbia, and has pertained overwhelmingly to Serbs, the ijekavian dialect was spoken in four of the Socialist Republics, and included Croats, Montenegrins, Muslim Slavs, and Serbs. Moreover, this point diminished the place of other ijekavian centers of literary activity, such as Dubrovnik, Sarajevo, and Cetinje.

These flaws became of paramount importance in the 1960s as the Novi Sad Agreement was becoming undone, and the republics were being given greater autonomy. For the Croats, fears of Serbian ekavian domination of their ijekavian variant resurfaced, while the Serbs sought to include their ijekavian-speaking kin in Croatia and Bosnia-Herzegovina within a Serbian cultural and linguistic sphere. When the prominent Croat linguist Ljudevit Jonke claimed that the ijekavian-speaking Serbs of Croatia belonged to the "Croatian cultural sphere," his Serb counterpart, Pavle Ivić, rejecting the notion, countered that the linguistic and cultural rights of Croatian and Bosnian Serbs had to be respected.[34] As discussed in Greenberg (1996: 404) this concern for the identity of the Croatian and Bosnian Serbs was a precursor to the nationalist rhetoric of the Serbian Academy's Memorandum and the uprising of the Croatian Serbs in 1990–5. Moreover, it was the driving force for Serb linguists' further documentation of the Serb ijekavian dialects within the ethnically mixed regions of Croatia and Bosnia-Herzegovina.

The increase in linguistic autonomy of the republics was affirmed in the 1974 Yugoslav Constitution, further undermining the Novi Sad Agreement. Article 171 of the Constitution recognized the right of each Yugoslav constituent people/ nation to use its own language at the republican and provincial levels. As a result, the Socialist Republics of Croatia, Bosnia-Herzegovina, and Montenegro declared their own "standard linguistic idioms" in their territories, yielding a unified language with three republican standard idioms alongside the Serbian (Eastern) standard variant. To complicate matters, the three republican idioms were all based on the Neo-Štokavian/ijekavian dialect type.

The final phase of the debates surrounding ijekavian is still ongoing. This dialect is currently considered to be at the core of the Bosnian, Croatian, and Montenegrin successor languages to Serbo-Croatian, and is one of the two official pronunciations of the Serbian language. Thus, while the unified Yugoslav state broke apart along the inter-republican borders, these borders have never corresponded to those of the various Štokavian sub-dialects, or the ethnic affiliations of the local populations. The nature of these contemporary claims

---

[34] Cf. Jonke 1969: 236, and Ivić 1971[1986]: 221.

and counter-claims to the ijekavian dialect will be discussed in the succeeding chapters.[35]

2.3.3 Standard pronunciations, variants, or idioms

The linguistic controversies in Tito's Yugoslavia invoked several terms used to denote the competing official varieties of the unified language. These terms included "variant" ("varijanta"), "idiom" or "expression" ("izraz"), and "pronunciation" ("izgovor"). The *Concise Oxford English Dictionary* defines these terms as follows:

- *variant:* "differing in form or in details from the one named or considered";
- *idiom:* "language of a people or a country";
- *pronunciation:* "a person's way of pronouncing words."

In Yugoslavia, all three terms have referred to the spoken, rather than written norms of the language, and each term could be modified by the adjective "standard." Most official grammars and handbooks stemming from the 1954 Novi Sad Agreement referred to the unified language as the "Serbo-Croatian or Croato-Serbian literary language," with its two "standard variants." Point 1 of the Novi Sad Agreement confirmed that the primary division within the joint literary language was that of the two standard variants, Western and Eastern. The separate reference in Point 4 to the ekavian and ijekavian pronunciations indicated that the two variants did not overlap with the two pronunciations. Therefore, at least theoretically, each of the halves (variants) could be rendered by the two official pronunciations, i.e., the Western and Eastern variants could both be realized in either the ijekavian or ekavian pronunciations. Indeed, Božo Ćorić, the author of a Serbo-Croatian textbook, confirmed this interpretation, when he wrote that

[t]he Serbo-Croatian language has many dialects and on the level of the literary language it has these variants: Eastern and Western. The Eastern variant has two pronunciations: ekavian and ijekavian. This textbook is based on the Eastern variant of the Serbo-Croatian literary language in its ekavian version.[36]

Such a tolerance of the two pronunciations for the Serbs within their Eastern variant served the purpose of drawing the ijekavian-speaking Montenegrins and Western Serbs into the sphere of the Eastern variant. By contrast, the Croats had no reason or desire to accept a Western variant with two pronunciations, since

---

[35] Cf. especially 3.1.2, 3.4, 4.1, 5.2.1, 6.3.1, and 6.3.2.

[36] This citation is taken from Ćorić (1995: 7): "Srpskohrvatski jezik ima više dijalekata, a na nivou književnog jezika ima ove varijante: istočnu i zapadnu. Istočna varijanta ima dva izgovora—ekavski i ijekavski. U osnovi ovog udžbenika nalazi se istočna varijanta srpskohrvatskog književnog jezika i to njena ekavska realizacija."

TABLE 1.   The Unified Language from 1954 to 1974

1954	1974
Western variant	Croatian standard idiom/ Croato-Serbian literary language
Eastern variant	
Ekavian	Eastern variant-ekavian pronunciation/ Serbo-Croatian literary language
Ijekavian	Eastern variant-ijekavian pronunciation/ Serbo-Croatian literary language
Ijekavian	Montenegrin standard idiom/ Serbo-Croatian literary language
Western variant plus	Bosnia-Herzegovinian standard idiom/
Eastern variant/ijekavian	Serbo-Croatian literary language

such a move would have been tantamount to giving the ekavian pronunciation an official status within Croatia. Such a move had been resisted in the first Yugoslav state, and the Croats vehemently opposed any moves to ekavianize their standard variant, fearing that such a policy would have represented a capitulation to perceived Serbian hegemonistic designs.

The complex interrelations of variants and pronunciations adopted through the Novi Sad Agreement were realigned under the influence of the 1974 federal Yugoslav and republican constitutions, which further loosened both the Yugoslav federation and the Serbo-Croatian language union. These constitutions effectively replaced the notions of variants and pronunciations with that of republican, i.e., territorially based, "standard linguistic idioms."[37] Table 1 illustrates the transformations that occurred.

As Table 1 indicates, the 1974 Constitution sharpened the distinction between the spoken standards and the literary languages. The Croats and Montenegrins adopted ethnic terms to designate their own standard linguistic idioms, while the ethnic groups in Bosnia-Herzegovina accepted the neutral republican designation "Bosnia-Herzegovinian standard linguistic idiom." By contrast, the Serbs maintained strict adherence to the terminology of the Novi Sad Agreement. Avoiding all references to a "Serbian standard idiom," they retained the terms "Serbo-Croatian" and "Eastern variant." The Muslim Slavs and Montenegrins, who had been left out of both the 1850 Literary Agreement and the 1954 Novi Sad Agreement, seized upon the opportunity to legislate their own standard idioms in Bosnia-Herzegovina and Montenegro, respectively. The authorities in Bosnia-Herzegovina were keen to downplay any hints of the link between ethnic affiliation and the republican standard linguistic idiom. For

---

[37] The drafters of the Novi Sad Agreement had made no provisions for "idioms."

instance, Vujičić (1984: 387) supported the notion that "Bosnia and Herzegovina must remain widely receptive to all positive linguistic currents from all sides, and the 'status of a basic principle' must be given to language tolerance." He asserted that the Bosnia-Herzegovina standard linguistic idiom represented an amalgam of features from the Republic's three main groups: Muslims, Serbs, and Croats. However, upon analysis of the features he listed for this idiom, it becomes obvious that the main distinguishing features of this idiom came primarily from the speech of the Muslim Slav population.

Although the official language union survived until 1991, the first signs of the impending four-way split were manifested in the 1974 Constitution. The Novi Sad Agreement was based on a pluricentric language unity model limited to two main variants, the 1974 Constitution created two more competing centers in Bosnia-Herzegovina and Montenegro.

2.4   The writing on the wall: Alphabets and writing systems

The dialectal discrepancies within the Central South Slavic speech territory might have been reconcilable had there been an early consensus on the use of scripts for the joint language. When Serbs and Croats signed the 1850 Literary Agreement, they made no explicit provisions regarding the alphabet. Rather, they implied that both the Cyrillic and Latin scripts would be used, since the Latin alphabet was traditional among the believers in the Western (Catholic) faith, and the Cyrillic alphabet was traditional for the believers in the Eastern (Orthodox) faith (see Point 3 of the Literary Agreement in Appendix A). In the 1954 Novi Sad Agreement, this biscriptalism was made explicit. Despite the consensus in these two agreements, the language planners of the joint language have engaged in recurring alphabet conflicts (2.4.1). The alphabet issue is also intrinsically linked with the political considerations of spelling rules and orthography (2.4.2).

2.4.1   *A multiplicity of alphabets*

To illustrate the multiplicity of alphabets in the Central South Slavic speech territory, Brozović (1995: 29) claimed that Croatian is the only language in Europe that has had three different alphabets in its history.[38] These alphabets include Glagolitic, used up to the twelfth century, Glagolitic and Cyrillic, used between the twelfth and

---

[38] At least one other language in Europe has had more than one writing system, namely Azeri, which has been written with Arabic, Cyrillic, and Latin scripts.

fourteenth centuries, and the Latin script used since the fourteenth century. He went on to suggest that the Arabic script (*arabica* also known as *arebica*), used in Bosnia-Herzegovina, could also be included among writing systems used by Croats. However, by the time of the national awakenings of the nineteenth century, the Croats had long been using the Latin script, while the Serbs had long been writing their literary works in the Cyrillic script.[39]

Two main alphabet controversies had arisen by this point for the unified language: (1) Vuk's struggle with the Vojvodina Serbs over his reformed Cyrillic alphabet, and (2) the provisions of the Novi Sad Agreement designating the Cyrillic and Latin scripts as official in Tito's Yugoslavia. The Literary Agreement was decisive in determining the manner in which the Latin and Cyrillic alphabets would be adapted to the requirements of the sound system of the Štokavian dialect, as it formalized both Vuk's reforms of the Cyrillic alphabet, and Gaj's modifications of the Latin script. Vuk's reforms included the introduction of the new graphemes ħ (ć), ђ (d/dj), љ (lj), њ (nj), џ (dž), and *j*, and the simultaneous elimination of several graphemes inherited from Church Slavonic but no longer phonologically relevant, such as the grapheme representing the old *jat*, Gaj was responsible for the introduction of diacritics to render palatal consonants in a modified Latin script for a Croatian standard. These aspects of the reforms roused much controversy, especially among the Serbs.

Three years before signing the Literary Agreement, Daničić (1847: 1) expressed his concern about the divisions among Serbs regarding the alphabet. He complained that

for those of us who use the Slavic [Cyrillic] script, there are as many literary figures as there are writing systems. Vuk's is but one, which is observed more than the others, while the remainder are darkness; neither their name nor number is known.[40]

At that time Vuk's modified Cyrillic had been rejected outright by the Serbs of Vojvodina, for whom the Orthodox religious elite still wielded great influence. One of Vuk's primary opponents in Vojvodina was the prelate Stratimirović, who publicly denounced Vuk and his reforms of the Serbian language. Much of his scorn was aimed at Vuk's introduction of the Latin grapheme /j/ into the Cyrillic script.[41] He considered the introduction of *j* to

---

[39] The literary languages for the Serbs included the Serbian recension of Church Slavonic in the medieval Serbian Kingdom, Russian Church Slavonic in the sixteenth through eighteenth centuries, and Slaveno-Serbian from the mid-eighteenth century through the mid-nineteenth century.

[40] "U nas, koji pišemo slavenskijem slovima, koliko je književnika toliko je i pravopisa. Jedan je samo Vukov kojega se više njih drži, a ostalijeh je tma, niti im se zna broja ni imena."

[41] The Cyrillic alphabets in Serbia-Montenegro and Macedonia still include the grapheme *j*, whereas the Cyrillic scripts in Bulgaria, Russia, and Ukraine render this sonorant

be a concession to the Catholic West, and a threat to the Orthodox East. Was Vuk's real agenda to weaken the power of the Orthodox Church, or even worse, to make concessions to the rival Catholic Church? The Vojvodinian elite felt threatened by Vuk's rejection of the graphemes that had long been part of the Church Slavonic and Slaveno-Serbian literary traditions, including the symbols for the so-called "reduced vowels," which centuries earlier either had transformed into the vowel a, or were simply dropped. These symbols are still found in Russian and Bulgarian, but in these languages they maintain a linguistic function; by contrast, in Serbian these vowels had absolutely no function other than a symbolic one—they asserted the link of the Serbian people with the other Orthodox Slavs and with the medieval Church Slavonic literary tradition. Over time the Serbs not only embraced the reformed Cyrillic alphabet, but also began increasingly to use the Latin script. Even in the nineteenth century, Daničić (1847: 1) suggested that the Serbs felt equally comfortable with both the Latin and Cyrillic scripts. Today in Serbia's urban centers both scripts are widely used, despite the efforts of some Serb nationalists to curb the use of the Latin script after 1991.

In Tito's Yugoslavia, the Croats used the alphabet issue for purposes of contrastive self-identification. In describing the differences between Serbs and Croats, Spalatin (1961: 3) gave prominence to the difference in scripts. He equated Serbs with Cyrillic/Greek Orthodoxy, and Croats with Latin/Roman Catholicism. The Novi Sad Agreement was explicit in its mandating the compulsory study of both scripts in schools throughout the country (see Point 3 of the Novi Sad Agreement in Appendix A). As Hammel (2000) pointed out, however, "[i]n Communist Yugoslavia, everyone who could read and write Cyrillic could also read and write Latinic, but the reverse was not always true, even though both Cyrillic and Latinic were taught in the schools." Many Croats resented being forced to learn Cyrillic, and considered it to be further evidence of Serbia's quest for domination over Croatian culture.[42] The Serbs believed that the Croats never enforced the provisions on the study of the Cyrillic script in their republic, lamenting that the Serbs of Croatia lacked the ability to read the Cyrillic script.[43] In Bosnia-Herzegovina, the population had to master both scripts, since many of the publications appeared in both alphabets, and the daily

consonant with ū or in the graphemes (Russian) e, ё, ю, я which in some positions represents *j* + vowel.

[42] I met numerous Croats in the late 1980s and early 1990s who claimed that they had forgotten how to read Cyrillic, or that they never studied it well enough to gain proficiency.

[43] Cf. Pantić (1995: 133) for the relevant passage in the 1986 "Memorandum" of the Serbian Academy of Sciences and Arts.

paper *Oslobodjenje* used to publish its newspapers with Latin and Cyrillic on alternate pages.[44]

Ultimately, none of the signatories to either the Literary Agreement or the Novi Sad Agreements were willing to compromise on the issue of the alphabets, and the unified language was born in 1850 on the basis of a single dialect, but with the two distinct alphabets. Such a situation resembles that of Hindi and Urdu, which were also based on a similar dialect, but employ two different alphabets.[45] However, unlike Hindi and Urdu, which became official languages of two different states, the Serbo-Croatian language emerged as a primary language in a single state. The unwillingness of both sides to compromise on the use of alphabets constituted a major impediment to the success of the joint language.

2.4.2   Spell-bound: Clashes over spelling rules

Early in the process of the implementation of a standard language, language planners needed to agree on their approach to orthographic or spelling rules. The possible approaches included: (1) an etymological writing system, which would tolerate archaic spellings inherited from earlier literary traditions or pronunciations; (2) a morphological writing system, preserving the integrity of roots, prefixes, suffixes, and grammatical endings, even if these elements may vary in their pronunciation depending on the word environment or the stress; and (3) a phonological system, whereby each distinctive sound of the language is represented by a single phoneme. In some languages, hybrid approaches are possible. Thus, while the writing system of the Macedonian language is mostly phonological, it also includes some rules that are typical of languages with the morphological approach.[46] By contrast, the Bulgarian and Russian writing systems combine elements of the etymological and morphological writing

---

[44] While Bosnian Muslim writers had employed a modified Arabic script during Ottoman times, there have been no credible calls to revive such a writing system for the new Bosnian standard. According to a recent textbook of the Bosnian language for foreigners, the Bosnian language may still be written in either the Latin or Cyrillic scripts (cf. Pelešić-Muminović 1997).

[45] According to Ford (2001: 40), "in Hindi and Urdu the use of the Arabic and Devanagari scripts...carried enormous symbolic power, with each alphabet deeply rooted in the religion and culture of its respective group."

[46] For instance, -*v* is the morphological ending of the Macedonian first person singular aorist tense, and is rendered in Macedonian Cyrillic as −в, even though it is pronounced as a devoiced consonant −*f* (-j). When such combinations or morphological and phonological principles are strictly observed, some linguists have spoken of "morpho-phonological" approaches to spelling; cf. Brozović (1995).

systems.[47] Before the establishment of the joint Serbo-Croatian language in 1850, the Serbs and Croats had had divergent approaches on writing systems, and despite their joint adoption of a phonological spelling system, the two sides never fully became unified on this issue.

In the Croat lands, where regional vernacular literatures had thrived, orthographic chaos prevailed,[48] whereas in the Serbian domains, the pre-Vukovian literary languages employed etymological approaches to writing. In the 1830s Gaj's priority was to simplify the orthography for Croatian writers, primarily for his native Kajkavian dialect (cf. Banac 1984: 217). He hoped that his reformed orthography with the diacritic marks taken from Czech would ultimately be adopted by all Croats. Simultaneously, Vuk and Daničić were defining a new phonological writing system, as they embraced the vernacular as the basis of a new standard language. They were keen to uproot the conservative and etymological writing system of Slaveno-Serbian, which was incomprehensible to the common citizen. For them, the adoption of the principle of "Write the way you speak and read the way it is written ("Piši kao što govoriš, i čitaj kao je napisano") was an integral part of their language ideology. Daničić (1847: 6) expressed this ideology by stating that "the best writing system" ("najbolji pravopis") is the one in which you can write with each letter the way you speak one sound after the next. Any other approach to writing is in his view "pitiful" ("žalostan"). He blasted the etymological approach, which in his view is a writing system of no value since in it "words are written differently from how they are spoken only because of roots... [and this] very notion is crazy." Ironically, Vuk and Daničić found their strongest opposition to the phonological orthographic rules from fellow Serbs in Vojvodina and Serbia, rather than from the Croat Illyrians. Belić (1949: 50) asserted that the "all-powerful prelate" Metropolitan Stratimirović of Vojvodina had contempt for "all... who dared to come near Vuk's orthography," and that he "went out of his way on matters concerning the defense of our nationhood and Orthodoxy from enemy attacks. And Vuk's orthography was considered to be just that."[49]

Initially rejected by his fellow Serbs, Vuk's orthographic system was praised outside of the Serbian principality and Vojvodina. The notable Slovene intellectual, Jernej Kopitar, was a staunch supporter of Vuk's reforms; the Germans,

---

[47] Prior to the 1917 reform of the Russian Cyrillic alphabet and the 1945 reform of the Bulgarian Cyrillic alphabet, both languages observed an etymological writing system for their respective standards.

[48] According to Brozović (1995: 28), the Croats had a long tradition of a phonological writing system, and only in the nineteenth century did some writers opt for an etymological one.

[49] The whole passage in Belić's account is as follows: "svi drugi koji bi se usudili prići Vukovoj ortografiji stajali su pod gnevom svemoćnoga prelata koji nije birao sredstva kada se ticalo odbrane naše narodnosti i pravoslavlja od neprijateljskih nasrtaja. A Vukova je ortografija tako smatrana."

Poles, and Russians were also favorably disposed towards Vuk's efforts. The Russian Tsar was so impressed with Vuk's reforms that he granted him a pension (Belić 1949: 54). Having received such a hostile reception among the Vojvodina Serbs, Vuk was pleased to find allies among the Croat Illyrians and the Montenegrins. The latter supported Vuk's choice of the Southern dialect as the basis of the literary language, and published his book of Serbian proverbs in Cetinje in 1836. It was only in the 1860s that Vuk's phonological writing system was accepted in Vojvodina and Serbia, some fifty years after it had first been conceived.

Under the fascist regime of Pavelić in Croatia (1941–5), the phonological writing system for the Croatian language was replaced by a strict etymological spelling (cf. Cipra and Klaić 1944). This switch away from the phonological system revealed a bias among Croat extremists. These individuals believed that only through an etymological writing system would Croatia regain its purity and authenticity, cleansing itself of the unwanted Serbian elements. After the establishment of Tito's Yugoslavia, the reunited Serbo-Croatian language was given back its phonological orthographic conventions. However, the perception remained among extreme nationalists in Croatia that this writing system was a Serbian import. After 1991, extreme nationalist legislators, such as Vice Vukojević, sought to pass legislation "restoring" the Croatian etymological writing system (cf. 5.3.2). Brozović (1995: 28) dismissed Vukojević as "an amateur" linguist who erroneously believed the phonological writing system to be "Serbian" and the etymological writing system to be purely "Croatian." He argued that prior to the nineteenth century, the opposite had been the case. Extreme nationalists in Serbia seemed better informed on the history of writing systems, advocating a return to a pre-Vukovian etymological writing system for the Serbian language (cf. 3.2).

In Tito's Yugoslavia Vuk was celebrated as a national hero, and became a symbol for Serb–Croat unity. Belić (1949) helped write the official Communist view on Vuk and his writing system. He spoke of Vuk's fervor and resolve as he fought a battle to bring literacy to the Yugoslav peoples, and how his actions helped cement the concept of "brotherhood and unity." In the same breath, Belić referred to the Croats as the "Western half of our people" and "our brothers of Roman faith." It is not surprising, therefore, that given this glorification of Vuk in Yugoslavia, the Croats after 1991 considered Vuk to be an agent of Serbian nationalism and the hero of Serbian linguistic hegemony. Since he was a Serb, his orthography was suspect even though his arch-enemies in the 1820s and 1830s had been the Serbs of Vojvodina.

As seen here, even the issue of spelling and orthographic norms was highly politicized during the period of language unity. Initially, the reforms of the Serbian alphabet and orthographic rules caused much consternation among conservative elements in Serbian society. Later on, these approaches became identified with the Serbian language, and some Croats sought to distance themselves from the Vukovian principles. Even after the 1954 Novi Sad Agreement and the publication of the 1960 *Pravopis*, the two sides could not agree fully on orthographic conventions. Thus, the future 'I will' would be written in the Western variant *bit ću*, while in the Eastern variant it was written as *biću*, even though in both variants the forms were pronounced identically. Such discrepancies suggest that both sides were keen on maintaining these minor differences, and resisted whenever possible any attempts to forge a true orthographic union of the Serbo-Croatian language.

As discussed in Chapters 3–6, Vuk Karadžić's legacy has figured prominently in the debates over the formation of the new successor languages to Serbo-Croatian. His writings have continued to inspire some post-1991 Serb linguists, who have found refuge in the literal interpretation of his ideas on orthographic matters (cf. 3.2). Some contemporary Bosniac, Croat, and Montenegrin language planners have viewed Vuk's phonological writing system suspiciously, considering it part of Vuk's agenda to assimilate non-Serbs into the Serbian people (cf. 4.2, 5.1.1, and 6.4).

2.5 Vocabulary: A reflection of divergent approaches to identity

Most observers of the evolution of the unified language have noted the centrality of lexical differences between what was traditionally the "Western" and "Eastern" variants of the language. Both the Serbs and Croats set out to base the joint literary language on principles reminiscent of those Fishman (1972[1989]: 111ff.) described as "stressed authenticity... [i.e.,] [n]ationalism's stress on authenticity-oriented belief, attitude, and behavior." In his view such stressed authenticity "may well be crucial in modern and modernizing mass-societies in order to reach, influence, and activate large numbers of individuals who actually lead quite different and separate daily lives and who only interact with a very small proportion of the total community." However, in the nineteenth century the Croats and Serbs had divergent approaches on how this authenticity should be manifested in the joint literary language. The Croats followed a policy of purism in issues of vocabulary, while the Serbs were largely concerned with remaining true to the vernacular language, and accepted mostly words found in the spoken dialects. For the Croats, purism has meant the introduction of often archaic, obsolete, or newly coined "native Croatian" words, while for the Serbs the achievement of authenticity was possible through the rejection of any words that were considered to be artificial, bookish, or radically divergent from words used in ordinary speech. These divergent approaches are discussed below in terms of: (1) the Croat embrace of purism, often at the expense of internationalisms or perceived Serbianisms; (2) The Serb preference for lexicon based on vernacular; and (3) divergence regarding borrowings from other languages.

2.5.1   Croatian purism

"[T]he enlightenment of nationalist purism in language planning...proceeds along many well-trodden paths: the differentiation between ethnic core and non-ethnic periphery, between technical and non-technical, the differentiation between preferred and non-preferred sources of borrowing, and, finally, the appeal to common usage among the masses" (Fishman 1972: 75). The Croats have been keen on ensuring that their language maintain elements of their own "ethnic core" even as they embarked on the joint language project with the Serbs. However, unlike Vuk and Daničić, the Illyrians did not seek inspiration for the new standard in rural dialects. Rather, as Thomas (1988: 70) noted, their movement was urban based, and since many components of the vocabulary in the areas of science, technology, arts, and humanistic studies were absent from the vernacular speech of that time, they were borrowed from other linguistic sources. Furthermore, Thomas suggested that the purism promoted by the Illyrians constituted: (1) a reaction to the significant number of German borrowings present in the Zagreb Kajkavian dialect; (2) a desire to emulate the Czech and Slovak models for language revival;[50] and (3) a means for introducing new words not associated with a specific region, so that they could be accepted by all Southern Slavs (cf. also 2.3.2).

Ultimately, the need to discover a Croatian language purer than that spoken in Zagreb motivated Gaj and his followers to choose the Southern Štokavian dialect as the basis of the new Croatian language in 1836. The Dubrovnik Štokavian dialect had been the source from which the most prestigious Croatian vernacular literature emerged during the sixteenth and seventeenth centuries. As Auty (1958: 398) has noted, the "[old literary] language of Dubrovnik...strongly affected the two foremost poets of the Illyrian movement, Ivan Mažuranić and Stanko Vraz." For these poets, the source of inspiration for the new Croatian standard was the Dubrovnik literature. By choosing the Dubrovnik dialect, these literary figures extracted and revived archaic forms from the Dubrovnik literature that had flowered some three hundred years earlier. These forms ensured a continuity of the Croatian literary language, and enhanced the prestige of the revitalized Croatian standard in the nineteenth century. The literary figures followed with this policy in the footsteps of Dobrovský, who revived Czech, and Kopitar, who codified the modern Slovene language (Auty 1973). Both the Czechs and the Slovenes had had vernacular literatures and grammars from the time of the Reformation, and for both languages codifiers have employed puristic principles in the development of new literary standards.[51]

---

[50] Croatian borrowed several of the Czech neologisms based on pure Slavic roots, including *časopis* 'journal', *pravnik* 'lawyer', and *okolnost* 'circumstance'.

[51] In contemporary standard Slovene—by contrast to Croatian or Serbian—puristic forms have been introduced for grammatical terminology, including *velevnik* 'imperative',

The period of extreme purism in Croatia was at the time of the Croatian Fascist state (1941–5), when Croatian was declared a separate language from Serbian. The regime embarked on a campaign both to eliminate from the Croatian language all perceived Serbian elements, and to ethnically cleanse Croatia of its Serbian population. In addition, many words of foreign origin were replaced by Croatian ones. The new words were either invented outright or revived from early Croatian literature. New Croatian words were added, such as *munjovoz* (literally 'lightning vehicle') replacing the foreign *tramvaj* 'tram', *osposoba* (instead of *kvalifikacija* 'qualification'), and *novačiti* 'to recruit, to conscript', rather than *regrutirati*.

In Tito's Yugoslavia the Croats abandoned the extreme purism of the fascist regime. Nevertheless, the Western variant of the joint literary language maintained distinctively Croat lexical items, when the Eastern variant would employ internationalisms or words of foreign origin. Examples included: (1) the native Croatian names for the months, e.g. *siječanj* 'January', *veljača* 'February', *ožujak* 'March' (vs. the Eastern forms *januar, februar, mart*); (2) words of Slavic origin in the Western variant as opposed to words of foreign origin in the Eastern variant, e.g., *tisuća* 'thousand' (vs. Eastern *hiljada*, of Greek origin), *tajnik* 'secretary' (vs. Eastern *sekretar*, of Latin origin), *susjed* 'neighbor' (vs. Eastern *komšija*, of Turkish origin), *rajčica* 'tomato' (vs. Eastern *paradajz*, of Germanic origin),[52] *tisak* 'press' (vs. Eastern *štampa*, of Romance origin), and *nogomet* 'football' (vs. Eastern *fudbal*, borrowed from English). In lexical items relating to the joint Yugoslav state, the two variants often employed identical administrative terms, although in some instances minor phonetic differences were observed, e.g., *lična karta* 'identity card', *pasoš* 'passport', *ambasada* 'embassy', *općina* (Western)/ *opština* (Eastern) 'county, municipality', *vijeće* (Western)/*veće* (Eastern) 'council', *jugoslavenski* (Western)/*jugoslovenski (Eastern)* 'Yugoslav,'" and *sekreterijat* 'secretariat'. After the break-up of Yugoslavia, the Croatian authorities replaced many such terms with forms consisting of South Slavic roots, which they considered to be native Croatian forms. Often these words were either neologisms or formerly obsolete words, including *osobna iskaznica* 'identity card', *putovnica* 'passport', and *veleposlanstvo* 'embassy'. Under Tudjman's regime (1990–9), a hypersensitivity to perceived Serbianisms and otherwise "non-Croatian" forms was prevalent. As a result, prescriptive manuals and dictionaries appeared with the aim of educating the public to speak proper Croatian. For instance, one

---

nedoločnik 'infinitive', and *glasoslovje* 'phonology' as opposed to Croatian *imperativ, infinitiv, fonologija*.

[52] The word for 'tomato' in both variants is based on the German form *Paradeis*, which corresponds to English paradise. In Vienna and eastern portions of Austria *Paradeis* has replaced standard German *Tomate*. The Serbs took the word directly from German, rendering it by *paradajz*, while the Croats preferred a Slavic translation of the German form (*raj*), followed by a Slavic diminutive suffix -*čica*, i.e. *rajčica* (cf. Czech *rajče*).

author exhorted readers to use Croatian forms, including *središte* 'center', which he considered to be proper Croatian, rather than the internationalism *centar* found in Serbian and other Slavic languages (cf. Russian *centr*, Macedonian *centar*).[53] In one speech Tudjman himself used the Serbian form *srećan* 'happy' rather than the Croatian form *sretan*. The Croatian opposition press found this slip of the tongue to be nothing less than scandalous, and was quick to report on how the state-run media carefully edited the president's blunderous speech in subsequent reports.

Edwards (1985: 27) argued that puristic tendencies in language implementation may predate language nationalism by several hundred years. Such was the case with the establishment of the Italian and French language academies in the sixteenth century with their goals of ensuring the purity of their respective languages. For the Croats, however, purism was inspired by the romanticism of the nineteenth century, and the national awakening of a people under foreign domination since the early twelfth century. While extreme nationalists have blatantly flaunted their puristic credentials, mainstream Croat language planners forwarded a moderately puristic agenda during the time of the joint language, and under nationalist pressures in 1991 reverted to more aggressive puristic interventions.

2.5.2   The supremacy of the vernacular for the Serbs

Once Vuk Karadžić's reforms triumphed throughout the Serbian lands in the 1860s, Serb language planners began consistently supporting Vukovian principles concerning the use of vocabulary. Their emphasis has been on incorporating words from the popular language into the standard, i.e., on deriving the vocabulary from below, rather than legislating it from above. Unlike the Croats, the Serbs had not had a tradition of literature written in the vernacular dialects; rather, they had a well-developed oral tradition consisting of epic and lyric poems, and a large corpus of folk tales. Vuk was instrumental in collecting these works of oral literature, and published numerous volumes using his reformed Cyrillic orthography.

Many of the language planners that followed Vuk did their utmost to adhere to Vuk's practices regarding vocabulary. Belić was a strong supporter of Vuk's reforms in Serbia, and influenced the development of the Eastern standard

---

[53] In the same manual, the author insists that Croats should say *Europa* for 'Europe', as opposed to the Serbian form *Evropa*, which due to the use of –v– is classified as a Greek borrowing that spread into Serbian and Czech (cf. Tanocki 1994: 26). According to Bašić (2001b: 91), some Croat linguists have rejected such prescriptivism, and have asserted that the doublets *Europa/Evropa* should be tolerated. For a more detailed discussion of this issue, cf. 5.2.2 and 5.3.

beginning in the early 1900s in the Kingdom of Serbia, and lasting through thefirst and second Yugoslav states. In the second edition of his orthographic manual, Belić deferred to Vuk for decisions on "standard" or "colloquial" usage. Thus, for vocabulary items containing the velar-fricative *h*, he affirmed:

The *h* is not pronounced among a large portion of our people. And up to 1836 Vuk Karadžić did not write it in his works. Then he began using it, having found it in popular use in the southwest regions (in Dubrovnik, Boka Kotorska, Eastern Montenegro), and from that time, the sound *h* has become an integral part of our sound system.[54]

In this manual, Belić's notion of "our people" included Serbs, Croats, Muslim Slavs, and Montenegrins, and even though most speakers had lost the phoneme /h/, it was still common in the areas from which Vuk took his standard. Belić was eager to keep with the spirit of Vuk's reforms, even if this choice meant including a phoneme that was frequently lost in the vernacular. Throughout the introductory sections of his orthographic manual, Belić's references to Vuk were juxtaposed with his own decisions regarding correct spelling and orthographic rules.

2.5.3 Divergent attitudes towards foreign borrowings

The inhabitants of the Central South Slavic speech territory came into contact with many peoples of non-Slavic origin as the result of foreign invasions, cultural ties, and migrations. The Croats lived under foreign rule for over 800 years, while the Serbs came under Ottoman Turkish rule from the fourteenth through the nineteenth century. German borrowings were more frequent in the territories formerly under Austro-Hungarian rule, while Turkish borrowings had greater frequency in regions that fell within the Ottoman domain.[55]

Some borrowings reflect the differences in religious affiliations of the Central South Slavic speakers. Hence the Catholic Croats tended to borrow religious and cultural terminology from Latin, the Orthodox Serbs looked to Greek, Russian, and Church Slavonic for such terms, and the Islamicized Slavs borrowed from

---

[54] (1930: 45): "U velikom delu našega naroda h se ne izgovara. I Vuk Karadžić ga nije pisao u svojim delima do 1836 godine. Tada ga je, našavši ga u narodnoj upotrebi u jugozapadnim krajevima (u Dubrovniku, Boci Kotorskoj i istočnoj Crnoj Gori), počeo upotrebljavati, i od toga je vremena taj glas postao sastavni deo našeg književnog glasovnog sistema."

[55] The influence of German can be seen not only in loanwords, but also in calques, including *pravopis* 'orthography' (cf. German *Rechtschreibung*), *stoljeće* 'century' (cf. German *Jahrhundert*), *pregled* 'survey' (cf. German *Ueberblick*), and *savjetodavac* 'counselor' (cf. *Ratgeber*).

Turkish or Arabic. For instance, in the rendering of proper names, the Croats often phonetically adapted forms from a Latin source, while the Serbs tended to adhere to phonological patterns typical of Greek. This phenomenon can be seen in the use of /b/ among Croats, as opposed to /v/ among Serbs, e.g., (Western) *Abraham* 'Abraham', *Betlehem* 'Bethlehem' vs. (Eastern) *Avram, Vitlejem* (Guberina 1940: 171 and Brozović 1995: 29). Otherwise, some features typical of Greek have spread to the Serb speech territory, but not to that of the Croats. One such feature is found in the verbal suffixes added to roots borrowed from other languages. Thus, the Serbs frequently admit the verbal suffix *–isa–* of Greek origin, while the Croats use the suffix *–ira–* of German origin, e.g., (Serbian) *formulisati* 'to formulate', *definisati* 'to define', *afirmisati* 'to affirm', and *distribuisati* 'to distribute', as opposed to (Croatian) *formulirati, definirati, afirmirati, distribuirati*.[56] Moreover, some of the so-called Balkan linguistic features typical of Greek, Romanian, Arumanian, Albanian, Bulgarian, Macedonian, and the dialects of Southeastern Serbia have crept into the Eastern variant and the new Serbian standard, but were absent from the Western (Croatian) variant of the joint language. These features include the loss of the infinitive, the use of the dative personal pronoun to denote possession, and the spread of a tense similar to the English present perfect formed by the auxiliary verb *imati* 'to have' and a past passive participle.[57]

Given the long period of Serbian/Croatian language unity, some borrowings spread from the Eastern variant into the Western one and vice versa. Examples include some Greek, Turkish, and Latin borrowings adopted by the Croats through the mediation of Serbs, Muslim Slavs, and Montenegrins, e.g., *hiljada* 'thousand' (a Greek loanword),[58] *hajde* 'come on!', a Turkism,[59] and the Latin names for the

---

[56] According to Radić (2002), internationalisms with the suffix in *–isa–* can be found in increasing numbers in the Serbian press since 1991. His examples include *da ispolemišu* 'that they polemicize' and *I Srbin se kinematografiše* 'And a Serb engages in cinematography' to illustrate the suffix's increased frequency. Otherwise, Serbs have used Turkish nominal suffixes for the most recent foreign borrowings. In particular, the suffixes *–džija* and *–lija* spread to several terms from the post-1991 period, often marked for "ironic and humorous" meanings, e.g., *nato-trupadžija* 'a person belonging to the Nato troops', *režimlija* 'regime supporter', and *dosmanlija* 'member of the Democratic Opposition of Serbia (DOS) political alliance'.

[57] Ibid. Radić's examples of the so-called "ima-perfect" include: *Banka ima plasirano 400 miliona* 'The Bank has placed 400 million', *Omladinska zadruga ima učlanjeno toliko članova* 'The youth organization has enlisted this many members'.

[58] Tanocki (1994: 13) urged Croats to abandon this form, even though it is frequent in the dialects of Eastern Slavonia. He insisted that this form is "not Croatian," and represents a marker of an "Orthodox [Serbian] identity." For further discussion, cf. 5.2.2.

[59] On the status of Turkish loanwords in Croatia today, cf. 5.2.2. Some typical Turkisms in Croatian include the exhortative particle *hajde* 'Move! Come on! Get on with it!', *čizma* 'boot', *šal* 'shawl', and *džep* 'pocket'.

TABLE 2. Lexical borrowings in ethnically mixed Southern Baranja (Croatia) based on Sekereš 1977

	German words	*Hungarian words*	*Turkish words*
Serbs	105	45	80
Croats	100	110	85

months of the year.[60] Similarly, borrowings adopted through German, such as *šnajderica* 'seamstress' and *telefonirati* 'to telephone' probably spread into the Serbian speech territory through Croatian. Often the Western and Eastern variants borrowed nearly identical forms; however, intentional borrowing or not, the two variants would exhibit minute differences in suffixation or phonetic variation. Examples of phonetic differences include: (Western) *šport* 'sports', *filozofija* 'philosophy', *milijun* 'million', *aktualan* 'contemporary', *konzul* 'consul', *demokracija* 'democracy', *španjolski* 'Spanish'; (Eastern) *sport, filosofija, milion, aktuelan, konsul, demokratija, španski*.[61] In addition, differences in suffixation are frequent in nouns for which the feminine forms were derived from the masculine, e.g., (Western) *kolegica* 'female colleague', *studentica* 'female student', *direktorica* 'female director', but (Eastern) *koleginica, studentkinja, direktorka*.[62]

Many of these differences were blurred in the dialects of Serbs, Croats, Muslim Slavs, and Montenegrins. For instance, in the Southern Baranja region of Croatia prior to the 1991 Serb-Croat war, Serbs and Croats lived in ethnically mixed towns and villages, and shared many dialectal features (cf. Greenberg 1998). As seen in Table 2, the main lexical differences in the dialects of the ethnic Serbs and Croats of that region were manifested in the number of Hungarian words each group borrowed; otherwise, the Serbs and Croats borrowed roughly the same number of words from German and Turkish (cf. Sekereš 1977: 369).

Such statistics would not satisfy prescriptivist linguists in either Zagreb or Belgrade after the break-up of the unified language; the Croats have tended to view Turkish borrowings negatively, while the nationalists among the Serbs have made known their bias against German loanwords.[63] Since 1991, political, social,

---

[60] These forms occur mostly in Croatian colloquial and dialectal speech.

[61] According to Guberina (1940: 171), the Western form *filozofija* reflects a phonetic rendering of the original Greek form, whereas the Eastern form *filosofija* better corresponds to the original Greek pronunciation. In Macedonian the preferred form after 1991 has also been *filosofija*, rather than *filozofija*, which had been common in Tito's Yugoslavia.

[62] In standard Serbian *direktorica* is also possible; in using the Google search engine, I discovered several newspaper articles from Serbia in which both *direktorka* and *direktorica* appeared intermittently in the same article.

and cultural considerations have guided many of the divergent choices regarding lexical borrowings among the four successor languages. As each successor language has developed independently, the language planners have looked to past practices for some of their preferences, such as the Croatian tradition of purism, the Bosniac preference for lexemes of Turkish/Arabic origin, and the Serbian incorporation of elements from the vernacular into the standard language. Even before 1991, these lexical preferences were significant, reflecting differences in corpus planning particularly in the development of the Western and Eastern standards of the joint language.

2.6   The turbulent history of the language union: A chronology

In the preceding sections the history of the unified language was treated thematically; what follows is a chronology of the main developments in the history of the unified language (see Table 3). Such a chronology presents the history of the joint literary language in a sequential and concise manner.

This chronology puts in doubt recent assertions that the unified language never truly existed, or had been imposed against the will of its speakers. The 1850 Literary Agreement was not imposed by the Austro-Hungarian regime, nor by any other regime. It was not universally accepted among Serbs and Croats, but gained the support of influential Serb and Croat linguists, literary figures, and politicians. From the late nineteenth century up to the 1920s, the unified language evolved without much controversy. However, the years 1930–41 were characterized by a breakdown of ethnic relations, shaking the foundations of the joint language. The chauvinist ideology of the Croat fascist regime quashed the joint language between 1941 and 1945, and thereafter the Serbs would associate a separate Croatian language with one of the darkest periods in Serb–Croat relations. Under Tito language union flowed as a continuation of the official Communist ideology of "brotherhood and unity." In retrospect such an ideology has been interpreted as "imposed" or "Bolshevik" (cf. Bašić 2001*b*: 87). However, such a policy—strictly imposed or not—received the support of Serbs, Croats, Muslim Slavs, and Montenegrins in the Yugoslav League of Communists. It broke down in the 1960s when centrifugal forces resurfaced, and the Yugoslav republics sought to loosen the bonds of the Federation.

The authors of a 1999 handbook on correct usage in the new Croatian language refrained from addressing whether a joint Serbo-Croatian written or

---

[63] Marojević (1995: 79) accused mainstream Serb linguists of maintaining a pro-Central European, pro-German prejudice, at the expense of the Serbian-Orthodox heritage.

TABLE 3. A sketch of the history of the joint literary language

Date	Development
1818	Publication of Vuk Karadžić's Serbian Dictionary
1836	Ljudevit Gaj chose the Dubrovnik-type Štokavian/ijekavian dialect for the Croats
1850	Literary Agreement signed in Vienna
1852	Publication of the second edition of Vuk's Dictionary
1860s	Vuk's orthography gained acceptance in Serbia
1867	Establishment of Yugoslav Academy of Sciences and Arts in Zagreb; Budmani published first grammar referring to language as "Serbo-Croatian"
1886	Founding of the Serbian Royal Academy of Sciences and Arts in Belgrade
1899	Publication of the first edition of Maretić's Grammar for the joint language in Zagreb
1913	Jovan Skerlić suggested a compromise on writing system and dialect to create a true language unity
1918	The Kingdom of Serbs, Croats, and Slovenes founded
1929	King Alexander renamed the country the Kingdom of Yugoslavia Publication of Belić's prescriptive orthographic manual
1941	Croatia, as a Nazi-puppet state, declared a separate Croatian language and introduced an etymological writing system
1945	Tito's victorious partisans restored language unity
1954	Signing of the Novi Sad Agreement reaffirming language unity with two equal variants (Western and Eastern)
1960	Publication of an orthographic manual for the joint literary language
1967	Dissemination of the "Declaration on the name and position of the Croatian literary language"
1970–1	Circulation of Dalibor Brozović's "Ten Theses of the Croatian Literary Language" and publication of his monograph *Standardni jezik* at the height of the Croatian Spring
1974	New Yugoslav constitution guaranteed language rights in all republics; new standard linguistic idioms adopted in Bosnia-Herzegovina, Croatia, and Montenegro
1990	Under Tudjman, Croatian became the official language in the republic of Croatia
1991	The official break-up of the unified language into Serbian and Croatian
1992	The codification of Bosnian and Montenegrin standards gained momentum

literary standard existed. They were, however, emphatic in their assertion that no unified spoken language could ever have existed:

On the characteristics of the Croatian language, and in general on the relationship between Croatian and Serbian we will say only the following: the Serbo-Croatian or Croato-Serbian language did not exist and does not exist as a concrete, spontaneous language, that is, the Serbo-Croatian or Croato-Serbian language did not exist and does not exist as a mother tongue, or more precisely, the Serbo-Croatian or Croato-Serbian language did not exist and does not exist as a standard language. What existed and exists are two concrete and spontaneous [standard languages], two mother tongues, two standard languages, Croatian and Serbian.[64]

How can these authors explain why many expatriates from the former Yugoslavia still believe that their native language is Serbo-Croatian? Can this belief be explained away as the results of Communist brainwashing, or a symptom of nostalgia for Tito's Yugoslavia (so-called "Yugo-nostalgia")? For whom is any standardized language truly "native"? Is it not common for standard languages to depart markedly from both rural and urban dialects?

The Serbs have rejected Croat claims that the unified language never truly existed. Rather, they have lamented the fate of the unified language during Tito's Yugoslavia, partially blaming themselves for bending over backwards to preserve the semblance of unity, even though this unity had been severely eroded. Brborić (1996: 26) complained about the erosion of unity, claiming that

> after 1945, [the unified language] became fragmented both in the way it was called and in its norms: it was called Serbian and Croatian, Croatian or Serbian, Serbo-Croatian and Croato-Serbian, Serbo-Croatian actually Croato-Serbian, Serbian or Croatian (most rarely), officially and unofficially, depending on when and where, although in SR Croatia between 1972 and 1990 both officially, i.e., in "public use" and for the [Croatian] Serbs the assimilative name "Croatian literary language" was in effect.[65]

Hence, the Serbs have admitted that they had virtually negotiated the unified language out of existence, and that for all practical purposes it had ceased to exist after the 1971 Croatian Spring and the 1974 Yugoslav Constitution. In such an analysis, the language break-up in 1991–3 was nothing more than a formality, since all sides had given up on unity in the 1970s. Nevertheless, during this period, while the strength of the internal identity weakened precipitously, the external identity remained strong, and observers from outside ex-Yugoslavia maintained the stance that Serbo-Croatian was a single unified language. This stance forced members of the four rival ethnic groups to continue certain collaborations, especially for international projects, such as the Common Slavic

---

[64] Barić et al. (1999: 9): "O posebnosti hrvatskog jezika i uopće o odnosu izmedju hrvatskog i srpskog jezika reći ćemo samo ovoliko: nije postojao i ne postoji srpskohrvatski ili hrvatskosrpski jezik kao konkretan i spontan jezik, tj. nije postojao i ne postoji srpskohrvatski ili hrvatskosrpski jezik kao materinski jezik ili još točnije nije postojao i ne postoji srpskohrvatski ili hrvatskosrpski jezik kao standardni jezik. Što je postojalo i što postoji to su dva konkretna i spontana, dva materinska, dva standardna jezika: hrvatski i srpski."

[65] "Objedinjeni jezik, posle 1945. godine, razjedinjavao se i u nazivanju i u normiranju: zvao se srpski i hrvatski, hrvatski ili srpski, srpskohrvatski i hrvatskosrpski, srpskohrvatski odnosno hrvatskosrpski, srpski ili hrvatski (najrede), službeno i neslužbeno, kako kad i kako gde, s tim što u SR Hrvatskoj, i za Srbe, od 1972 do 1990, i službeno, tj. u 'javnoj upotrebi', važio asimilativni naziv 'hrvatski književni jezik'."

Linguistic Atlas, and for the assembling of national delegations to international conferences, such as the International Congress of Slavists.

Such a consistently strong external identity of the unified language was partially a result of the long years of cooperation between Serb and Croat linguists. Many linguists had invested much time and effort in creating dictionaries, handbooks, and studies for the unified language. These works, such as Maretić's grammar (1899), the Yugoslav Academy's Dictionary (*Rječnik* 1880–1975), Belić's descriptions of Croatian Čakavian dialects (1935), Ivić's survey of the Štokavian dialects (1958), and Skok's Etymological Dictionary (1971–4), have become classic works for students of the Central South Slavic speech territory. Skok's dictionary incorporated much data ranging from the Croatian Kajkavian territory in the northwest through the Serbian Torlak dialects in the southeast, and still constitutes an excellent resource for understanding the origin of the vocabulary of the formerly unified language.

This chapter has further established that the Croats and Serbs had had radically different literary and cultural traditions prior to the 1850 Literary Agreement, and the break-up of the unified language into two of its components—Serbian and Croatian—in itself was not surprising, given the unwillingness of both sides to give up their respective dialects, alphabets, writing systems, and approaches on issues related to vocabulary. The Montenegrins and Muslim Slavs had little impact on these Serb/Croat language controversies. Their sense of identity was enhanced in Tito's Yugoslavia, when both groups were recognized as distinct nations/peoples of Yugoslavia, albeit without their own full-fledged "variants" of the unified language. With the 1974 Yugoslav Constitution, the Montenegrins and the Muslim Slavs officially adopted new sub-variants of the unified language, and the link between ethnicity, identity, and language was strengthened. According to this scheme, each of the six nations/peoples of Yugoslavia had the right to a home republic, a separate socio-cultural identity, and their own version of the Central South Slavic language. Thus, four embryonic successor languages were created as a result of the new constitution. Such fragmentation would seem unjustified, since all of these embryonic languages were based on nearly identical dialects. However, in the 1980s, this linkage of language and ethnic identity became irreversible with the rise of nationalism in ex-Yugoslavia. Ethno-linguistic nationalism arouses emotional reactions, not logical ones. After 1991, Croatian, Serbian, Bosnian, and Montenegrin have all emerged. Each of these languages has officially adopted the Štokavian/ijekavian dialect either as the sole literary dialect, or as a co-official literary dialect. In order for each of these languages to gain legitimacy as full-fledged standard languages, not a "BCS" (Bosnian/Croatian/ Serbian), language planners in the successor states have had to resort to various kinds of language engineering, creative corpus planning, new grammars and dictionaries, and new relations with speakers of the other successor languages. In the succeeding chapters, these issues, as seen in the first decade after the break-up of Yugoslavia, will be scrutinized and analyzed.

3

Serbian: Isn't my language your language?

Although individuals or groups in their professional or private capacities may on occasion promote rather extreme positions regarding purism, script, orthography and so on, with or without quiet support from certain academic circles or institutions, organized measures to this effect are certainly no part of official language policy in Serbia. ... So the overall verdict could be that there is considerable tolerance in the linguistic reality of Serbia today. The switch from "Serbo-Croatian" to "Serbian", then, has inevitably had some consequences but it has not caused radical shifts in linguistic legislation or practice.

(Ranko Bugarski 2000: 199)

3.0 Introduction

In April 1992 Montenegro and Serbia joined together to form the Federal Republic of Yugoslavia (FRY). This state proved to be one of Europe's least stable entities. Under Slobodan Milošević, it was isolated, subject to international sanctions, and the target of the NATO bombing campaign in 1999. The FRY was barred from most international organizations and institutions. Internally, some Montenegrins and most Kosovo Albanians had sought to secede from the federal state. In February 2003, the FRY was dissolved and became a loose federation known as Serbia and Montenegro; this arrangement lasted for "three years". On 21 May 2006, a slim majority of Montenegrins (55.5%) voted in favor of independence from the joint state, and an independent Montenegro was established on 13 July 2006. The FRY was originally conceived to be a single state with a single official language—Serbian. As Serbia and Montenegro drifted apart, especially in the late 1990s, the prospects for a two-state, two-language scenario grew. This chapter will focus on status and corpus planning for the Serbian language, which was the official language of Serbia-Montenegro, and retains a diminished official status in independent Montenegro, Chapter 4 will focus on (1) language debates in Montenegro during the 1990s and (2) the attempts to separate a Montenegrin standard from Serbian. Such a standard has received official language status in independent Montenegro.

Initially, the FRY continued the system of government of post-1974 Socialist Yugoslavia, whereby the two constituent republics enjoyed autonomy regarding local matters.[1] Such autonomy was enshrined in the republican constitutions, parliaments, governments, police, and other republic-specific institutions. This new state also inherited some of the language policies set forth through the 1974 Yugoslav Constitution, which had placed language legislation primarily on the republican level (cf. 2.1.3, 2.3.2, 2.3.3). Indeed, as discussed below (3.1.1), the Serbian and Montenegrin post-1991 republican constitutions have diverged slightly regarding the designation of the official scripts and pronunciations of the language, although in both constitutions the Serbian language is named as the official one. The differences in the two constitutions may seem minor to a casual observer; however, in ex-Yugoslavia, seemingly minor language issues have aroused emotional debates in scholarly journals, emergency meetings among scholars, and the scandal pages of *Politika* and *Naša borba*. In 1993, a national debate erupted over the status of the dialect spoken by Bosnian Serbs, resulting in a veritable schism among the FRY's linguists (see 3.2). This schism was further manifested in opposing views on orthographic matters (see 3.3), and emotional debates over whether the Serbian language should have one or two standard pronunciations (see 3.4). Finally, the Serbs formed the Committee for the Standardization of the Serbian Language in 1997, with the aim of creating a forum for reaching consensus on the future path for the new Serbian standard (see 3.5).

3.1   One language, two variants

After the break-up of the Socialist Federal Republic of Yugoslavia (SFRY) in 1991, the new Serbian-Montenegrin state was often called the "rump Yugoslavia" or the "third Yugoslavia." In the minds of the FRY's leaders, the preservation of the name "Yugoslavia" gave legitimacy to the FRY as the successor state to the SFRY. Their new state was to maintain the notion of "nations" and "national minorities" set up in Tito's Yugoslavia. In the FRY, the two Slavic peoples—Serbs and Montenegrins—were the constituent nations ("narodi") of the new state, and agreed to live in equality and mutual respect. The FRY's language policy maintained the pluricentric unity model espoused by Tito and the Yugoslav League of Communists (cf. 2.1.3). In this scheme, the language—like the state—would be a direct descendant of the Serbo-Croatian unified language as elaborated

---

[1] One difference between the FRY and Tito's Yugoslavia concerned the status of Kosovo and Vojvodina, which were given enhanced autonomy in 1974. Milošević stripped Kosovo of its autonomy in 1989, and rallied the Serbian people with a claim that this act would restore Serbian unity and re-centralize the Republic of Serbia.

through the 1954 Novi Sad Agreement. This Serbian "successor" language would have two official alphabets and two official pronunciations. Whereas the Serbo-Croatian/Croato-Serbian language of the 1950s admitted two official variants (Western and Eastern), the Serbian language admits two official pronunciations, which de facto became identified as the Belgrade-Novi Sad (ekavian) dialect and the Montenegrin-Western Serbian (ijekavian) dialect. The FRY's Constitution of 1992 was explicit in this regard, declaring "in the Federal Republic of Yugoslavia in official use is the Serbian language of the ekavian and ijekavian pronunciations and the Cyrillic script, while the Latin script is in official use in accordance with the Constitution and law" (Article 15).[2] Such an official sanctioning of two language varieties within a single federal state proved to be unworkable in Tito's Yugoslavia, as the unified language endured one crisis after another. In the 1990s the Serbian language adopted the characteristics of the formerly unified Serbo-Croatian language, as it served to bring together the Serbian and Montenegrin peoples. This new incarnation of the unified language has been a source of tension between Serbs and Montenegrins, and aroused controversies among the FRY's linguists.

Before discussing these controversies, I first summarize the constitutional status of the Serbian alphabets (3.1.1) and pronunciations (3.1.2).

3.1.1   The two alphabets

Serbs and Montenegrins are linked to other Orthodox Slavic peoples through their use of the Cyrillic script. Had the FRY authorities insisted that everyone use Cyrillic exclusively, they would have risked alienating members of minority groups, such as the Albanians, Bosniacs, Croats, Slovaks, Hungarians, and Roma. These groups considered the Cyrillic script to be part of the Orthodox Slavic heritage, and a rallying call for Serb nationalists. This perception was reinforced through the 1986 Memorandum of the Serbian Academy of Sciences and Arts, the 1990 publication of the "Position of the Serbian Academy of Sciences and Arts on Language",[3] and some concrete decisions by the FRY's government after 1992.[4]

---

[2] "U Saveznoj Republici Jugoslaviji u službenoj je upotrebi srpski jezik ekavskog i ijekavskog izgovora i ćiriličko pismo, a latiničko pismo je u službenoj upotrebi u skladu sa ustavom i zakonom."

[3] Cf. "Stav SANU o jeziku," which appeared in *Naš jezik*, 27/4–5 (1990), p. 197.

[4] Soon after Croatia and Slovenia declared their independence in June 1991, rumors abounded in Belgrade that letters mailed domestically would only be delivered if they were addressed in the Cyrillic script. I personally heard this rumor from several individuals in August 1991 when I visited Belgrade.

In its 1986 "Memorandum," the Serbian Academy of Sciences and Arts linked the use of the Cyrillic script with Serb identity in Croatia, stating that:

The practical meaning of such statements as: "the Cyrillic script should be taught more widely in Croatia" can be assessed only in the light of the actual policy on language which is being pursued in the Socialist Republic of Croatia. The fanatic zeal to create a separate Croatian language countervailing any idea of a common language of the Croats and Serbs in the long run does not leave much hope that the Serbian people in Croatia will be able to preserve their national identity (Pantić 1995: 133).

The Memorandum's message was that the Serbs of Croatia were not properly versed in the use of the Cyrillic script, and that this situation reflected the strong anti-Cyrillic bias of the majority Croat population in that republic. This statement elevated the issue of the script to paramount importance—seemingly trumping such issues as the Orthodox religion and Serbian culture—as a marker of Serb identity. The Academy reaffirmed its stance in Point 1 of its position paper on language, claiming that "the right of each person to his/her own language and its free use, and to his/her own script, constitutes one of the basic civil rights."[5] Such a formulation implied that for Serbs living in Croatia "his/her own script" could only be Cyrillic, and that the Latin script was necessarily "Croatian." Given the Serbian Academy's influence on government policy, it is not surprising that the Constitution of the Republic of Serbia adopted in 1990 downgraded the status of the Latin script, as can be seen in Article 8: "In the Republic of Serbia the Serbo-Croatian language and the Cyrillic script are in official use, while the Latin script is in official use in a manner confirmed by law."[6] This article implied that the use of the Latin script would be subject to further legislation, whereas the official use of the Cyrillic script was mandated by the Constitution and not subject to further discussion or regulation. When the FRY was established in 1992, the name of the official language was changed, but the hierarchy of scripts was maintained. The new Serbian Constitution modified the article on language by replacing "Serbo-Croatian" with "Serbian." And the supremacy of the Cyrillic script over Latin was manifested with the printing of the FRY's Cyrillic-only banknotes.[7] Bugarski (1997: 107) condemned the government's Cyrillic-only policy, noting that a proposal to return the Latin script to the banknotes was rejected by the government as "anti-constitutional" ("protivustavan"). Bugarski considered this decision to be part of a government-sponsored drive to promote

[5] "Pravo svakoga čoveka na svoj jezik i njegovu slobodnu upotrebu i na svoje pismo jedno je od osnovnih ljudskih prava."

[6] "U Republici Srbiji u službenoj je upotrebi srpskohrvatski jezik i ćiriličko pismo, a latiničko pismo je u službenoj upotrebi na način utvrdjen zakonom." Cf. also Hayden (1992) and Brborić (1996).

[7] Newer dinar banknotes, introduced in 1999, were printed in both Cyrillic and Latin. The former SFRY's banknotes were written in Serbo-Croatian (Cyrillic), Croato-Serbian (Latin), Macedonian, and Slovene.

a policy of Cyrillic-only for Serbian, and that such a policy reflected the Milošević regime's underlying agenda of advancing the cause of a Greater Serbia.[8]

This emphasis on the Cyrillic script reversed a trend that had evolved over many years, whereby the Latin alphabet was gaining wider acceptance in Serbia. Prior to 1991, the Latin and Cyrillic scripts were interchangeable for the writing of the Eastern variant of the unified language especially in the urban centers of Serbia, Vojvodina, and Montenegro. According to Naylor (1978: 459), the Latin script was especially common in Belgrade, and books were increasingly published there in the Latin script during Tito's times (p. 463). Magner (1988: 117) estimated that in the 1980s in Serbia's urban centers, the Latin script was used more often than Cyrillic, but that in "small settlements" Cyrillic was used all the time. In both rural and urban Vojvodina the Latin script was preferred over Cyrillic, given the province's large Hungarian minority.

The Cyrillic script in the FRY's other republic, Montenegro, was not given preferential treatment. The Republic of Montenegro enforced strict equality of both the Latin and Cyrillic scripts on its territory. According to the Montenegrin Constitution both the Latin and Cyrillic scripts were in "official use."[9] Nikčević (1993: 90) confirmed that in Montenegro, unlike Serbia, the two scripts were completely "equal" ("ravnopravna pisma"). Such equality of the two scripts followed the traditions of the 1850 Literary Agreement and Vuk Karadžić, who had elevated the Neo-Štokavian/ijekavian dialect spoken in northwestern Montenegro/Eastern Herzegovina to literary status. In this manner, the Montenegrin authorities rejected the prevailing tendency within Serbia to favor Cyrillic, in what Bugarski (1995: 166) called the politics of Serb nationalism, and of "Cyrillic-ekavian" (cf. 3.4). Rather, as in many other policies, the Montenegrins sought to chart their own future. The embrace of both Latin and Cyrillic had practical importance for Montenegrins. In this manner they not only differentiated themselves from their Serb neighbors, but they also symbolically hoped to ingratiate themselves with Western nations, underscoring their desire to attract foreign investment, to develop their tourism industry, and to reach out to their Bosniac and Albanian minorities for whom Cyrillic was identified as the alphabet of their main regional foes, the Serbs.

---

[8] For instance, in the Memorandum of the Serbian Academy of Sciences and Arts (1986), the Serb academicians claimed that "[t]he large sections of the Serbian people who live in other republics, unlike the national minorities, do not have the right to use their own language and script; they do not have the right to set up their own political or cultural organizations or to foster the common cultural traditions of their nation together with their co-nationals." Cf. also Hammel (1993: 19).

[9] The Montenet website (**www.montenet.org**) also specifies that according to the Constitution of Montenegro, in municipalities with a majority or substantial minority belonging to a designated "national minority," the minorities' languages and alphabets are co-official with Serbian.

Despite the status differences of the two alphabets in post-1991 Serbia and Montenegro, the handbooks of the Serbian successor language to Serbo-Croatian confirm that the Serbian language can be written in both the Cyrillic and Latin alphabets. Still, an overwhelming majority of language books published since 1991 have been printed in Cyrillic. The official sanctioning of the two alphabets for Serbian continued the policy of official biscriptalism implemented for the unified Serbo-Croatian language in Tito's Yugoslavia. The issue of whether it is practical for a modern standard language to have two official scripts has been a subject of recurring debates. Some Serbs have felt strongly that only Cyrillic should be protected and promoted, and they have responded to real or perceived threats to the status of this script. One such threat apparently arose in late 2002, when rumors spread that the Microsoft Corporation was planning to omit Serbian Cyrillic in one of its versions of Windows. The following urgent e-mail entitled "let's save Cyrillic" was sent across the Internet:

The Microsoft Company announced that it had officially started translating its Windows XP Professional operating system, and its next versions of the business software package Office 11, into Serbian. What was deliberately omitted from this seemingly good news was that the local [Serbian] version would be done using the Latin script. This is the last chance for us to organize ourselves and take a stance for our script. If we do not advocate for a Cyrillic translation now, all our efforts to maintain Cyrillic will have been in vain. Cyrillic and a part of our history would be banished.[10]

With all other languages using the Cyrillic script, the release of a version of Windows with the Latin script would be unthinkable. However, the orthographic identity of Serbian has remained nebulous despite the break-up of Yugoslavia, the rhetoric of Serb nationalism, and the constitutional advantages given to the Cyrillic script.

3.1.2 *The two pronunciations*

The handbooks of Serbian published since 1991 refer to the language's two official pronunciations—ekavian and ijekavian—and this policy was confirmed in the FRY's 1992 constitution. However, as with the issue of scripts, the constitutions of Serbia and Montenegro within the FRY differed with regard to the designation of the types of pronunciation in official use. Thus, whereas the

---

[10] I received an e-mail with the following text on 18 November 2002 from a colleague in Belgrade: "Kompanija Microsoft objavila je da je i zvanično započela prevođenje na srpski jezik operativnog sistema 'Windows XP Professional' i naredne verzije poslovnog softverskog paketa 'Office 11'. Ono što u ovoj naoko dobroj vijesti namjerno nije rečeno je da će lokalizacija biti uradjena na latinici. Ovo je poslednja prilika da se organizujemo i izborimo za naše pismo…Ako se sada ne izborimo za ćirilični prevod, sav naš trud na održavanju ćirilice biće uzaludan. Ćirilica i deo naše istorije će biti prognani."

Montenegrin Constitution declared that the official language in Montenegro was "Serbian in its ijekavian pronunciation," the Serbian Constitution simply omitted references to any of the official pronunciations. This omission raised suspicions in Montenegro and among Serbs who supported the ijekavian pronunciation. They considered it to reflect an official preference within Serbia for the Belgrade-Novi Sad ekavian pronunciation.

From the perspective of Montenegrin literary figures and politicians, the non-specification of an official pronunciation in Serbia was a source of anxiety, and the issue was brought up in the Montenegrin parliament in 1994. When debating amendments to the Law for High Schools, Montenegrin parliamentarians expressed their outrage at Serb hegemonistic designs on Montenegro through the use of ekavian as an official pronunciation. Dr Radoslav Rotković of the Liberal Alliance reportedly complained that the law being discussed mentioned the Serbian language, but without specifying the ijekavian pronunciation. He stressed that such a formulation was inconsistent with that of the Constitution of Montenegro, and that the omission of references to the ijekavian pronunciation reflected the policy to eliminate ijekavian "little by little":

> [Rotković] brought photocopies of a book cover of an edition of Stjepan Mitrov Ljubiša's short stories and said that Ljubiša did not write "pripovetke" [("tales" in the ekavian pronunciation)], but "pripovijesti" [("tales" in the ijekavian pronunciation)] of Montenegro and the coastal area. In his view the title "Pripovetke" is tantamount to "impudence and political imperialism". ... The legislators agreed that in all laws it is necessary to put an emphasis on "the Serbian language in the ijekavian pronunciation".[11]

As seen below (3.4), the Montenegrin legislators had some grounds for their anxiety; several prominent linguists in Serbia supported moves towards a single, unified, ekavian standard for the Serbian language.

With its two alphabets and two pronunciations, the Serbian language has displayed what Bugarski would have called a "weak internal identity," i.e., an identity prone to disputes and controversies.[12] While many efforts have been made to strengthen this identity, the divisions within Serbian linguistic circles since 1991 have been an obstacle to a coherent language-planning process for the Serbian language. These divisions are the subjects of the next section.

---

[11] The article "Uz 'srpski jezik' uvek 'ijekavskog izgovora'" ("Together with the 'Serbian Language' Always 'of the Ijekavian Pronunciation'") appeared in the Belgrade daily newspaper, *Politika*, on 27 July 1994: "[Rotković je] doneo...fotokopije korica jednog izdanja pripovetki Stjepana Mitrova Ljubiše i rekao da Ljubiša nije pisao pripovetke, već pripovijesti crnogorske i primorske. Po njemu, naslov 'Pripovetke' je 'bezobrazluk i politički imperijalizam'...Poslanici su se složili da u svim zakonima treba naglašavati: 'srpski jezik ijekavskog izgovora'."

[12] Cf. 2.0–2.1. Bugarski considered the Serbo-Croatian language also to have a weak internal identity.

3.2 The factions in Serbian linguistic circles

As discussed in Greenberg (2000), three main factions of linguists have been engaged in acrimonious debates about the future of the Serbian language. These factions include:

(1) The status quo linguists, who consider that Modern Serbian is an outgrowth of Serbo-Croatian, and also believe that it should evolve naturally from the former Eastern variant of the joint language.

(2) The neo-Vukovite linguists, who advocate the return to the pure principles of the nineteenth-century Serbian language reformers Vuk Karadžić and Djura Daničić.

(3) The Orthodox linguists, who espouse an ideology of extreme nationalism, and seek an "Orthodox Serbian" language and orthography.

The status quo linguists have included mostly researchers of the Institute for the Serbian Language of the Serbian Academy of Sciences and Arts and professors of the Philosophy Faculty of Novi Sad University. Pavle Ivić, widely respected at home and abroad, was the most prominent academician in this group. He gained stature in the 1960s and 1970s when the Novi Sad Agreement was in serious jeopardy (cf. 2.2.2). Ivić, a leading dialectologist, formulated the Serbian response to the Resolution of the Zagreb Linguistic Circle of 1967. He was instrumental in promoting Yugoslav participation in the Common Slavic Linguistic Atlas project (cf. Ivić 1961). In his dialect study on the speech of the Gallipoli Serbs (1957), he used linguistic criteria to prove that the Slavs in the area of Gallipoli were indeed Serbs. Such concern for documenting the dialects of Serbs outside of Serbia became widespread among Serb dialectologists after the 1960s, and had political ramifications (cf. 2.3.2). A firm believer in the unified Serbo-Croatian language, Ivić was the author of an influential monograph describing the Serbo-Croatian Štokavian dialects as spoken in Croatia, Bosnia-Herzegovina, Montenegro, and Serbia (1958). In a 1991 interview, Ivić admitted that he had tried to convince his Croat colleagues to continue the language union, claiming that:

I had on many occasions polemicized with the Croatian colleagues, and would remind them to be reasonable and to keep their interests in mind. They would reject this as my interference in their internal affairs. I would assert that we all lose because of the destruction of the cultural environment. I would tell [them] they were acting unwisely when they distanced themselves from the Serbs in Croatia and from Bosnia and Herzegovina, but they did not want to hear about these arguments.[13]

---

[13] Cf. "Hrvatska će izgubiti rat," published in the Belgrade weekly *Intervju*, no. 265 (2 August 1991), 4–7: "Više puta polemisao sam sa hrvatskim kolegama, podsećao ih na razum, na njihove interese. Oni su to odbijali kao moje mešanje u njihove unutrašnje stvari. Tvrdio sam da razbijanjem kulturnog tržišta gubimo svi. Govorio sam da čine nerazumno kad se udaljavaju od Srba u Hrvatskoj i od Bosne i Hercegovine, ali oni za argumente nisu hteli ni da čuju."

Ivić greatly influenced his colleagues at Novi Sad University and the Serbian Academy of Sciences and Arts. At the Academy, he was on the editorial board of the *Srpski dijalektološki zbornik* ("Serbian Dialectological Journal"), where many of the dialect studies of Serbs residing in Croatia and Bosnia-Herzegovina were published (cf. Greenberg 1996). Two of his colleagues at the Academy—Mitar Pešikan and Slobodan Remetić—also played leading roles in the journal, and shared many of Ivić's views on language-planning matters. Born in Montenegro, Pešikan was one of the authors of a 1994 orthographic manual for the Serbian successor language to Serbo-Croatian, published by the Matica srpska (cf. Pešikan et al. 1994). Remetić, born in Eastern Bosnia, has served as the director of the Institute for the Serbian Language of the Serbian Academy of Sciences and Arts. Although Remetić is a native ijekavian speaker, he supported moves in Bosnia's Serb-held areas to switch to the Belgrade ekavian standard in 1993–4 (cf. Djurović 1995).[14] Hence, this group of linguists has reportedly been lobbying for the abandonment of the ijekavian pronunciation, and unifying Serbian under a single official pronunciation. This process of ekavianizing the Serbian language has occurred naturally over the years, since ekavian is the dialect of Serbia's primary urban centers, and native ijekavian speakers who have moved to Belgrade frequently switch to the ekavian pronunciation.[15] Given the entrenched Vukovian tradition of basing the standard on extant living dialects, language planners have resisted overly prescriptivist interventions. In accordance with this tradition, the status quo linguists have refused to make any radical changes to the Serbian standard, and for this position they have had the support of much of the population.[16]

The Neo-Vukovite group of linguists has consisted mostly of scholars at the Philology Faculty of Belgrade University and the Philosophy Faculty in Nikšić of the University of Montenegro. These linguists have challenged the authority of the status quo linguists, and argued that those who cooperated with the Croats in elaborating upon the joint Serbo-Croatian language had rendered the Serbian people a disservice. They rejected the 1954 Novi Sad Agreement and the joint Orthographic Manual of 1960. In their view, the Novi Sad process constituted a betrayal of the ijekavian-speaking Serbs of Croatia and Bosnia-Herzegovina. These Serb linguistic and cultural rights were allegedly negotiated away through

---

[14] According to Djurović, Remetić expressed his "understanding" ("razumevanje") regarding the Bosnian Serb decision in the print media.

[15] In Belgrade in 1997 and 1998 I met many Montenegrins, and Serbs from ijekavian-speaking regions, who use ekavian forms in all contexts. Most of them do not code-switch between ekavian and ijekavian.

[16] I have relied on anecdotal evidence for this observation, especially resulting from consultations I have had with my colleagues in Serbia. Many non-linguist acquaintances have also expressed their disbelief and dismay over what they have perceived as excesses of the Croatian government in forcing unnatural changes to the Croatian language.

the compromises made by the drafters of the Novi Sad Agreement, which in their view identified the ijekavian pronunciation with the Western, rather than Eastern variant of the joint language. The Neo-Vukovites believed that the Croats intended to assimilate Serbs living on Croatian territory by forcing them to accept the Croatian literary language for everyday communication.

Led by Radoje Simić, Miloš Kovačević, Branislav Ostojić, and Živojin Stanojčić, this faction has vigorously defended the ijekavian dialect, and has employed nationalistic rhetoric in their writings. In particular, Simić, a Belgrade University professor in the Philology Faculty, has been vociferous in his opposition to the status quo linguists, especially academicians such as Pešikan. In his view, Pešikan "thunders from his Academic Olympus" ("grmi sa svog akademskog Olimpa"), has lost touch with the needs of students, and has prevailed because of government support.[17] He claimed that the status quo linguists had fashioned themselves as the defenders of the Serbian fatherland, and likened his own group of Neo-Vukovites to Socrates, who had dared to challenge authority:

When we begin to look deeper into the past we will find enough ominous examples of the reasoning for and the consequences of such divisions into "patriotic" scholarship and "anti-establishment" scholarship. Whoever has read, for instance, Socrates' *Defense*, knows that at the very beginnings of scholarly and pedagogical work with "helpless students" stands the most terrible example: the wise man … had to drink poison because of the accusations that he "warped the youth".[18]

Simić made these comments in 1994 when he was defending his own ortho-graphic manual, which he co-authored with other Neo-Vukovite linguists from Belgrade and Nikšić (cf. Simić et al. 1993). Simić and other Neo-Vukovites demonstrated their support of the ijekavian-speaking Serbs and Montenegrins by teaching on a part-time basis at both the Philosophy Faculties in Republika Srpska (Pale and Banja Luka) and Montenegro (Nikšić).

Another Neo-Vukovite linguist, Miloš Kovačević, a Bosnian Serb, left the Philosophy Faculty at the University of Sarajevo at the beginning of the Bosnian war, and became one of the staunchest defenders of the Serbian language. In his 1997 monograph, "*U odbranu jezika srpskoga*" (In Defense of the Serbian Language), Kovačević complained that the status quo linguists have even had difficulty accepting the term "Serbian language." He noted that in the Matica

---

[17] Cf. Simić (1994: 79).

[18] Ibid.: 78: "Kada zagledamo dublje u prošlost, naći ćemo dovoljno opominjućih primera o tome kakav je smisao i kakve su posledice tih podela na 'otadžbinsku' i 'antidržavnu' nauku. Ko je čitao npr. Odbranu Sokratovu, zna da na samim počecima naučnog i pedagoškog rada sa 'bespomoćnim studentima' stoji najstrašniji primer: mudrac … morao je ispiti otrov zbog optužbe da je 'kvario omladinu.'"

srpska Orthographic Manual, the term "Serbian language" was avoided at all costs, and that instead its authors referred to the language as "the Serbian standard linguistic idiom" or "Serbian speech patterns."[19] He considered this reluctance to embrace the term "Serbian language" to be part of the policy of Serbian self-denial, arguing that this policy began in Socialist Yugoslavia, when the Serbs had insisted that "Serbo-Croatian" was their language, even though the Croats had long negated this term, and called their language "Croatian." He believed that by avoiding the term "Serbian language," the status quo linguists were living in the past, and neglected the task of developing a distinctly Serbian standard language.

The extreme nationalist faction of linguists has been ideologically aligned with the policies of the Serbian Radical Party. The height of these linguists' influence was between June 1998 and February 1999, when their primary proponent, Radmilo Marojević, served as the Dean of the Philology Faculty at Belgrade University.[20] Marojević virulently opposed the status quo linguists, claiming that Ivić and his followers had sought to move Serbian into a Central European, pro-German milieu and away from its Orthodox Slavic cultural heritage. Marojević was instrumental in the publication of the "Declaration about the Serbian Language" (cf. Marojević et al. 1998), which unabashedly asserted that all Štokavian speakers, i.e., most Croats, all Bosniacs, and all Montenegrins, are Serbs. The "Declaration" (p. 17) supported this notion by claiming that:

Vuk considered that the Serbian language included the whole Štokavian dialect and proved, by using a linguistic criterion, that all the Štokavian-speaking people were Serbs and that all the Serbs were Štokavian. The fact that the Serbs, like other peoples, belong in various confessions, there being Orthodox, Catholic and Moslem Serbs (or as Vuk used to say, the Serbs of Greek, Roman, and Turkish faiths), does not influence the ethnic or linguistic reality of that people. Under such a logic, the use of the ekavian and the ijekavian is not and cannot be a distinctive trait differentiating between the Catholic and Moslem variants of the Serbian language. The ijekavian variety of the Serbian language and the ekavian one are equally Serbian. The Serbian standard language has two alphabets: Cyrillic and Latin. The Cyrillic and the Latin alphabets are not a distinctive trait separating the Serbian standard language from its regional, confessional variants.

Already, three years earlier, Marojević (1995: 79) alleged that Ivić was "fighting against" ("borio [se] protiv") the Serbian name of the Serbian language, and was

---

[19] Cf. Kovačević (1997: 129–36), and the chapter entitled "Za i protiv (ne)srpskog pravopisa" ("For and against the (un)Serbian Orthography"). The sub-heading of this chapter is more explicit in its attack on the status quo linguists: "(Ne) srpski pravopis Matice srpske" ("The (un)Serbian Orthographic Manual of Matica srpska").

[20] Marojević's policies were unpopular at Belgrade University, and after student protests against his deanship in February 1999 he was suddenly dispatched to Moscow.

objecting to Serbian Cyrillic as a national script, insisting on some kind of biscriptalism.[21] A specialist in Old Russian, Marojević proposed a return to an Orthodox-Cyrillic etymological writing system, which would reintroduce some of the Church Slavonic letters eliminated by Vuk. He vowed to cleanse the Serbian alphabet of the Latin *j*, which had roused much controversy in Vojvodina in the mid-nineteenth century (cf. 2.4.1), and was considered to be emblematic of the compromises Vuk and Daničić had made with the Croat Illyrians. Since 1991, the most extreme of the nationalists in Serbia have gone as far as to distort the facts relating to Vuk and his reforms, claiming that Vuk had been a spy for the Austrian government, and that his real agenda had been to help the Croats "steal" the Serbian Štokavian dialect.[22]

Marojević and 14 others signed the "Declaration about the Serbian Language." Among them were two of the co-authors of the Neo-Vukovite orthographic manual, Miloš Kovačević and Božo Ćorić. The overlap of some of the Neo-Vukovite and extreme nationalist linguists suggests that the two factions were united against the status quo group, and at times worked together to counteract it. However, with the ousting of Milošević on 5 October 2000, the influence of the extreme nationalist faction has declined. As seen in the following sections, the controversies on writing systems and the choice of dialect reached their climax in 1994, when the Neo-Vukovite linguists openly attacked the status quo linguists.

3.3 Orthographic chaos: 1993–1994

An orthographic manual (*Pravopis*) typically provides rules for the correct spelling, capitalization, and punctuation in the standard language. A narrative section is usually followed by an orthographic dictionary, in which the correct spelling and accentuation of the words is provided without additional information, such as definitions or synonyms.[23] In the former Yugoslavia, such manuals have been widely circulated, and are required of all those who aspire to write the language properly, ranging from schoolchildren to journalists. Having a similar role to the Merriam Webster *Collegiate Dictionary* for American

---

[21] Marojević et al. (1998: 27). The passage is quoted directly from the English translation provided by the authors of the Declaration.

[22] These claims were made by Samardžić (1995), who wrote about Vuk's "secret reforms."

[23] Henceforth I will refer to orthographic manuals in the context of the Central South Slavic speech territory with the term *Pravopis* (literally 'correct writing'), which is the term used by Serbs, Croats, Bosniacs, and Montenegrins for their orthographic manuals.

students, in the former Yugoslavia a *Pravopis* was an essential item for pupils in elementary school, in high school, and at university level.

At various stages in the history of the Central South Slavic speech territory, the *Pravopis* has been politicized, and manipulated as a tool for unifying peoples either under the banners of the joint language or dividing them into speakers of the new separate standards. For instance, in 1930, a year after King Alexander assumed absolute rule in the first Yugoslavia, Belić's prescriptive *Pravopis* appeared with the following declaration:

> Having envisioned the need for a single Orthographic manual for all [areas] of our school instruction, the Ministry of Education entrusted to a commission of experts [the tasks of] carrying out the standardization of the ways of writing used until now and proposing that which is today applicable and useful. That commission devised the Rules, which the Ministry of Education has published, and has directed that they be used in all our primary, secondary, and specialized schools.[24]

Hence, the appearance of a *Pravopis* in the former Yugoslavia has historically aroused contentious debates, since such manuals tended to be the most prescriptive of the instruments of codification, and they were frequently reissued to reflect a continuous refining and revising of both the orthographic norms, and the underlying political needs.[25] Linguists and philologists in the former Yugoslavia have historically regarded orthographic manuals as the first official instrument of codification for the standard language of the day. These manuals appeared well before official dictionaries or grammars. Thus, Broz's 1892 orthographic manual was published some seven years before Maretić's 1899 grammar was published. The 1960 joint Serbo-Croatian/Croato-Serbian orthographic manual was published simultaneously in Zagreb and Novi Sad heralding the new linguistic arrangements put forth in the 1954 Novi Sad Agreement, predating the production of the first volume of the joint dictionary in 1967. The same pattern can be seen in post-1992 Bosnia-Herzegovina, where Halilović's Bosnian orthographic manual came off the press in 1996, while his grammar of Bosnian appeared in 2000.[26]

In the Yugoslav successor states the publication of a *Pravopis* becomes a media event. Media attention is even greater when two rival manuals appear within months of one another. Such was the state of affairs in late 1993 and 1994, when the Pešikan–Jerković–Pižurica manual (henceforth the Matica srpska manual) and

---

[24] "Ministarstvo prosvete, uvidjajući potrebu jednog pravopisa za celu našu školsku nastavu, poverilo je komisiji stručnjaka da izvede ujednačenje dosadašnjih načina pisanja i predloži ono što je u tom pravcu danas ostvarljivo i korisno. Ta komisija je izradila Uputstvo koje je Minastarstvo prosvete objavilo i izdalo naredbu da se njega drže sve naše osnovne, srednje i stručne škole."

[25] For instance, Boranić's manual was published in ten editions between 1921 and 1951, while Belić's manual was printed in five editions between 1923 and 1952.

[26] Cf. Halilović et al. (2000).

the Simić–Ostojić–Ćorić–Stanojčić manual (henceforth the Neo-Vukovite manual) were published. When the Matica srpska manual was about to appear, the daily *Politika* featured the event with the following report:

In the National Library of Serbia the new Orthographic Manual of the Serbian Language, which was prepared by Mitar Pešikan, Jovan Jerković, and Mato Pižurica, was introduced yesterday. The manual was published jointly by the Matica srpska, the National Library of Serbia, and the Library of the Serbian Academy of Sciences and Arts; its reviewers were the academicians Pavle Ivić and Dr Drago Ćupić. Thanking the Matica srpska for its forty years of work on an Orthographic manual for our language, the director of the National Library, Dr. Milomir Petrović, stated that "the book has great significance for the culture of the Serbian people, since it represents a comprehensive study of the orthography and orthographic norms". The academician Pavle Ivić stressed that, without equal, the new Orthographic Manual of the Serbian Language is the best and most solid orthographic manual that has ever appeared in our midst.[27]

Such reports spurred numerous media articles, scholarly publications, and public debates on the new "war" for a Serbian writing system.

These two competing manuals were sent to their respective publishers in 1993, the year the FRY experienced unprecedented hyperinflation, and the country's economy was decimated by economic sanctions. As a result, the publication of the Matica srpska manual was halted due to a shortage of funds, but not for long. The Serbian government quickly rescued the project on 16 February 1994, deciding to provide the necessary funds to complete production of the manual (Brborić 2001: 250). This decision was undoubtedly made more urgent by the appearance of the rival Neo-Vukovite manual. It also reflected the government support of the status quo linguists and their views. On two crucial issues, however, the two manuals ostensibly were in agreement: (1) the Serbian language can be written in either the Cyrillic or Latin scripts; and (2) the Serbian language admits two official pronunciations: ekavian and ijekavian.[28] Ironically, both manuals were published exclusively in Cyrillic. On closer examination, however,

---

[27] The article, entitled "The New Orthographic Manual of Matica Srpska is Introduced" ("Predstavljen je novi pravopis Matice srpske"), appeared on 23 June 1994: "U Narodnoj biblioteci Srbije predstavljen je juče novi 'Pravopis srpskog jezika' koji su priredili Mitar Pešikan, Jovan Jerković i Mato Pižurica. Pravopis su zajednički izdali Matica srpska, Narodna biblioteka Srbije i biblioteka Srpske akademije nauka i umetnosti, a recenzenti su akademik Pavle Ivić i dr Drago Ćupić. Zahvaljujući Matici srpskoj na četrdesetogodišnjem radu na pravopisu našeg jezika, direktor Narodne biblioteke Milomir Petrović je istakao da 'knjiga ima veliki značaj za kulturu srpskog naroda, jer predstavlja celovitu studiju o pravopisu i pravopisnim normama'. Akademik Ivić je naglasio da je novi 'Pravopis srpskog jezika', bez premca, najbolje i najsolidnije ortografsko delo koje je ikada kod nas nastalo."

[28] The Matica srpska manual was printed in May 1994 in two versions—ekavian (4,000 copies) and ijekavian (1,000 copies). The Neo-Vukovite manual, however, was printed only in ekavian.

the two manuals diverged on these two issues in subtle, but significant ways. The Neo-Vukovite manual proposed the adoption of Daničić's Latin-Serbian alphabet, which differs from the Croatian alphabet in the writing of three phonemes: |lj|, |nj|, and |dž|. In the view of the manual's authors, none of the Serbian Cyrillic graphemes can be rendered by two Latin graphemes, as in (Latin) *dj, lj, nj, dž* for (Cyrillic) ђ, љ, њ, џ, respectively. Such a principle would violate one of Vuk's basic tenets, whereby a single grapheme should have represented a single phoneme. They identified the practice of writing the two Latin graphemes to render a single phoneme as a Croatian-inspired system, and recommended the return to Daničić's single graphemes: đ, ļ, ń, ǧ.[29] In this manner, they believed they would restore the Vukovian spirit, and render a perfect correspondence between the Latin-Serbian and Cyrillic-Serbian scripts. In addition, although both manuals asserted that Serbian is a language with two equal variants (ekavian and ijekavian), the authors of the Neo-Vukovite manual accused the authors of the Matica srpska manual of favoring the ekavian pronunciation. This viewpoint was supported by many intellectuals in Montenegro, including those Montenegrins, led by Vojislav Nikčević, who argued for the complete separation of the Montenegrin and Serbian languages. Outlining Montenegrin grievances regarding perceived Serbian linguistic excesses, Nikčević (1997*a*: 593–4) asserted that the Matica srpska manual was anti-Montenegrin in that it provided examples mostly in their ekavian forms. He considered this fact to be proof of Belgrade's hegemonistic designs on spreading an ekavian-only policy to ijekavian-speaking Montenegro.

The two manuals revealed much about the conflicting attitudes regarding the future path for the standardization of Serbian. These differences were reflected in all aspects of each manual, from the writing style to the formulation of rules of punctuation. The Neo-Vukovite linguists were particularly critical of the Matica srpska manual's verbose prose, and its emphasis on complicated and often incomprehensible rules. Evoking Vukovian principles on ensuring that the Serbian writing system be understood by the common person, Kovačević (1997: 114ff.) accused the authors of the manual of being over-scholarly and inaccessible to the non-specialist.[30] In his view, the rival Neo-Vukovite manual was preferable, since it was written in a more comprehensible style, which avoided scientific terminology, and strove towards maximal simplicity through the establishment of only

---

[29] Of these graphemes, the Croats accepted only Daničić's đ into their orthography.

[30] One of the proponents of the Matica Srpska manual, Branislav Brborić, considered the Matica srpska manual to be the more appropriate for university students who study the Serbian language in depth. He said that most other university students and some high school students should use the simplified "School Edition" of the manual, which appeared in 1995, and which was also produced by Matica srpska with the same authors as the official scholarly manual (Pešikan et al. 1995).

88 succinct orthographic rules with few exceptions. The Neo-Vukovite manual's radical proposals shocked the scholarly community. Its innovations included: (1) a new way for writing compound words, (2) revised rules on the use of the comma, and (3) changes in the writing of consonant clusters admitting voicing dissimilation in foreign borrowings into Serbian.[31] For voicing dissimilation, the Neo-Vukovite manual rejected the practice prescribed in the Matica srpska manual, whereby consonants in foreign borrowings are rendered non-phonetically, e.g., *gangster* 'gangster' and *nokdaun* 'knock-down'. The Neo-Vukovite manual advocated an adherence to Vuk's "Write the way you speak" ("Piši kao što govoriš"), and recommended the phonetic spellings *gankster* and *nogdaun*. Similarly, the Neo-Vukovite manual invoked Vukovian principles in the writing of the comma, whereby a comma can be placed wherever a pause occurs in the utterance of a sentence. With such a rule, speakers of the language would have a completely phonological writing system, where even the comma would be placed whenever the speaker sensed that a pause in speech was required. The Neo-Vukovites were iconoclastic when it came to the orthographic decisions made in Yugoslavia between 1960 and 1989. In their view, the break-up of the unified language has given Serb linguists the flexibility to standardize the Serbian language without outside interference, allowing them to find inspiration in the work of the reformers of the language, Vuk and Daničić.

On behalf of the status quo linguists, Pešikan (1994: 68) claimed that work on the Matica srpska manual had begun in 1987 and represented the culmination of thirty years of work by Serb linguists. He argued that the Neo-Vukovite manual lacked all legitimacy, since it had only been announced that fall (1993). Its contents and conceptual framework had not been subjected to appropriate peer review, and had been kept away from the consideration of the experts in the field. He complained that the first indication that a new manual was forthcoming came with the appearance of a pamphlet with rules in October 1993 just a few months before the publication of the entire book. In his view, the Neo-Vukovite manual's

[m]ost radical innovations (in consonant clusters and the writing of compound words together or separately) had never before arisen over the thirty years of discussions on orthographic matters. Even two of the co-authors of the [Neo-Vukovite] Pravopis,[32] who had been participating in the volume *Prilozi pravopisu* [1989] or the Inter-Academy Commission [for the Study of Orthographic and Orthoepic Problems],[33] had never raised these issues.[34]

[31] Kovačević 1997: 114.

[32] The two authors are Branislav Ostojić of the Nikšić Faculty of Philosophy and Živojin Stanojčić of Belgrade University's Philology Faculty.

[33] The Commission was founded in Sarajevo in 1986.

[34] "Njegove najradikalnije inovacije (u suglasničkim grupama i u spoj. i odv. pisanju) nijesu bile ni predmet tridesetogodišnjih pravopisnih rasprava, jer ih niko nije pokretao. Nijesu ih pokrenuli ni dva koautora PSJ učestvujući u radu oko *Priloga pravopisu* [1989] i u Medjuakademijskom odboru [za proučavanje ortografske i ortepske problematike]."

The volume *Prilozi pravopisu* constituted a Serbian addendum to the 1960 joint Matica srpska/Matica hrvatska orthographic manual (cf. Ivić et al. 1989), and appeared at a time when politically saving the joint Serbo-Croatian language seemed virtually impossible. However, this work represented the link between the compromises negotiated through the 1954 Novi Sad Agreement and the 1994 Matica srpska manual.

In addition to this fundamental flaw in the Neo-Vukovite manual, Pešikan found the rival manual to be harboring other shortcomings, which included:

(1)   issues not adequately explained, including the transcription of foreign words, and whether or not the consonant *h* should be written;

(2)   the lack of cross-referencing in the orthographic dictionary, and no discussion of alternative spellings such as *Skoplje/Skopje* 'Skopje';

(3)   the lack of all references to the relationship between Serbian and Croatian standards, and Eastern vs. Western variants. The Neo-Vukovite manual "completely leaves out any discussion or explanation about the relationship between the Serbian and Croatian standards, and the Eastern and Western variants";[35]

(4)   inaccuracies in spelling of individual words, and omission of specific items requiring a capital letter;

(5)   no explanations given for the writing of two-word expressions: should they be written as two separate words (*uza sve* 'all in all') or joined as a single word *uzasve*?[36]

As in past discussions of orthographic matters in the former Yugoslavia, the 1994 controversies over minute details, such as whether *na jesen* 'in the fall' should be written as a single word or not, became emblematic of a deeper political agenda and personal animosities. In his criticism, Pešikan revealed that he was still a believer in Yugoslav linguistics, intent on maintaining references to the old order of Eastern and Western variants, and using comparisons between Serbian and Croatian. The Neo-Vukovite manual, by contrast, attempted to make a clean break from the immediate Yugoslav past, and to rediscover the true Serbian language not "corrupted" by the years of the joint Serbo-Croatian language.

---

[35]   Cf. Pešikan (1994: 69): "ispušta svaku raspravu ili objašnjenje o odnosu srp. i hrv. standarda i istočnih i zapadnih varijanata."

[36]   In his criticism of the rival manual, Pešikan cited the numbers of pages or lines devoted to a particular subject in three manuals, including the 1960 manual, the Neo-Vukovite manual, and his own manual. On the proper writing of foreign words the Neo-Vukovite manual devoted only 5 pages, as opposed to the 1960 manual with 32 pages, and the 1994 Matica Srpska manual with 78 pages. Pešikan believed that the rival manual's inferior quality was underscored by its briefer treatment of specific topics.

The publication of the two competing manuals created confusion and crisis in Serbian linguistic circles for the next few years. Serving as the government's Deputy Minister of Culture, Branislav Brborić (2001: 248) described the years 1993–4 as a journey through "minefields," and a period in which the Neo-Vukovite linguists launched a spirited campaign against the Matica srpska manual. Brborić described this campaign in terms reminiscent of Communist-era rhetoric, calling the Neo-Vukovite manual a "counter-*Pravopis*," evoking the notion of a "counter-revolution":

The opponents of the new *Pravopis*, especially some unscrupulous and impassioned people, organized a large number of protest gatherings, where the aim was not to prove dispassionately and in a manner acceptable to science the advantages of the "counter-*Pravopis*" and the shortcomings of the Matica srpska *Pravopis*, but to discredit all those who deserved credit for its long preparation and studious editing and review, that is, for its publication.[37]

One of the gatherings organized by the Neo-Vukovites was held at the Philosophy Faculty in Nikšić on 14 April 1994. The four authors of the "counter-Pravopis" presented papers to an audience that conspicuously lacked the presence of any of the authors of the Matica srpska manual. Although Mitar Pešikan had been invited, he declined his invitation to attend, for health reasons. The organizers published all papers from the conference in *SPONE*, a Montenegrin journal for literature and the arts. Many of the participants sought to break the monopoly of the establishment linguists, as exemplified by Dragomir Vujičić's (1994: 14) comment that

it is not necessary to interpret the appearance of the two orthographic manuals as some kind of evil thing, since it is not good to maintain a monopoly in any specialized or scholarly endeavor. That is one thing, and another is that it is logical to understand that it is a big advantage to be in a situation of choosing the better of the two manuals. I do not believe that this leads to chaos and illiteracy, since illiterate people are not only those who do not know writing, but, above all, those who not know how to think.[38]

However, few of the participants were concerned about literacy; their chief goal was to lead a revolt against the establishment. A prominent speaker at the Nikšić

---

[37] "Protivnici novog pravopisa, naročito nekoliki bezobzirni i ostrašćeni ljudi, organizovali su veći broj protestnih skupova, čija svrha nije bila hladnokrvno i nauci primereno dokazivanje prednosti 'kontrapravopisa' i slabosti Matičinog pravopisa, nego osporavanje svih onih koji su bili zaslužni za njegovo duže pripremanje i studiozno priredjivanje i recenziranje, odnosno i za njegovo objavljivanje."

[38] "pojavu ova dva pravopisa ne treba shvatiti kao nekakvo zlo, jer monopol ni u jednom stručnom i naučnom poslu nije dobro održavati. To je jedna stvar, a druga stvar je to što je logično shvatiti da je veliko preimuštvo biti u situaciji da se od dva pravopisa bira bolji. Ne vjerujem da to vodi u haos i nepismenost, jer nepismeni ljudi nisu samo oni koji ne znaju pisma, nego—prije svega—oni koji ne znaju misliti."

meeting, Radoje Simić, led this assault. He presented the conference's conclusions in his forceful attack on Pešikan in his paper "False Concern Over False Problems: Conclusions from the Meeting of Scholars." Simić suggested that Pešikan was not truly interested in the needs of students, professors, and the general public (cf. 3.2).

Several weeks before the Nikšić conference, the Institute for the Serbian Language of the Serbian Academy of Sciences and Arts officially endorsed the Matica srpska manual. By December 1994, Novi Sad University's Philosophy Faculty, the Serbian Academy of Sciences and Arts, and the Niš Philosophy Faculty had followed suit in supporting the Matica srpska manual. As Brborić (2001: 264) noted, however, these actions were unsuccessful in silencing the supporters of the "counter-*Pravopis*," who were backed by Belgrade University's Philology Faculty and the Nikšić Philosophy Faculty. The Neo-Vukovite linguists formed a Society for the Study and Preservation of the Serbian Language ("Društvo za proučavanje i negovanje srpskog jezika"), which represented the institutionalization of their counter-current in Serbian linguistics. Brborić dismissed this society as a fringe group lacking any authority. In his view, such a "society" had few chances of competing with the work of the mainstream linguists, who formed in 1997 the Committee for the Standardization of the Serbian Language ("Odbor za standardizaciju srpskog jezika").[39]

The government of Serbia became embroiled in the orthographic controversies in late 1996 and 1997. Based on the comments of the leading institutions dating back to 1994, the government took the unprecedented measure of declaring the Matica srpska manual the "official" Serbian *Pravopis* in August 1997:

The Ministry of Education and the Ministry of Culture of the Republic of Serbia inform you that the conditions have been achieved whereby Matica Srpska's Orthographic Manual of the Serbian Language from 1993 replaces the Orthographic Manual of the Serbo-Croatian Language of the two Maticas [from 1960].[40]

The government involvement in orthographic matters was reminiscent of the actions taken by the interwar government, which had led to the publication of Belić's *Pravopis* in 1930. Even the Matica srpska/Matica hrvatska joint orthographic manual had not been officially mandated as the manual to be used exclusively in the country. While Brborić called this decision the "making official" ("ozvaničenje") of the Matica srpska manual, he denied the claims of the Neo-Vukovites, who accused the government of issuing a decree (p. 248). Once the government decision was made, the Neo-Vukovite manual was removed from bookstores in Serbia. However, the Montenegrin government did not make

---

[39] Cf. 3.5 for a discussion of this committee's work.

[40] Cf. Brborić (2001: 246): "Ministarstvo Prosvete i Ministarstvo Kulture Republike Srbije obaveštavaju vas da su stekli uslovi da *Pravopis srpskoga jezika* Matice srpske (iz 1993) zameni *Pravopis Srpskohrvatskoga književnog jezika* dveju Matica [iz 1960]."

a similar decision; after all, the Nikšić-based publisher Unireks had published the Neo-Vukovite manual, and one of its co-authors was Branislav Ostojić, a professor in the Nikšić Philosophy Faculty.[41] The preference in Montenegro for the Neo-Vukovite manual reflected dissatisfaction in the republic with the perceived favoring of the Belgrade-Novi Sad standard with its ekavian pronunciation and bias in favor of the Cyrillic script.

By the end of the 1990s, the status quo linguists clearly had the upper hand regarding the competing orthographic manuals. Through the Committee for the Standardization of the Serbian Language, they formed a sub-committee charged with solving all remaining orthographic issues for the Serbian language. The Committee and its various sub-committees were given no time limit for the completion of their work, and therefore, orthographic issues will continue to be discussed in Serbia. In the meantime, little or no progress has been made in bringing the Montenegrins on board for the standardization process, even though two Montenegrin representatives are part of the 19-member Standardization Committee. It became evident that the orthographic controversy for the Montenegrins is merely a symptom of a more fundamental suspicion that the Serbian language can no longer fully support its two "equal" pronunciations—ekavian and ijekavian.

3.4 The battle between the ekavian and ijekavian dialects

The internal debate among the Serbs regarding the co-official status of the ekavian and ijekavian dialects/pronunciations has a long and emotional history. Vuk's initial choice of the Southern dialect inflamed passions among the Serbs of Vojvodina and Serbia proper who spoke the Eastern dialect. These speakers of the Eastern dialect had long dismissed ijekavian as a provincial dialect spoken primarily by uneducated country folk, inhabiting the backward villages in the hinterland. Nevertheless, they could not deny the value of the literary materials produced by speakers of the Southern (ijekavian) dialect. Many of these works have become classics of Serbian literature, including the folk poems collected and published by Vuk, and works of authors such as Njegoš. In the most prescriptivist period of the joint literary language during the years of absolutism in the first Yugoslavia, the "literary status" of the Southern dialect was still officially sanctioned. Hence, Belić (1930: 29–32) devoted several pages of his prescriptivist orthographic manual to the two "literary pronunciations" of Serbo-Croatian, although the ijekavian pronunciation was given much less prominence than ekavian.

---

[41] For more details on Ostojić, cf. 4.2.1.

The FRY's Constitution revived Belić's notions of two standard or literary "pronunciations," by contrast to the Yugoslav socialist formula of two equal but separate "variants." However, the term "pronunciation" ("izgovor") is problematic, since it minimizes the differences between two distinctive Neo-Štokavian dialect types, by implying that differences lie in the mere pronunciation of the single inherited vowel *jat'* (cf. 2.3, 2.3.3). Rather, the "ijekavian pronunciation" is characterized by a myriad of other features as well. Thus, this pronunciation is in fact the Eastern Herzegovina-type dialect, spoken in Northwestern Montenegro, Southern Dalmatia, much of Bosnia-Herzegovina, among Serbs in Croatia, and Western Serbia. After the wars in the 1990s, the non-Serb speakers of this dialect became part of the Croatian or Bosnian linguistic spheres. Thus the speakers of ijekavian who would identify themselves as speakers of Serbian currently include a significant number of Montenegrins, Bosnian Serbs, some Serbs remaining in Croatia, and Serbs in a small portion of Western Serbia. These geographically disparate groups maintain several key dialectal commonalities beyond the reflexes of *jat'*, including accentual features, the maintenance of unstressed long vowels, and a frequent use of aorist/imperfect past tense forms. Nevertheless, their dialect is not uniform; for instance, regional differences can be found in the speech of a Montenegrin living in the Nikšić area as compared to a Serb from Banja Luka in Western Bosnia.

The two "pronunciations" are not mirror images of one another. The ijekavian pronunciation is found in a geographically diffuse territory, and used today in various entities and countries, i.e., Croatia, Republika Srpska, the Croat-Bosniac Federation, Montenegro, and Serbia. Reflexes of *jat'* represent a least common denominator, which can be used to unite the Serbs in these different administrative units. By contrast, the Neo-Štokavian ekavian-speaking area is much more compact, and is limited to the territory of the Republic of Serbia and is centered in the Šumadija-Vojvodina dialect region, where Serbia's main cultural centers are located. As discussed in 2.2.1, the ijekavian dialect was the first to be elevated to literary status by Vuk in the nineteenth century, and perhaps for this reason Serb linguists have resisted any attempts to abandon this dialect in favor of ekavian. In the post-1991 period, however, they came closer than ever before to declaring the ekavian dialect as the new Serbian standard. This action was prompted in the fall of 1993 by a purely political decision of the Bosnian Serbs.

In September 1993 the Bosnian Serb leader, Radovan Karadžić, imposed the ekavian dialect as the official pronunciation in Serb-held territories of Bosnia-Herzegovina.[42] This decision was designed to maximally distinguish the speech of Bosnian Serbs from that of the Bosnian Croats and Bosniacs. Such a decree was unprecedented, since it required that Bosnian Serbs change their dialect

---

[42] According to Brborić (2001: 140), this idea originated with Karadžić's ally from the Serbian Democratic Party (SDS), Momčilo Krajišnik.

from the native ijekavian to the ekavian of Belgrade and Novi Sad overnight. Through this politically motivated decision, the Bosnian Serb territories would be linguistically more rigid than any other Serbian speech area. The Bosnian Serb newscasters in Pale, for instance, had great difficulties properly employing ekavian pronunciation. A reporter for *Le Monde* described this decision in the following manner:

A grotesque example of linguistic separatism occurred in the Serb area a few years ago. The Republika Srpska government issued a decree in an attempt to force staff of its radio and television stations to speak the Ekavian variant of Serbo-Croatian. This is the variant spoken in Serbia, as opposed to the Ijekavian variant spoken by all communities in Bosnia and Herzegovina, Croatia and Montenegro.... Ranko Risojević, a writer from Banja Luka, is amused at the fact that the journalists themselves lost their Serbian: "As they didn't know how to speak it any more".[43]

This policy was consistent with the government-imposed unity model described in 2.1.2, and such efforts have historically been short-lived in the former Yugoslavia. While language is a powerful symbol, the imposition of a new norm by such an extremist political leader immediately evoked fierce opposition, even among the Bosnian Serbs themselves. The respected Belgrade University professor, Ranko Bugarski (1995: 166) wrote that the decision of the Bosnian Serb leadership was "a political decree without precedent, a special kind of violence against the language and its speakers, based on the ideology of a Cyrillic and ekavian Greater Serbia."[44] With mounting pressure from within the Serb-held areas of Bosnia-Herzegovina and from across the border in the FRY, in November 1994 the Bosnian Serb Assembly rescinded this decree, once again allowing for both ekavian and ijekavian pronunciations to be in official use in Republika Srpska. This episode, however, pitted the Neo-Vukovite linguists against the status quo linguists on the issue of the position of the ijekavian dialect within the Serbian standard. In a 1994 presentation given at a conference of Serb intellectuals, "The Serbian Question Today" ("Srpsko pitanje danas"), Ivić reacted cautiously to Radovan Karadžić's ruling. He stated that the ijekavian speakers should have the right to decide on the status of their own dialect, much to the anger of the Neo-Vukovite faction. In these statements, Ivić was accused of publicly endorsing the "unification" of the Serbian language under the dominant ekavian dialect. Another advocate of the "unification" of standard Serbian, Brborić (2001: 155) rejected the ijekavian pronunciation, since in his view only a few linguists can truly speak Vuk's "standard ijekavian" and most Serbs in Bosnia would frequently make mistakes with the reflexes of *jat*. The Neo-Vukovites interpreted these statements as support for the Bosnian Serb

[43] Cf. André Loersch, "Conflict in the Balkans: Language of Ethnicity" (1999) available at www.mondediplo.com/1999/06/09loersh.

[44] "To je politički dekret bez presedana, svojevrsno nasilje nad jezikom i njegovim govornicima, zasnovano na ideologiji velike Srbije, ćirilične i ekavske."

stance, and implicated the Serbian Ministry of Culture, Novi Sad University, and the Institute for the Serbian Language in a plot to quash the ijekavian pronunciation, sacrificing it on the altar of a Greater Serbia. Only two months after their conference on orthographic matters, the Neo-Vukovite linguists convened another meeting in Nikšić to defend the ijekavian dialect from possible domination by its stronger ekavian counterpart. This conference was sponsored by the University of Montenegro and the Montenegrin Republican Division for Instruction, and was held on 17 June 1994.

The 17 conference papers, published in the Montenegrin journal *Vaspitanje i obrazovanje*, were unanimous in their opposition to the downgrading of ijekavian to non-literary status, and called for a policy of tolerance towards linguistic variation in the Serbian speech territory. In defending ijekavian, many presenters pointed to the rich cultural heritage that the ijekavian dialect has brought to standard Serbian. Božo Ćorić (1994: 60), a co-author of the Neo-Vukovite manual and one of the signatories of the extremist "Declaration on the Serbian Language," considered language diversity to be an "important part of any language," and that for Serbian the traditional ekavian/ijekavian bi-dialectism needed to be preserved in all spheres of the language—from literature to oral communication.

The Bosnian-born linguist, Milorad Dešić (1994: 48), argued against the imposition of ekavian in his native republic. He rejected the view of ekavian speakers, who considered the ijekavian dialect as characteristic of uneducated villagers of the Serbian, Bosnian, and Croatian hinterlands, noting that the overwhelming majority of Bosnian Serbs—including the most educated and intellectual elite—speak exclusively the ijekavian dialect.[45] Simultaneously, among Montenegrins, the perceived threat to the ijekavian dialect became a rallying call for the pro-independence forces in Montenegro. Their fears of Serbian linguistic hegemony echoed those so commonly felt in Croatia during the decades of the language union. Other Serbian supporters of ijekavian worried that the potential downgrading of ijekavian would inevitably lead to the formation of a separate Montenegrin language, and the further splintering of Serbian speech territory (cf. Djukanović 1996: 86). Indeed, Nikčević (1997a: 592), gained support for his separate Montenegrin language, especially after Ivić expressed support for the spread of ekavian to the Bosnian Serbs. He called Ivić an "adamant fighter against the Montenegrin language" ("žučni borac protiv crnogorskog jezika").

Nevertheless, the status quo linguists included among their ranks prominent Bosnian Serb and Montenegrin linguists, who recognized the anomaly of a standard language spoken by a population of some ten million with two official pronunciations. Such a situation is not tolerated in most other European

---

[45] According to Dešić, only a negligible number of Bosnian Serb intellectuals had chosen to adopt the ekavian of Belgrade and Novi Sad.

countries. However, given the pressure mounted by the Neo-Vukovites, the linguistic establishment had to maintain the equality of the two pronunciations, at least for the time being. In an impoverished country, the publication of parallel ekavian and ijekavian texts can be an expensive proposition, and many observers have worried about its ultimate practicality. The supporters of ekavian have often claimed that ekavian is the dialect of "linguistic economy." Such economy is achieved in ekavian texts, since it is possible to shorten an ijekavian text by replacing either *ije* or *je* with a single *e*—hence, the economic benefit for the publishers. Ekavian speakers felt that it was redundant to publish parallel materials in both dialects. Referring to the publication of the extreme nationalist "Declaration on the Serbian Language" in Serbian ekavian, Serbian ijekavian, and five other languages, Brborić (2001: 345) mockingly noted that this text was "translated from Serbian to Serbian, from ekavian to ijekavian" ("preveden sa srpskog na srpski, s ekavskog na ijekavski").

The tension between the ekavian and ijekavian dialects or pronunciations for Serbian has been a recurrent theme in Serbian linguistics. This theme was first brought to the forefront when Vuk chose the Southern (ijekavian) dialect as the basis for the new standard language in an action which particularly angered the ekavian-speakers of Vojvodina. Since Vuk's times, the Serbs have used two standard dialects, and resisted the adoption of a compromise "super-dialect" or the imposition of a single norm. A rational compromise for unifying at least the orthography of the two dialects has also been proposed repeatedly over time. This compromise has involved the reintroduction of a special grapheme to denote the old *jat'*. Such a grapheme would violate Vukovian principles of a phonological orthography, since the letter would be pronounced *e* by ekavian speakers, and *ije/je/i/e* by ijekavian speakers. Ironically, such a proposal has gained the support of two linguists from two opposing camps: Brborić (2001: 146–7), from the status quo group, and Marojević (1995), from the extreme nationalist group. For Marojević, the reintroduction of the original Cyrillic grapheme *ѣ*—together with the simultaneous dropping of the Latin *j*—would return the Serbian language to its Orthodox Slavic roots. For Brborić, the reintroduction of a special grapheme for *jat'*, which could be rendered by the grapheme *ě* in both the Latin and Cyrillic scripts, would eliminate the necessity for expensive parallel editions of dictionaries, grammars, school textbooks, and government publications.[46] The supporters of the ijekavian dialect have rejected such solutions, since the reflexes of *jat'*, a salient differentiating feature of the two Serbian pronunciations, is not the sole distinguishing characteristic of the two dialects.

While the leadership in Republika Srpska reversed its initial decision to impose the ekavian pronunciation, the entity's government under the

---

[46] The grapheme *ě* is already used in Czech for some of the Czech reflexes of the original *jat'* phoneme.

domination of the nationalist Serbian Democratic Party passed a language law in 1996, which explicitly favored the ekavian pronunciation. In this respect, Republika Srpska has gone farther in setting language policy than either Serbia or Montenegro, by passing the "Law on the Official Use of Language and Script" ("Zakon o službenoj upotrebi jezika i pisma"). This law institutionalized the Bosnian Serb leadership's preference for the ekavian dialect, even though officially both the ekavian and ijekavian pronunciations were sanctioned in the entity. For instance, Article 5, subsection 2 stated that "authors" texts and programs are published or broadcast in the pronunciation from the previous section [(ekavian)], unless the author requests otherwise."[47]

Symptomatic of the Republika Srpska's preference for a Cyrillic-ekavian union with Serbia was the limited class time devoted to the teaching of the Latin script in Bosnian Serb elementary schools. Pupils were exposed to the Latin alphabet only beginning in the second grade, and then only in one class session per week.

After the 1998 elections and the change of government in Banja Luka, a new series of debates arose surrounding the ijekavian–ekavian controversy. According to the Bosnian Serb Minister of Information, Rajko Vasić, the Bosnian Serb educational system stressed the ekavian pronunciation and the Cyrillic alphabet. He complained that pupils were taught the Latin alphabet poorly. In his view, this neglect of the Latin script would harm the chances for the Bosnian Serbs to join Europe, leaving them in a Balkan backwater. In a letter to the newspaper *Nezavisne novine* in May 1998, Vasić summarized the negative consequences of the previous government's policies on language in Republika Srpska:

The consequences [of the law] are also catastrophic. Our children have already ruined their native ijekavian, and now—like their parents—they are ruining the ekavian pronunciation, since those who are born into an ijekavian milieu can never learn nor assimilate into their linguistic genes the melody, rhythm, accent, and feeling for the ekavian pronunciation. Our radio and television journalists whine, wail, screech, howl, and stutter—they do everything but use the ekavian pronunciation.[48]

The preference for ekavian and Cyrillic has not dissipated in Republika Srpska, as the nationalists regained strength in the 2002 elections. Nevertheless, the attempt to impose a dialect proved that it is futile to force an entire population

---

[47] "autorski tekstovi i programi štampaju se, odnosno emituju izgovorom iz prethodnog stava, ukoliko autor ne zahtijeva drukčije." This text is reprinted in Brborić (2001: 167).

[48] Ibid.: 168: "Posledice su takodje katastrofalne. Naša djeca su već iskvarila svoj maternji ijekavski, a sad i kvare, kao i odrasli, i ekavski izgovor. Jer neko ko je rodjen u ijekavštini nikada ne može naučiti i u svoje jezičke gene primiti melodiku, ritmiku, akcenat i osjećaj za ekavski izgovor. Naši televizijski i radio novinari kukumavče, leleču, cijuču, zavijaju i mucaju—sve samo ne izgovaraju ekavskim izgovorom."

to change its way of speaking. The Bosnian Serbs were unable to switch to the ekavian pronunciation, and have kept their native ijekavian dialect. Such a situation has dismayed some of the status quo linguists. Thus, Brborić commented that Serbian is now the only language in the Balkans that has not unified its standard, while all the other peoples/nations were able to agree upon a single dialect in forming a unified standard. In his view, the Croats abandoned Kajkavian and Čakavian in the nineteenth century, the Albanians chose a Tosk standard in the 1960s, and the Greeks unified their standard language in 1974. Rather, the trend for Serbian has been to retain two standard dialects, as seen in the decision by the members of the Committee for the Standardization of the Serbian Language, which in one of its first decisions (1997) formally recognized the equality of ekavian and jekavian. The Committee refused to address issues of the relationship between ekavian and ijekavian, since this issue had been a Serb/Croat controversy, and therefore the Committee's members felt that this issue is finally resolved, and has no place in future discussions about the Serbian standard (Brborić 2001: 130).

3.5 The triumph of the academies

Given the bruising controversies over orthographies and pronunciations, the first decade of the reborn separate Serbian standard was so turbulent that a radical reappraisal of language policies had to be undertaken. Since the days of Vuk and the creation of the joint literary language, the Serbs have avoided the implementation of a centrally monitored model, whereby an academy would ensure adherence to a consistent, official codification of a standard language. Their only previous flirtation with such a model was in the first years of absolutism in Royalist Yugoslavia in the early 1930s. Hence, the formation of the Committee for the Standardization of the Serbian Language on 12 December 1997 was a triumph for the Academies of Sciences and Arts. Once again, academics took the leading role in language planning and the formulation of language policy for the Serbian language.

The three academies in the Serbian speech territory—the Serbian Academy of Sciences and Arts (SANU), the Montenegrin Academy of Sciences and Arts (CANU), and the Academy of Sciences and Arts of Republika Srpska (ANURS)—initiated the formation of the Committee for the Standardization of the Serbian Language. The Committee consists of 19 members, nominated by their home institutions, which included the three academies, Matica srpska, and the major universities in Serbia-Montenegro and Republika Srpska. The overwhelming majority of Committee members were from Serbia (14), followed by Republika Srpska (3), and Montenegro (2). Moreover, the make-up of the Committee was such that the institutions of the status quo linguists predominated; the strongholds of the Neo-Vukovite faction, Belgrade University's Philology Faculty and the Nikšić Philosophy Faculty, had a total of 3 members on the Committee.[49] To underscore the dominance of the status quo faction, the first president of the Committee was Pavle Ivić, who served in this capacity until his death in September 1999.[50] Under such circumstances, the influence of the Neo-Vukovites has been significantly reduced within Serbian linguistic circles.

The main tasks of the Committee were elaborated upon in Article 1 of the Committee's Charter. Given the fissures in Serbian linguistic circles, it was not surprising that this Article opened with the word "objedinjavanje" ("unification")—not of the language but of specialists who will standardize the Serbian language. The Article then described the Committee's goal as

[t]he systematic regulation of the Serbian language, with [its] ekavian and ijekavian pronunciations, both comprehensively and on particular matters, and the preparation of appropriate documents and handbooks, as well as the enacting of measures which would secure the implementation of recent innovations in normativistic and linguistic practice.[51]

The proof of the envisaged government involvement in language matters is found in Article 4 of the Committee's Charter, which stipulates that ministers from the governments of Serbia, Montenegro, and Republika Srpska can participate in the meetings of the Committee. The justification given is that "language standardization is not only a linguistic process, but also the broadest societal, socio-cultural, and civilizational process."[52]

Since its inception, the Committee has made several decisions, ranging from relatively minor linguistic issues, such as the correct use of *sat* vs. *čas* 'hour', to the publication of a new orthographic manual for elementary schools. Ironically, in one of its early rulings, the Committee for the Standardization of the Serbian Language considered an ostensibly non-Serbian issue, namely the status of the new Bosnian standard language (cf. 6.1), rejecting the term "Bosnian" in favor of "Bosniac." In

---

[49] The larger institutions, including the Serbian Academy of Sciences and Arts, the Institute for the Serbian Language, Matica srpska, Belgrade University's Philology Faculty, and Novi Sad University's Philosophy Faculty, appoint two members each to the Committee. The other institutions—the Montenegrin Academy of Sciences and Arts, the Academy of Sciences and Arts of Republika Srpska, the Nikšić Philosophy Faculty, the Niš Philosophy Faculty, the Priština Philosophy Faculty, Serbian Sarajevo's Philosophy Faculty, Banja Luka Philosophy Faculty, and Kragujevac University—appoint one member each.

[50] Pavle Ivić was succeeded by his wife, Milka Ivić, an influential linguist at Novi Sad University.

[51] Text taken from Brborić (2001: 328): "sistematsko normiranje srpskog jezika, s ekavskim i ijekavskim izgovorom, sveobuhvatno i u pojedinostima, i izrada odgovarajućih dokumenata i priručnika, kao i donošenje akata koji bi obezbedjivali prohodnost nedavnih inovacija u normativistici i jezičkoj praksi."

[52] Ibid.: "Jezička standardizacija nije samo lingvistički nego je i najširi društveni, sociokulturni i civilizacijski process."

1998, attention was turned to internal Serbian discord on language matters, as the Committee censured the extreme nationalist "Declaration on the Serbian Language" at a time when Radmilo Marojević, one of the pamphlet's authors, was still the Dean of the Belgrade University Philology Faculty. The Committee rejected the stance of the authors of the "Declaration" that all Štokavian speakers are Serbs, including the Catholics and the Muslims in Croatia and Bosnia-Herzegovina. According to Brborić (2001: 344ff.), who served as the Committee's Secretary, the Committee discussed the "Declaration" because its main proponents ("nosioci") were the "Dean of a certain Faculty" and two university professors, "one of whom is a member of the Committee."[53] The Committee was particularly candid in condemning the "Declaration," claiming that it helped perpetuate the world's "satanization of the Serbian people" (ibid.: 344).

The Committee for the Standardization of the Serbian Language has served as the decision-making body for the future of the language. Currently, the Committee has seven Sub-Committees ("komisije"), each focusing on an area of specialty, including phonology, morphology, syntax, lexicon, orthographic matters, historical perspectives on the development of Serbian, and relations with the public. By its second full year of operation (1999), the Committee's deliberations were already often heated, leading one member to call the body the "Committee for the Satanization (rather than 'standardization') of the Serbian Language" (ibid.: 352). Nevertheless, the publication of new handbooks, grammars, and dictionaries can be expected in the next few years as a direct result of the work of the Committee. Notwithstanding its problems, such a Committee, should it remain influential, has the potential of formally directing the future path for the Serbian language, and could serve as a scholarly forum for resolving future language controversies.

3.6 Conclusions

Language planning and language policy in the FRY proceeded in an unpredictable manner after the break-up of Socialist Yugoslavia in 1991. Unlike their Croat counterparts, Serb linguists were ill prepared for the new linguistic order. The new Serbian language represents an outgrowth of the former Eastern variant of Serbo-Croatian, and did not undergo significant changes during the 1990s, despite the vocal clamoring in some circles. Throughout the 1990s, the status quo group of linguists maintained a position of dominance. The formation of the Committee for the Standardization of the Serbian Language, with its open-ended mandate, suggests that the status quo linguists will continue to direct language policy for Serbia. The most significant threats to the unity of the Serbian language could come from either Republika Srpska or Montenegro, where politicians and linguists have accused the

[53] The name of the Committee's member not mentioned here was Miloš Kovačević, who was the representative from "Serbian Sarajevo."

status quo linguists of favoring the ekavian pronunciation at the expense of ijekavian. The Neo-Vukovites and extreme nationalists within Serbia have similarly expressed opposition to a perceived ekavian-only agenda. These factions are ideologically driven. They invoke Serbia's rich cultural heritage and advocate the disavowal of the compromises made with the Croats, and a return to the pure Serbian roots of the Serbian language. The Neo-Vukovites have found allies among pro-Serbian Montenegrin linguists, for whom the preservation of the ijekavian pronunciation of the Serbian language has been of paramount concern. As Brborić lamented, in his 2001 monograph, the Montenegrins had still not accepted the Matica Srpska orthographic manual, preferring instead the Neo-Vukovite manual published in Belgrade and Nikšić in 1993. Even more on the fringe, the extreme nationalists, with their support of a Cyrillic-only Serbian language, have remained active. Table 4 provides an overview of key events in the recent history of the Serbian language.

TABLE 4.   Chronological summary of Events Affecting the Standardization of Serbian in the 1990s

Date	Event
1993	• Bosnian Serbs impose ekavian pronunciation in Serb-held regions of Bosnia-Herzegovina
	• Belgrade-Nikšić Orthographic Manual published
1994	• Matica srpska orthographic manual appears
	• Pavle Ivić and status quo linguists support the Bosnian Serb decision on ekavian
	• Meetings in Nikšić to discuss "orthographic chaos" (14 April) and the status of ijekavian (17 June)
	• Bosnian Serb parliament reinstates ijekavian, but ekavian has preferred status
1996	• The Matica Srpska *Pravopis* is officially sanctioned in Serbia
	• Rival Neo-Vukovite *Pravopis* adopted in Montenegro
	• Republika Srpska adopts Law on the Official Use of Language and Scripts, formalizing preferred status for ekavian pronunciation in the entity
1997	• Formation of the Committee for the Standardization of the Serbian Language
	• Djukanović elected president in Montenegro and prospects grow for an independent Montenegrin state and language
1998	• Publication of the "Declaration about the Serbian Language" with its extreme nationalist viewpoint
	• Republika srpska switches allegiances and moves to restore the ijekavian pronunciation
1999	• Committee for the Standardization of Serbian rejects the extremist "Declaration on the Serbian Language"
	• The death of influential Serb linguist Pavle Ivić

The above discussion reveals that towards the end of the 1990s an attempt was made to create a Serbian language policy that would be applicable to all Serbs and Montenegrins regardless of their physical location. This task has not been simple, since the Serbian language planners currently face a complex situation, as the Serbs in the Balkans no longer reside within the borders of a single state and many have been displaced. Undoubtedly, in order to preserve Serbian unity under such circumstances, the language planners have perpetuated the two-pronunciation formula for the standard language. Given the dissolution of the joint state of Serbia and Montenegro in 2006, the unified Serbian language in its current fractured form is likely to endure new stresses. With the secession of the ijekavian-speaking Republic of Montenegro, will the linguists in Serbia be under increased pressure to abandon the ijekavian pronunciation altogether? Even though the Serbian language has retained a diminished official status in Montenegro, it is still difficult to distinguish linguistically between Montenegrin and Serbian. As the next chapter demonstrates, the political divorce between Serbia and Montenegro has already occured, but the linguistic one might be more difficult to achieve.

4

Montenegrin: A mountain out of a mole hill?

The inclusion of the Serbian language in the Constitution of Montenegro is absurd. Montenegrins cannot exist, can have neither an independent state, nor be a people and nation speaking a foreign tongue.

(Vojislav Nikčević)[1]

4.0 Introduction

According to the 1954 Novi Sad Agreement, the unified Serbo-Croatian language was shared by Croats, Serbs, and Montenegrins. In this formula, the single language had only two variants, i.e., the Western variant (Zagreb) and the Eastern variant (Belgrade). This agreement explicitly mentioned the Montenegrin people, but it did not provide for a third official variant that may have developed in the southwestern areas of the Štokavian speech territory, or around the cultural or administrative centers of Montenegro. The Yugoslav language planners may have justified such an omission by claiming that the Western variant was based on an Eastern Herzegovina (Southwestern) dialect, which was precisely the same dialect spoken in Northwestern Montenegro. Nevertheless, the Western variant of the unified language was typically written only in the Latin alphabet, and included many elements of the Croatian speech territories, many of which would have been alien to educated Montenegrins. Thus, even though the language of the Montenegrins was phonologically akin to that of the Croats,[2] it was characterized by a lexicon similar to that used in Serbia, and some morphological features typical of the ijekavian dialects of Bosnia-Herzegovina or Western Serbia.[3] When the Croats began questioning the language union in the

[1] Cf. **www.danas.org/programi/interview/2000/12/20001213134113**: "Unošenje srpskog jezika u ustav Republike Crne Gore je apsurd. Ne mogu Crnogorci postojati i imati svoju samostalnu državu i biti narod i nacija na tudjem jeziku."

[2] The phonological similarities apply only to the Neo-Štokavian ijekavian dialects of Northwestern Montenegro. The Southeastern Montenegrin dialects exhibit old Štokavian accentuation, and have no clear corollaries within the Štokavian speech territory.

[3] These morphological features include the frequent use of the aorist and imperfect tenses.

late 1960s, some Montenegrins quickly followed suit. They had been left out of the Novi Sad formula, and felt compelled to assert their own ethnic and linguistic identity. In 1968 several Montenegrin intellectuals gathered at a "Symposium on Montenegrin Culture and Paths towards its Development" ("Simpozium o crnogorskoj kulturi i putovima njenog razvoja"). According to Nikčević (1997a: 585), "in the context of pursuing a Montenegrin identity as a general movement, they also began to raise the Montenegrin language from the dead."[4] With the suppression of the Croatian Spring in 1971, such language resuscitation had to be suspended under pressure from the Yugoslav League of Communists, who tried to preserve both the unified language and the unified federal state. The most Montenegro's would-be linguistic separatists could achieve in Tito's Yugoslavia was recognition of a Montenegrin "standard linguistic idiom," a subvariant of the unified language, through the 1974 Constitution of the Socialist Republic of Montenegro.

Unlike the Croats, the Montenegrins did not produce any separate grammars, orthographic manuals, or school handbooks for their language during the years of Socialist Yugoslavia. The impetus for the birth of a separate Montenegrin language remained dormant until 1994, after it became obvious that Serbo-Croatian no longer existed, and after the Bosnian Serbs had attempted to impose the Belgrade ekavian norm upon their territories in Bosnia-Herzegovina (cf. 3.4). Led by Vojislav Nikčević—a professor of Slovene literature from Nikšić's Philosophy Faculty—the Montenegrins advocating a separate Montenegrin language became louder and politically more palatable after 1997, when Milo Djukanović was elected president of Montenegro, and the republic began moving towards secession from the FRY. While the adoption of the new Constitutional Charter on the restructuring of relations between Serbia and Montenegro in February 2003 put Montenegrin independence on hold until 2006, the new constitutional arrangement granted Montenegro many of the trappings of an independent state. During the time of this short-lived arrangement, pressure mounted within Montenegro to accept as official the Montenegrin language. Only two weeks after the ratification of the new Charter, a representative of the Democratic Party of Socialists suggested that the language of Serbia and Montenegro be called "Serbo-Montenegrin or Montenegro-Serbian." In his view, this name was to represent a compromise solution that would have satisfied pro-Serbian forces in Montenegro, who insisted that the Montenegrin Constitution continue to name the language "Serbian," and the pro-independence camp that long advocated calling the language "Montenegrin." After achieving independence for Montenegro in 2006, the ruling political parties succesfully lobbied for the official sanctioning of a separate Montenegrin language.

[4] "U okviru Cnrogorstva kao opšteg pokreta, počeli su i jezik crnogorski dizati iz mrtvih."
[5] Cf. the Radio Free Europe/Radio Liberty website, **www.danas.org** for 18 February 2003 and the news item entitled "SCG/CGS: Srpsko-crnogorski/Crnogorsko-srpskijezik?"

In Fishman's formulation (1993), when language planners discuss the establishment of new standard languages, their task is both to define the characteristics of the new language, and to establish the differentiating features of the new language as opposed to other closely related or competing languages. Thus, planners at the first congress on a language such as Catalan defined the features of the Catalan language, and how Catalan was different from Spanish. As the successor languages of Serbo-Croatian emerged after 1991, the language planners had to focus on the linguistic features that justified the establishment of a new standard language, taking into consideration if and how Montenegrin differed from the formerly united language (Serbo-Croatian), and from the other successor languages. For instance, language planners for the Bosnian language have had to convince the skeptics that the new Bosnian standard is neither Serbian, nor Croatian, nor Serbo-Croatian, nor a "standard dialect/idiom" of one of the other languages. For Nikčević, the focus was less on how Montenegrin is neither Croatian nor Bosnian, but rather on what differentiated Montenegrin from Serbian. This focus on Serbian had two primary reasons: (1) linguists in Croatia and Bosnia-Herzegovina, unlike their counterparts in Serbia, have not challenged the legitimacy of a separate Montenegrin language, and (2) many Serbs have long considered Montenegrins and Serbs to be a single people, sharing the Orthodox religion, the language, and the literary tradition. Thus, the prominent Croat linguist, Radoslav Katičić, asserted,

[t]he more the Serbian standard became coloured by the Belgrade vernacular and was in consequence felt as an expression of metropolitan mentality, the less acceptable it was to Montenegrins who had a quite different mentality and continued to remember their own statehood. A substantial number were not willing to accept a projection of this colour and this mentality on themselves. They had inherited the tradition of Serbian culture and literary language, but they had found their own way to literary usage based on their vernacular independently from Karadžić's reform (Katičić 1997: 178–9).

Similarly, the primary Bosniac linguist, Senahid Halilović, has unquestionably accepted the notion that Serbo-Croatian has four legitimate successor languages, including Montenegrin, while his colleague, Josip Baotić (1999: 92), who was lukewarm in his acceptance of a Bosnian language, nevertheless referred to development of a "Montenegrin language."[6] By contrast, many of the linguists in Serbia have expressed their belief in the unity of Serbs and Montenegrins. For instance, when discussing issues that divided linguists in the FRY, Djurović (1995: 73) asserted that all the Serbian and Montenegrin linguists agreed on the "ethnic, cultural, and spiritual unity of Serbs and Montenegrins" ("za etničko, kulturno i duhovno jedinstvo srpskog i crnogorskog naroda"). Therefore, the current debate on whether Serbian and Montenegrin are a single language or two languages can be interpreted as the final phase in the dissolution of the joint Serbo-Croatian language. By the end

---

[6] Halilović's assessment was quoted in Magner and Marić (2002: 61).

of the wars in Croatia and Bosnia-Herzegovina (1995), this unified language had officially splintered into Bosnian, Croatian, and Serbian. International organizations have adopted the term "BCS" ("Bosnian/Croatian/Serbian") to refer to this new linguistic reality; however, the Montenegrin language has not achieved such recognition, and could remain on the fringes for some time to come.

This chapter analyzes the complex language situation in Montenegro, focusing on the dialects and literary traditions (4.1), the debates surrounding the official language of Montenegro (4.2), and the characteristics of a separate Montenegrin language (4.3). The nature of the Montenegrin language is still on the one hand, affected by its past links with Serbian and, on the other hand, increasingly shaped by the political agenda of the leaders of the newly-independent Montenegrin state[7].

4.1 Montenegro's dialects and its literary traditions

Historically, the Montenegrin speech territory has long been considered to be an integral part of the Serbian, Orthodox Slavic speech community. Thus, one of the two dialect types in Montenegro—the Neo-Štokavian/ijekavian dialect—is nearly identical to that spoken by the Serbs residing west of the Drina River. In 1814, Vuk chose this dialect as the basis for his reformed Serbian literary language, and this same dialect was embraced by the Serb and Croat signatories of the 1850 Vienna Literary Agreement. During the twentieth century, Montenegrin dialects were nearly always considered in the context of Serbian dialectology, and most scholarly studies of the Montenegrin dialects appeared in the Serbian Dialectological Journal published by the Serbian Academy of Sciences and Arts in Belgrade.[8] The pro-independence Montenegrin intellectuals have labored to reconstruct all the trappings of a separate Montenegrin identity, through the highlighting of the Montenegrin ethnogenesis, references to the glorious Montenegrin past, and the uniqueness of Montenegrin culture. Among the most relevant of these identity markers to justify a separate Montenegrin language are the claim that the dialects spoken in Montenegro are Montenegrin and not Serbian (4.1.1), and an assertion of the distinctly Montenegrin—and not Serbian—nature of the nineteenth-century literary tradition, which developed on Montenegrin soil (4.1.2). The pattern of Montenegrin identity creation since 1945 resembled that of the other former Yugoslav peoples/nations, and included the following stages: (1) the attainment of recognition as a constituent "nation" of Yugoslavia; (2) the trend toward political control over its own territory; and (3) the

---

[7] For further discussion, see the Postscript section at the end of this work.

[8] Moreover, many prominent Serbian linguists and dialectologists have been natives of Montenegro, including Mihailo Stevanović, Mitar Pešikan, and Drago Ćupić.

adoption of a national narrative on the origins of its culture and people. For this latter stage, the people of Montenegro have been unable to agree on a common national narrative; some Montenegrins have traced a distinctly Montenegrin ethnicity, culture, and language back to the sixth century, while others continue to view Montenegrins as part of the Serbian nation. At the same time, the Serbs have rejected the Montenegrin pro-independence narrative that in their view would appropriate their culture, literature, and language.

4.1.1   *The sociolinguistics of dialect geography*

The Republic of Montenegro is divided into two distinct speech territories: Northwestern Montenegrin and Southeastern Montenegrin. The northwestern dialects are Neo-Štokavian/ijekavian, while the southeastern ones are known as Old Štokavian/ijekavian, displaying an archaic system of accentuation, and are typically called "Old Montenegrin" or "Zeta-Lovćen" dialects.[9] Montenegro's current political boundaries do not correspond to either the dialectal or the ethnic ones. The Northwestern Montenegrin dialects are similar to those across the border in Eastern Herzegovina and southernmost Croatia (Dubrovnik). As seen in 2.3, these dialects make up the so-called "Southern" dialects on which the joint literary language was based in the nineteenth century. In a similar fashion, the Southeastern Montenegrin dialects extend across the international border into the Serbian Sandžak region and to the Slavic populations in northern Albania. Ethnically, these southeastern dialects are spoken mostly by Montenegrins, but also by some Serbs and Bosniacs of the Sandžak region. Map 4 depicts the primary division within Montenegrin dialectology between Northwestern (Neo-Štokavian ijekavian) and Southeastern Montenegrin (Old-Štokavian ijekavian) dialects.

The ijekavian reflexes of Common Slavic *jat'* represent the primary unifying linguistic feature of the two Montenegrin dialect types. Thus, unlike any of the other ethnic groups in the Štokavian speech territory, the Montenegrins are all ijekavian speakers.[10] The differences between the two Montenegrin dialects are found most notably in the areas of phonology and morpho-syntactic constructions. Hence the Northwestern Montenegrin dialects are characterized by the Neo-Štokavian accent retractions found in the contemporary Croatian, Bosnian, and Serbian standards. By contrast, the southeastern dialects reveal more archaic non-retracted accentual patterns. As a result, the pronunciation of many words differs markedly in the two dialects; for instance, *ruka* 'hand' would be pronounced with a long rising accent on the first syllable in Northwestern Montenegro, while in much of Southeastern Montenegro the first syllable

---

[9] The latter term is purely geographical, referring to the River Zeta and Mount Lovćen.

[10] Cf. Greenberg (1996: 400) for a table showing the correlation of Štokavian sub-dialect type and ethnic group in the former Yugoslavia. Bosniacs and Croats are both ijekavian and ikavian speakers, while Serbs are both ijekavian and ekavian speakers.

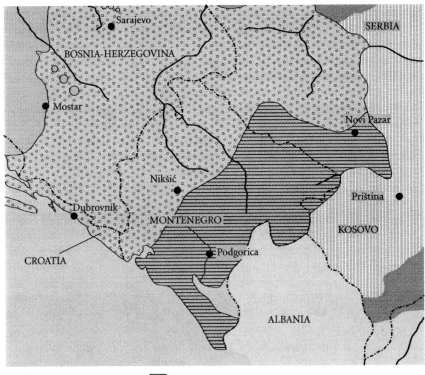

[ ] Neo-Štokavian ijekavian   [ ] Old Štokavian ijekavian

MAP 4. Map of the Southwest Štokavian dialect

would be pronounced as a long vowel, and the accent would fall on the final syllable. The Southeastern dialects also include so-called "Balkan" features shared with neighboring Slavic and non-Slavic languages and dialects. [11]

Sociolinguistically, the northwestern dialects link Northwestern Montenegrins to members of the three other ethnic groups, who speak what is termed the former Serbo-Croatian language,[12] while the southeastern dialects are overwhelmingly Montenegrin, shared only with speakers of the neighboring

[11] Cf. Greenberg (1994) for a discussion of the Balkan features within the Zeta-Lovćen dialectal zone. The Balkan features constitute structural similarities in the Balkan speech community (*Sprachbund*), which includes speakers of Albanian, Arumanian, Bulgarian, Greek, Macedonian, Romanian, and Southeastern Serbian dialects. These features spread through extensive Balkan language contact, and are generally absent in the dialects of Croatia, Bosnia-Herzegovina, Northwestern Montenegro, Vojvodina and the Šumadija region of Serbia.

[12] This Eastern Herzegovinian dialect type was described by Vušović (1927) and Peco (1964).

Sandžak region. These southeastern dialects encompass the old Montenegrin capital of Cetinje, and the current administrative center and capital of Montenegro, Podgorica. Ironically, however, the would-be codifiers of a new Montenegrin standard language have not chosen these distinctly Montenegrin dialects around the capital as a basis for the new Montenegrin language. Rather, they have officially sanctioned the Northwestern dialects, those same dialects that form the phonological core of the new Croatian, Bosnian, and Serbian in its ijekavian pronunciation. Had they chosen the Podgorica dialect, they would have elevated the dialect type most radically opposed to that of any other of the rival standard languages. However, these codifiers conceived of the entire dialectological division of Montenegro as an interpretation put forth especially by Serb linguists with the aim of dividing and conquering the Montenegrin speech territory. Thus, Nikčević (1997a: 602ff.) rejected the division of the Montenegrin dialects according to the types of accentuation (Neo-Štokavian vs. Old Štokavian). For him, these dialect divisions were artificially constructed so as to deny the existence of a "spoken Montenegrin language" ("crnogorski govorni jezik"), allegedly common to the majority of Montenegrins. He postulated that such a spoken Montenegrin language consists of three main elements: (1) South Slavic/Proto-Slavic or Štokavian elements, shared with Croats, Serbs, and Bosniacs; (2) "inter-dialectal" or "super-dialectal" Montenegrin elements; and (3) distinctly Montenegrin regionalisms and provincialisms which have arisen through contact with non-Slavic languages, or as a result of the differentiation of Montenegrin tribes or religious groups. It is unlikely that a single Montenegrin dialect admits all these clusters of features. However, as seen below, the phonological features making up his proposed standard are taken primarily from the Northwestern Montenegrin dialects (cf. 4.3). He combined these features with archaisms that were typical of the language of Montenegro's most prominent poet, Petar II Petrović Njegoš. In this manner he created a super-dialect on which he based his new standard (cf. 4.3).

4.1.2   The literary traditions in Montenegro

In the nineteenth century Montenegro became a center of literary activity. The genre of epic poetry flourished at that time, using the local Štokavian/ijekavian dialect. Montenegrin nationalists have hearkened back to this literature when justifying their claims on the uniqueness of a Montenegrin linguistic identity, and have disputed Serbian claims that these literary works should be counted among the classics of a Serbian, rather than a Montenegrin, culture.

The literary activities in Montenegro reached their heights in the epic poetry of Petar II Petrović Njegoš (1813–51), who in 1830 inherited his uncle's positions as the head of both the Church and the State in the Montenegrin lands. In 1847,

Njegoš published his most famous work, *The Mountain Wreath* ("Gorski vijenac"). In the divisive atmosphere prevalent in post-1991 Serbia and Montenegro, both Serbs and Montenegrins have claimed Njegoš as their own. Thus, while Serbs have asserted that Njegoš is a great Serbian writer, the Montenegrin nationalists have affirmed that he was Montenegrin through and through, and that he had expressed Montenegro's aspirations to be a people and a nation. The Serbian point of view can be seen in Mihailovich (2000), who stated that *The Mountain Wreath*

epitomizes the spirit of the Serbian people kept alive for centuries; indeed, there is no other literary work with which the Serbs identify more. It gave Njegoš an opportunity to formulate his own philosophical views, views which also reflect and further inspire those of his nation. Finally, in this work the author reaches artistic heights seen neither before nor since in Serbian literature. These are the main reasons for the universal reverence for and high estimation of *The Mountain Wreath*, the highest achievement in all of Serbian literature.

By contrast, Nikčević and his supporters have considered the language of Njegoš's works to be authentically Montenegrin. At a conference held in Podgorica in November 2000 dedicated to "Štokavian Literary Languages in the Family of Slavic Standard Languages" ("Stokavski knjizevni jezici u porodici slovenskih standardnih jezika"), Nikčević, together with some other Montenegrin academicians and professors, proclaimed that *The Mountain Wreath* was written not merely with "Montenegrinisms" ("crnogorizmi") as Serbs might argue, but in the Montenegrin literary language. Moreover, he was quoted claiming that

"The Serbs could not translate Njegoš's works into Serbian" and that for this reason "they printed them in the form of tales," and that [therefore] the "Serbian and Montenegrin linguistic systems are two completely different organic systems."[13]

This belief has been staunchly defended in Montenegrin nationalist movements and associations both inside and outside Montenegro since 1993. For instance, the Montenegrin Association of America contends that:

Before the South Slavic linguistic reforms begun in 1863, the traditional Montenegrin language was used freely, naturally and spontaneously and so developed to a high level of creative expressiveness, as manifested in the rich oral literature and in the works of the genius poet Njegoš. Njegoš's writing captured this original Montenegrin language. His work included local dialects, provincialisms and neologisms. He exercised wide freedom

---

[13] Cf. the website of the Media Club of Montenegro, www.medijaklub.cg.yu/kultura/arhiva/11-00/27-1.htm: " 'Srbi Njegoševo djelo nijesu mogli da prevedu na srpski', da su ga zbog toga 'svojevremeno objavili u obliku pripovjetke', te da su 'srpski i crnogorski jezički sistemi dva potpuno organski različita sistema.'" This site includes a brief report on the Podgorica conference.

in the use of language—like all great writers, who are essentially creators of language and for whom anything artistically functional is correct and beautiful.[14]

While it is true that Njegoš wrote his poetry in Montenegro, and many linguistic features typical of the Montenegrin speech territory can be found in his work, the current debate on whether or not he wrote in Montenegrin or Serbian is speculative. Nikčević and his supporters have attempted to establish Njegoš's purely Montenegrin credentials. However, in both his politics and his writings, Njegoš viewed himself as part of a broader Slavic community. Thus, at the time of his rule, there were no references to a separate Montenegrin language, and his policies suggested that he had identified himself with Serbian culture. For instance, he instituted a curriculum in the Serbian language in the schools in Montenegro. Politically he supported the freeing of the Serbs from Ottoman Turkish rule, and sought to join with Serbs in an independent state. Like the Croat Illyrians, he had endorsed notions of Southern Slavic unity. His belief in pan-Slavic culture, rather than a narrowly defined Montenegrin one, was reflected in his love of Russian culture. Njegoš was so enamored with Russia that he made two visits there. On his first visit in 1833 he was ordained Bishop of Montenegro, while his second trip in 1837 "contributed even further to the recognition of Montenegro as a sovereign state, and to the security of its borders. He remained a loyal admirer of Russia all his life, even when Russia had to make peace with his arch-enemy, Turkey" (Mihailovich 2000).

In his writing, Njegoš was strongly influenced by the ijekavian epic and folk poetry. He shared a love of these folk traditions with his contemporaries, including Vuk Karadžić. Indeed, Njegoš had the opportunity to meet Vuk twice in 1833 in Vienna. Njegoš "gave Vuk some of his writings to be published," while Vuk encouraged Njegoš to continue with his literary endeavors (ibid.). As Ostojić (1989: 11–13) suggested, the mutual admiration between Vuk and Njegoš allowed for Vuk's language reforms to be accepted in Montenegro much earlier than in either Serbia or Vojvodina. Indeed, Vuk's early successes in Montenegro were due to the following factors: (1) the artificial Slaveno-Serbian language used in Vojvodina had not penetrated into the Montenegrin lands; (2) Vuk had favored both the dialect and epic poetry close to that of the Montenegrins; and (3) Njegoš, like Vuk, believed that the standard language should be based on the language of ordinary people. This evidence gives credence to the view of Nikčević's opponents, who believed that Njegoš contributed to the development of Vuk's Serbian language, rather than to the evolution of a separate Montenegrin one.

In addition to Njegoš, Nikčević considered Stefan Mitrov Ljubiša and Marko Miljanov Popović to be two more classic writers, whose works prove the existence of a separate Montenegrin literary tradition and language. As seen in 3.1.2, some

---

[14] Cf. www.montenegro.org.

parliamentarians in Montenegro have felt threatened by Serbian renditions of Ljubiša's works, resolutely rejecting Belgrade's ekavian versions of his tales. Their main argument for claiming these writers as Montenegrin is that they wrote in the Montenegrin-ijekavian vernacular, even if their themes tended to be Serbian, including the glory of Serbia's medieval past, Serbian heroism at the 1389 Battle of Kosovo, and the Orthodox Slavic struggles against the Ottomans. Thus, nineteenth-century Montenegrin literature has been part of a broader South Slavic Orthodox tradition, and therefore intertwined with the literary tradition of Serbia. In this way, it differs from the Croat vernacular literary traditions or the Bosnian Muslim Alhamijado literature, which could truly be classified as separate from the South Slavic Orthodox literary patrimony. The above discussion reveals that in their quest for legitimization of the separate Montenegrin language and identity, Nikčević and his followers have selectively emphasized certain facts while ignoring others. The importance of the Montenegro-born writers has been paramount in their establishment of the Montenegrin language, whose existence Nikčević "proved" through "thirty years of research" ("po mojim istraživanjima, koja traju preko trideset godina").[15] He did not seem concerned that no single historical figure ever took on the task of writing a grammar or dictionary of such a "separate" Montenegrin language.

4.2 Montenegro's two factions

Language planning in Montenegro since 1992 has followed two opposite trajectories: (1) a pro-Serbian group, mostly with a Neo-Vukovite orientation; and (2) a pro-Montenegrin group, poised to make official the separation of Montenegrin from Serbian. The former group includes the linguists of Nikšić's Philosophy Faculty, while the latter is comprised of non-linguists, including writers, academicians, and professors.[16]

The two factions have diametrically opposed opinions on the role of Vuk Karadžić in the formation of a standard language for Montenegrins. As described in 3.2, the Neo-Vukovites have sought to transform the new Serbian successor language through the reintroduction of practices developed by Vuk Karadžić and Djura Daničić. These linguists have been advocates of the ijekavian dialect, and in 1994 argued that owing to the Vukovian traditions ijekavian has retained its position as a standard variant of the Serbian literary language (cf. 3.2). They

---

[15] Cf. the interview on the Montenet website at **www.montenet.org**.

[16] Here I refer to the groups currently active within the Republic of Montenegro. Many prominent Montenegrins had long been residing in Serbia, and recently have been active in the shaping of the contemporary Serbian language. These linguists—including Mitar Pešikan, Drago Ćupić, and Mato Pižurica—have subscribed to the views of what I called the "status quo" group of linguists; cf. 3.2.

recalled Vuk's family ties to the East Herzegovina/Northwestern Montenegrin area of Piva and Drobnjak, from where Vuk chose the dialectal base for his new standard.[17] By contrast, for the Montenegrin nationalists this action represented Vuk's desire to realize his "mono-genetic theory" ("monogenetska teorija") about the wholly Serbian nature of the Štokavian dialect and its literature (Nikčević 1997*a*: 588). They alleged that in such a theory the rights of the Croats, Bosniacs, and Montenegrins for a separate identity were denied.

4.2.1   The Neo-Vukovites

In the early 1990s, linguists based in Montenegro joined forces with Serb linguists in the debates on the future of Serbian, and have thus far accepted as a given that the Montenegrin dialects belong to the Serbian speech territory.

Branislav Ostojić, a co-author of the Neo-Vukovite *Pravopis*,[18] has been one of the main Nikšić-based linguists to participate in both the discussions surrounding the future of the Serbian ijekavian pronunciation, and the controversies surrounding Serbia's competing orthographic manuals. Reacting to the 1993 Bosnian Serb decree to impose ekavian in Republika Srspka, he complained that no people should be forced to speak a dialect that is not their native speech, and believed in the cause of defending the status of the ijekavian pronunciation within the Serbian language. He conceded that as a result of fear of ekavian domination, the Montenegrins have over-ijekavianized their language, especially in the writing of *je* following the sonorant consonant *r*.[19] As one of only four members from ijekavian-speaking regions, Ostojić was appointed in 1998 to be Montenegro's representative to the Committee for the Standardization of the Serbian Language.[20] With the formation of the Committee, the proposals and rules introduced by the Neo-Vukovites were both discredited and ignored. Given the dominance of the status quo linguists, the Montenegrin Neo-Vukovite linguists found themselves on the losing side of the debate on the future standardization of the new Serbian language. This defeat did not result in the defection of the Montenegrin Neo-Vukovites to the pro-independence side advocating a separate Montenegrin language. Rather, it alienated them from mainstream Serbian linguistic circles, and made them more vulnerable to attacks from the pro-independence faction. Indeed, the

---

[17] Vuk was born in Tršić in Western Serbia, but his family migrated there from the Piva/Drobnjak region, and the East Herzegovina-type dialect was his native idiom.

[18] Cf. Simić et al. (1993).

[19] Cf. Ostojić (1994: 5–8). In these environments, the historically short South Slavic *jat'* was usually realized as *e*, rather than *je*, e.g., *vrijeme* 'time', where *ije* resulted from a long *jat'* vs. *vremena* (not **vrjemena*) 'times', where a short *jat'* yielded *e*.

[20] The remaining 15 members of the Committee are from ekavian-speaking regions.

debates within Serbian linguistic circles outlined in Chapter 3 buoyed the true Montenegrin linguistic secessionists, who viewed the work of the Committee to be anti-Montenegrin. They further contended that the Neo Vukovites such as Ostojić had failed to protect Montenegrin linguistic interests, and that their policy had represented a "middle path" destined to crumble under Serbian-ekavian pressure. Thus, Nikčević (1997a: 593) described Ostojić's activities in the following manner:

Dr Branislav Ostojić ... is at the halfway point, the midpoint between the Karadžić-Belić "Serbian/Serbo-Croatian" vernacular and standard language as a single system and a single norm, on the one hand, and the Montenegrin spoken and literary language, which in his view is a sub-variant and idiom ... of [that Serbian/Serbo-Croatian] language, on the other hand.[21]

The Serbian government's decision to declare the Matica srpska ortho-graphic manual to be official in the territory of Serbia propelled Ostojić closer than ever to the pro-independence camp. It was reported that Ostojić, in an interview published in *Pobjeda*, called this decision "the separation of the Serbian language according to republican boundaries" ("cijepanje srpskog jezika po republičkim granicama").[22] Given that this boundary is now an international, and not a republican boundary, some younger linguists in Montenegro have already joined forces with those individuals who had long been advocating for the establishment of a separate Montenegrin language.[23] The nature of this language, however, remains uncertain.

4.2.2 Nikčević and his supporters

The Montenegrin nationalist faction, led by the late Vojislav Nikčević, has included literary figures from the Montenegrin affiliate of the PEN Center and members of the Matica crnogorska, a Montenegrin cultural society. Nikčević (1997a: 586) contended that his group has opposed the pro-Serbian faction since the end of the 1960s, when

two polarized approaches in the linguistic life of Montenegro have led a parallel existence, and have clashed among themselves in the fight for prestige. The first has been the

---

[21] "Dr Branislav Ostojić ... se nalazi na pola puta, na sredokraći izmedju karadžićevsko-belićevskoga 'srpskog/srpskohrvatskog' narodnoga i standardnog jezika kao jednoga sistema i kao jedne norme, s jedne, i crnogorskog govornoga i književnog jezika, po njemu, kao podvarijante i izraza ... [toga srpskog/srpskohrvatskog] jezika, s druge strane."

[22] Cf. *Republika*, no. 152 (1996), "Radovanom po Vuku," available at **www.yurope.com/zines/republika/arhiva/96/152/152-9.html**.

[23] One such linguist, Adnan Čirgić, succeeded the late Vojislav Nikčević as director of the Institute for the Montenegrin Language and Linguistics in 2007. Čirgić has been called the "first doctor of the Montenegrin language."

Karadžić-Belić approach ... under the protection and powerful support of the current government. ... The second, which has supported the authenticity and origin of the independent Montenegrin language from the works of the Montenegrin masters, of the greatest writers ... has had heretical status.[24]

Like other nationalists, members of the pro-Montenegrin faction have supported their claims for a sovereign Montenegrin nation-state by emphasizing its peculiar cultural heritage, history, literature, ethnic origins, and language. In their search for authenticity, they have made some outlandish claims on the special origin of the Montenegrin people. In an interview posted on the Montenet website entitled "Does a Montenegrin Language Exist?" ("Da li postoji crnogorski jezik") Nikčević made the highly dubious claim that "the prototype for the Montenegrin language is the Polabian language," having based these unfounded assertions on "hundreds" of Montenegrin place names. Even more unlikely is his assertion that the ancestors of the Serbs came from an "ekavian-speaking" area of southeastern Poland, and that their ekavian reflexes of *jat'* are somehow linked to those found in Bye-lorussian. For him, the Montenegrins are the sole authentic ijekavian speakers in the Balkans, and other peoples in the area (Serbs, Croats, Bosniacs) had acquired ijekavian speech "secondarily." There is no credible evidence to justify any of these claims. The Montenegrins would be as connected to the Polabians as any other Southern Slavic people, and toponyms in the Southwestern Balkans can usually be traced to substratum languages or to South Slavic influences, rather than West Slavic ones. Moreover, while it is true that ijekavian was spread from the South-west to other parts of the region, this dialect was found among many indigenous Serbs from Eastern Herzegovina, and Croats in southern Dalmatia, including most Croats living on the Peljašac Peninsula.

Nikčević's allies in the Montenegrin affiliate of the PEN Center for writers have been actively promoting a separate Montenegrin language. In 1993, they disseminated their "Declaration on the Legal and Constitutional Position of the Montenegrin Language" ("Deklaracija o ustavnopravnom položaju crnogorskog jezika"). This Declaration emphasized that

from the scientific standpoint, there is no scholarly reason, and from the standpoint of the interests of Montenegro there is no political reason, for the Montenegrin language not to be called by its own name, both in the scientific realm, and in the legal-constitutional one.[25]

---

[24] "U lingvističkom životu Crne Gore ... paralelno žive, medjusobno se sukobljavaju i bore za prestiž dva jako polarizovana pristupa. Prvi je tradicionalistički, karadžićevsko-belićevski ... pod zaštitom i sa snažnom podrškom aktuelne vlasti ... Drugi pristup, koji se zalaže za izvornost i autentičnost samosvojnoga crnogorskog jezika iz djela crno-gorskijeh klasika, najvećih pisaca ... ima jeretički status."

[25] Cf. "Jezik Cnrogoraca je crnogorski jezik" from *Naša borba* (20 January 1996): "sa stanovišta nauke ne postoji naučni razlog, a sa stanovišta interesa Crne Gore politički razlog, da se crnogorski jezik ne imenuje, naučno i ustavno-pravno, svojim imenom."

After the orthographic controversies that dominated linguistic discourse in the FRY in the mid-1990s (cf. 3.3), the PEN Center issued a strongly worded statement reaffirming its conviction that the "language of Montenegrins is Montenegrin." Once the Matica srpska manual was officially endorsed by the Serbian government, members of the PEN Center defiantly declared that

[t]hese days the linguistic passions of Serbian provenance are bursting into flames. [On the one hand,] the Greater Serbian options have been keen on imposing confusion through an orthographic order for the entire "heavenly people" by means of pale adaptations of the so-called Novi Sad Agreement and Vuk's literary language to the new stipulations of the "Žabljak Constitution" [of the FRY]. On the other hand, Matica srpska has clearly and unambiguously brought forth the *Pravopis srpskog jezika* according to the specifications of its own people, and their linguistic needs—among other things, the Cyrillic alphabet and the ekavian pronunciation. ... The Serbian state has finally supported [the authors of the *Pravopis*] in this effort with its decree, which calls for the obligatory acceptance of Matica srpska's *Pravopis srpskog jezika* on the territory of Serbia from 1 January 1997. ... With this, Montenegro and its people are confronted with yet another fateful challenge on the subject of national identity, culture, and even statehood. Space is becoming all the more restricted for hermaphroditism, for split personalities and manipulation, for using a Montenegrin first name and a Serbian last name, for mythomania and irrational attitudes.[26]

Such arguments played into fears of a Serbian cultural takeover. The failed compromises of the past, including the Novi Sad Agreement and the Literary Agreement, caused the emergence of "weak hybrid identities," which in the view of the members of the Montenegrin PEN Center were designed to assimilate the Montenegrin people, denying them the right to a distinct Montenegrin ethnolinguistic identity. Ironically, in 2003, seven years after the PEN Center's statement was issued, the FRY's April 1992 "Žabljak Constitution" was officially discarded, and the new state of Serbia-Montenegro was established. This

[26] Ibid. "Ovih dana rasplamsavaju se jezičke strasti srpske provenijencije. [S jedne strane,] velikosrpske opcije teže da nametnu galimatijas pravopisnog odredjenja za sav 'nebeski narod' blijedim prilagodjivanjem tzv. Novosadskog dogovora i Vukovog književnog jezika novim uslovima 'Žabljačkog Ustava'. S druge strane, Matica srpska, jasno i nedvosmisleno, prezentira *Pravopis srpskog jezika* prema mjeri svoga naroda i njegovih lingvističkih potreba—pored ostalog, pismo ćirilica i ekavski izgovor ... u tome [je], konačno, podržala [autore Pravopisa] i srpska država, svojim dekretom koji zahtijeva obaveznu primjenu *Pravopisa srpskog jezika* Matice srpske na teritoriji Srbije, od 1. januara 1997 godine. ... Time su Crna Gora i njen narod suočeni sa još jednim sudbinskim izazovom na planu nacionalnog identiteta, kulture, pa i državnosti. Sve više se sužava prostor za hermafroditizam, dvoličnost i manipulisanje, za ime crnogorsko i prezime srpsko, za mitomaniju i iracionalno ponašanje."

development marked the final demise of Yugoslavism as both an ideology and an identity construct, allowing for the inevitable strengthening of separate Montenegrin and Serbian identities, and the emergence of an independent Montenegrin state in 2006.

The Constitutional Charter which created the state of Serbia and Montenegro contained no provisions on official use of languages or scripts. The question of an official endorsement of a separate Montenegrin language was put on hold until the status question was resolved through the referendum on independence held on 21 May 2006. Controversy persisted surrounding the designation of the official language(s) in the new Montenegrin Constitution; ultimately on 19 October 2007 the parliament charted a new constitution proclaiming Montenegrin as the primary official language and Serbian as one of four secondary official languages.[27]

4.3 The proposed standard

While Nikčević made bizarre claims for authenticity, he went further than any other Montenegrin academic towards codifying a new Montenegrin language. His publications on the Montenegrin language include a preliminary orthographic manual (1993), a more comprehensive *Pravopis* (1997b), and a two-volume work on the Montenegrin language published by the Matica crnogorska (1997a). The latter is an ambitious work which covers the "genesis, typology, development, structural characteristics, and function" of the Montenegrin language, and includes a list of the typically Montenegrin linguistic features, which justify the claims of legitimacy for yet another language based on the Neo-Štokavian ijekavian dialect. These features include (p. 603ff.):

(1) The Štokavian/ijekavian base of the language, including the system of four tonal accents, phonological and morphological structures, and core vocabulary shared with other Štokavian-based languages (Bosnian, Croatian, and Serbian).
(2) Consistent ijekavian reflexes of Common Slavic *jat'*; this feature unites all speakers of Montenegrin.
(3) Phonological features, including the development of innovative "Montenegrin" phonemes /dz/, /ś/, and /ź/, some non-contracted forms, and new jotations.
(4) Admittance of Montenegrin-specific morphological endings for some adjectival and pronominal declension types.

Nikčević devoted little time to explanations of the first two types of linguistic features, since these have been precisely those features that link the Montenegrin speech territory with that of the Croats, Bosniacs, and ijekavian-speaking Serbs. Rather, he focuses on the Montenegrin-specific features listed under (3) and (4). These features have some far-reaching symbolic functions, since, as seen below,

---

[27] This issue is addressed further in the Postscript section of this volume.

they required a modification in the inventory of the Montenegrin Cyrillic and Latin alphabets, and the revival of some archaic endings found in the writings of the Southwestern Štokavian area in the nineteenth century.

4.3.1 New letters and new pronunciations

The would-be Montenegrin language reformers have argued that the Montenegrin standard language requires the introduction of three new consonants. These consonants are shown in the following table:

Cyrillic grapheme	Latin grapheme	Approximate pronunciation
ѕ	з	/dz/, as in (English) 'lan**ds**'
ć	ś	soft /sh/, almost like (English) '**sh**eer'
з́	ź	soft /zh/, almost like (English) 're**g**ime'

The two palatal sounds, ś and ź, arose primarily in the Northwestern Montenegrin and East Herzegovinian Neo-Štokavian/ijekavian dialects.[28] These dialects obtain such forms through a process referred to as "new jotations," which occurs when the dental consonants *s, z, d, t* were followed by *j* resulting

Montenegrin	Bosnian
śedi	sjedi 'sit!'
źenica	zjenica 'pupil (of eye)'
đevojka	djevojka 'girl'
ćerati	tjerati 'to drive out'

from the ijekavian renditions of the short *jat'.* In the ijekavian dialects spoken by Bosniacs and Croats such jotations are completely absent; they may only be found among Serbs of East Herzegovina and Montenegrins. Compare the following Montenegrin-ijekavian and Bosnian-ijekavian forms:
Nikčević and his followers have advocated the elevation of these geographically restricted dialectal forms to the status of the Montenegrin literary norm. While these new jotations are found in the territory of Montenegro, they are neither pan-Montenegrin nor uniquely Montenegrin, since East Herzegovinian Serbs also admit such a feature.[29] Moreover, the occurrences of the new jotations **sj* and **zj*, which produced

---

[28] For instance, these phonemes are regularly noted in the dialect of the Uskoks (Stanić 1974), and in the dialects of Piva and Drobnjak (Vuković 1938–9).

[29] Vuk mentioned the new jotations for *dj* and *tj*, but did not consider them part of the standard pronunciation for his literary standard.

the new phonemes and their corresponding graphemes in the proposed new Montenegrin alphabets, are relatively infrequent. Nikčević provided no proof that these sounds qualify as distinctive phonemes, whose proper notation in the language would serve to distinguish meanings of words. For these reasons, the introduction of the new graphemes has had mostly symbolic value, since they bring to the Montenegrin language two letters unique to the Montenegrin alphabet within the Southern Slavic context.

The third new grapheme, (Latin script) з/(Cyrillic script) ѕ, also serves to distinguish the Montenegrin language from the three other Serbo-Croatian successor languages. However, unlike the other two phonemes, this one was present in Old Church Slavic texts, and has been incorporated into the orthography of the Macedonian literary language. This phoneme is largely absent from the Northwestern Montenegrin dialects, which admit the new jotations; rather, it is more frequent in the so-called Zeta-Lovćen dialects of Southeastern Montenegro and the Serbian Sandžak. The same phoneme is found in the dialects of Albanian and Western Macedonian.[30] Nikčević decided to include this phoneme based on such dialectal forms as *bendzin* 'petrol', *brondzin* 'bronze pot', *jedzero* 'lake'.[31] In all these cases, the phoneme /dz/ replaced an original /z/. This development is inconsistent within the speech territory, and is hardly considered to be a typical "Montenegrin" feature. By including such a marginal and questionable phoneme in his inventory, Nikčević succeeded in fashioning a kind of Montenegrin "super-dialect" that integrates the new jotations from the northwest with the phoneme /dz/ from the southeast.

4.3.2 The expansion of ijekavian features

In addition to the new letters, Nikčević has sought to reintroduce archaic morphological endings reflecting the practices frequent in the Northwestern Montenegrin Neo-Štokavian/ijekavian dialects.[32] Nikčević has called this phenomenon "phonological and morphophonemic ijekavianisms," since all these features involve the continuants of the Common Slavic *jat*'. The Montenegrin-Eastern Herzegovinian ijekavian dialects—called by many linguists the "Southern" Štokavian dialects—differ from the other Štokavian dialects in that these are specific adjectival and pronominal endings in which the vocalic element was *jat*' (e), rather than *i* or *o*. These differences can be seen in the following

---

[30] Elsewhere I have attributed this phenomenon to a probable Balkan Romance substratum, cf. Greenberg (2001*b*).

[31] These examples are taken from Southeast Montenegrin/Sandžak dialects, cf. Vujović (1969) and Barjaktarević (1966).

[32] In addition, Nikčević included in standard Montenegrin one high-frequency ijekavian form which has long been perceived as a typical Montenegrin feature, namely the negative forms of the verb 'to be': (Montenegrin) *nijesam* 'I am not' vs. (other Štokavian) *nisam*. This feature can be commonly heard in the speech of Montenegrins.

examples of the masculine singular and plural genitive endings and the endings for the dative-locative-instrumental plural:

Montenegrin dialects	Other Štokavian dialects
ovijeg	*ovog* (genitive singular) 'this'
dobrijega	*dobroga* (genitive singular) 'good'
šezdesetijeh	*šezdesetih* (genitive plural) 'sixties'
svijem	*svim* (locative plural) 'all'[33]

Belić (1930: 32) believed that precisely these "Southern Štokavian" forms should be avoided and did not belong in a standard ijekavian pronunciation. However, these endings were typical in the Štokavian/ijekavian literary works of Njegoš, and for this reason Nikčević incorporated them into his new Montenegrin language.[34]

To summarize, the elements that Nikčević combined in creating the unique features of the Montenegrin language included: (1) dialect-specific phenomena, especially those reflecting Montenegrin phonological changes, and (2) the kinds of phonological and morphological characteristics found in nineteenth-century literary works written by Montenegrin writers, but inconsistently found in living dialects. Consequently, he created an artificial and idealized language for the Montenegrins, which is not native to any of its citizens. In doing so, he hoped to prove that Montenegrin is fundamentally different from the other ijekavian-based standard languages (Croatian, Bosnian, and Serbian/ijekavian), but simultaneously he ran the risk of alienating Montenegrins unwilling to make radical changes in their language. Without broad support for his proposed standard, he could ultimately fail to be the founder of a fourth vibrant successor language to Serbo-Croatian.

4.4 Conclusions

Magner and Marić have suggested (2002: 55–6) that the separate standards in the Serbo-Croatian speech territory emerged when distinct, but mutually intelligible dialects rose to the status of standard languages as a result of socio-political factors. The Montenegrins observed how these factors, including

[33] The Montenegrin plural forms derived from the so-called hard-stem pronominal declension types found in Old Church Slavic, as seen in (Old Church Slavic) *těxX* (genitive plural) 'that'. The other Štokavian dialects generalized the soft-stem pronominal endings as in (Old Church Slavic) *v'sixX* (genitive plural) 'all'. For the Montenegrin dialects, the *jat'*-from the plural has spread analogically to the genitive singular, which in Old Church Slavic pronominal declensions was –*ogo*/-*ego*.

[34] The original text of the 1850 Literary Agreement is replete with such morphological endings (see Appendix A).

nationalist-inspired ethnic polarization and the resulting ethnic conflicts, caused the initial break-up of the unified language into Bosnian, Croatian, and Serbian. Since Montenegrins chose to remain federated with the Serbs in 1992, the socio-political factors did not initially favor the emergence of a separate Montenegrin standard. However, in the FRY, the loosely federated state of Serbia and Montenegro, and in independent Montenegro, the pressure mounted for the official acceptance of the linguistic separateness of the Montenegrin language. This pressure to differentiate the Montenegrin language from the Serbian language gained momentum due to the disputes surrounding the future of the Serbian language as described in Chapter 3; these disputes had been particularly acrimonious in non-ekavian regions, such as Republika Srpska and Montenegro. The controversies that strained the unity of the Serbian language included:

(1) The Bosnian Serb decree on the implementation of the Belgrade-Novi Sad ekavian pronunciation in their territories, rather than their native ijekavian. As a result, Montenegro remained the last administrative unit where the ijekavian pronunciation was officially mandated.

(2) The support given by Pavle Ivić and Serbia's status quo linguists to the Bosnian Serb decision to downgrade ijekavian. As a result, the Montenegrins of all persuasions—pro-independence or Neo-Vukovites—rallied in support of the ijekavian pronunciation, since ijekavian was the ethnolinguistic marker for inhabitants of Montenegro.

(3) The decision of the Serbian government to require the use of the Matica srpska *Pravopis* in Serbian territory in all schools and institutions of higher learning. This decision caused many in Montenegro to believe that the Serbian language was splintering along the Serbian-Montenegrin republican boundary.

(4) The election of Milo Djukanović as Montenegro's president in 1997; this election provided a political boost to the pro-independence forces in Montenegro, who sought to institute their version of a separate Montenegrin standard.

Despite these fissures in the unity of the Serbian language, most Serbs and a significant segment of Montenegrin society continue to oppose the legitimization of the independent Montenegrin standard or literary language.[35] For his part, Nikčević and his pro-independence cohorts have claimed that every people deserves to

---

[35] I found several articles in the Montenegrin press from March and April 2007 that expressed opposition to Montenegro's designation of the Montenegrin language as an official language of the country. In one article from 24 April, Jelica Stojanovic, professor of the Philosophy Faculty in Nikšić is quoted as claiming that "in Montenegro, the Serbian language has always been spoken, and that is also how it was called. . . . Not a single dialect or speech variety ends on the borders of Montenegro" ("u Crnoj Gori se uvijek govorio jezik srpski, a tako se i imenovao. . . .nijedan govor, ili dijalekat, ne završava se na granicama Crne Gore"). The text of this article from *Pobjeda* is available at www.pobjeda.co.yu/naslovna.phtml?akcija=vijest&id=116928. For a more detailed discussion of this and other articles, see section 8.4

have its own language, and that a Montenegrin language is justified by its nineteenth-century literature and its distinctive brand of ijekavian. The Serbs and pro-Serbian Montenegrins rejected such claims, and considered both the Montenegrin literary tradition and the ijekavian pronunciation to be elements of the Vukovian heritage, and therefore a part of a Serbian cultural heritage. Thus, while the Serbs grudgingly accept the emergence of the separate Croatian and Bosnian languages, they stand firm against Montenegrin efforts towards linguistic separation. The drive for a separate Montenegrin language has been further complicated by the dialectal diversity of Montenegro. The ijekavian dialect in the republic, with its two main sub-dialects, is not uniquely Montenegrin. Across the former Yugoslavia, the dialectal boundaries have not corresponded with republican borders, and the ijekavian pronunciation, despite its political setbacks in the 1990s, is still widely spoken outside Montenegro, i.e., by Serbs in Bosnia-Herzegovina, the Sandžak, and a section of Western Serbia.

The discussion above demonstrates that even with the Constitutional designation of the official use of the Montenegrin language in the newly-independent Montenegrin state, the nature of that language remains uncertain. In terms of Radovanović's (1996: 5) ten phases of language planning, the pro-Montenegrin faction has proceeded through only the first four phases, including "selection," "description," "prescription," and "elaboration". They are currently winning the battle for the fifth stage- "acceptance". Only after passing through this phase can they assume supremacy in the language-planning process in Montenegro. Should Nikčević's norm prevail, either through the acceptance of the political elite, or the acquiescence of the pro-Serbian forces, the Montenegrin language can continue relatively unimpeded through the final five crucial phases of language planning, including "implementation" and "cultivation." Simultaneously, the pro-Serbian faction among language planners in Montenegro has thus far failed to gain acceptance for the Neo-Vukovite agenda, especially regarding orthographic matters and the status of the ijekavian pronunciation in the standard Serbian language. Given the victory of the status quo linguists in Serbia and the work of the Committee for the Standardization of the Serbian Language, the small Montenegrin group of linguists have had only limited influence on language planning within Montenegro. While they have superior linguistic credentials *vis-à-vis* Nikčević and his cohorts, they have lagged behind politically within the power structures of the independent Montenegrin state. The Nikčević group, through the PEN Center and the Matica crnogorska, have been far more vocal in their pursuit of a separate Montenegrin language, and spearheaded an official change in the constitutional status of the Montenegrin language.

With the establishment of the independent Republic of Montenegro, more than ever the future of a separate Montenegrin language hinges on political factors. Currently, the ruling coalition headed by the Democractic Party of Socialists is supporting efforts to standardize the Montenegrin language. In the 2003 census, only approximately 22% of Montenegrins claimed their mother tongue to be Montenegrin, while nearly 64% claimed it to be Serbian.[36] While the Montenegrin language has become a reality through official sanctioning, such a Montenegrin language may not necessarily be the one proposed by Nikčević. Rather, it is possible that Montenegrin linguists will become more actively engaged in the language standardization processes in the country, potentially choosing a standard that is closer to the "Montenegrin standard linguistic idiom" that developed during the latter decades of Socialist Yugoslavia. Ultimately, the future path of the Montenegrin language remains uncertain, and it is still unclear if and to what extent it will be accepted outside Montenegro's borders.

[36] These census data are available at www.monstat.cg.yu/Popis1.htm.

5

Croatian: We are separate but equal twins

The Croatian language has existed...at least since approximately the end of the eighth century, and since then it has never been the case that the Croatian language has not existed.

(Katičić 1995: 16)[1]

5.0 Introduction

In the nineteenth century, the codifiers of a standard Croatian language were faced with the challenge of creating a unified literary language for the Croat people. Led by Ljudevit Gaj of the Illyrian Movement, these language planners insisted upon the elevation of the Neo-Štokavian/ijekavian dialect as the single literary standard for all Croats. This choice of dialect was not an obvious one, since for several centuries prior to 1830 various other regional dialects had also boasted literary traditions in the Croat lands.[2] Moreover, the different regions of Croatia had long developed their own cultural and linguistic identities, especially Istria, Dalmatia, and Slavonia. After the defeat of Napoleon, and the unification of the Croat lands under Austro-Hungarian rule, the tensions between region-alism and centralism reached a decisive phase. In this phase, the members of the Illyrian movement sought to unify the Croatian people through language.

Gaj and his followers in the Illyrian Movement achieved for the Croatian people a linguistic union well before the attainment of a political union. Thus, they "brought centuries-old trends to a victorious conclusion by bridging the linguistic gap between kajkavian Croatia [around Zagreb] and the rest of the Croat lands" (Banac 1984: 216). This "victorious" conclusion prevented linguistic fragmentation among the Croats, and therefore language has served a unifying

[1] "Hrvatskoga jezika bilo je...barem od tamo negdje pred kraj osmoga stoljeća. I od tada nikad nije bilo da ne bi bilo hrvatskoga jezika."

[2] According to Guberina (1940[1997]: 2), the tradition of writing literature in the vernacular began in the fourteenth century.

function for the Croat people. Recently, Croat linguists have emphasized the role of the Illyrians in securing the unity of the Croatian language, while downplaying their simultaneous support for the language union with the Serbs. Thus, in Point 4 of his "Ten Theses on the Croatian Standard Language," Brozović asserted that

[i]n the early thirties of the 19th century the Croatian (Illyrian) National Movement unified all the Croatians linguistically through... [the] New Štokavian standard language. Two or three decades afterwards the Ikavian aspect was abandoned, and the New-Štokavian Ijekavian koine became the homogeneous Croatian standard language.[3]

For Brozović, then, the Illyrian Movement was noted for creating a language to unite the Croats, even though they achieved this goal through the 1850 Literary Agreement with the Serbs. Spalatin (1975: 8ff.) echoed this sentiment, when suggesting that the Illyrians had set aside "the two peripheral Croatian standards, Čakavian and Kajkavian,... [in favor of] the central Croatian standard, based on the Štokavian dialect, for the common Croatian standard language. That dialect instead of becoming a general South Slavic standard became only a Croatian standard."[4]

Given the Croats' prolonged autonomous linguistic and literary traditions, it is natural to ask why contemporary Croat linguists have been preoccupied with proving that Croatian and Serbian are full-fledged separate languages. This question is tackled in a discussion of the link between language and politics in the history of the Croat people during the last two centuries (5.1). Croats have considered this history to be characterized by the struggle of the Croatian nation for independence and sovereignty. The final obstacle for such sovereignty was the Yugoslav People's Army and the rebellion in 1991 of Croatia's Serb minority. Given this attitude, the Croats felt that their language, like their people, became emancipated when Croatia seceded from Yugoslavia. Therefore, Croatia's contemporary language planners labored to create a Croatian standard language separate from the Serbian standard language swiftly and completely. After analyzing these efforts (5.2), I demonstrate that the task of standardization of the new Croatian language has not been without controversy, especially on orthographic matters (5.3).

---

[3] This quotation is taken from Spalatin (1975: 12), who provided the translation of Brozović's original text.

[4] As seen below (5.2.1), the Kajkavian and Čakavian dialects were not ignored in the standardization of the ijekavian standard developing around Zagreb after 1836. Spalatin argued that the Illyrian Movement had a pan-Croatian orientation, symbolized by the diverse backgrounds of its leaders, who included a native Kajkavian speaker (Ljudevit Gaj), a Čakavian speaker (Antun Mažuranić), and a Štokavian speaker (Vjekoslav Babukić). He concluded that for this reason the phonological, morphological, and syntactic basis for the modern Croatian language is Štokavian, but the vocabulary includes numerous Čakavian and Kajkavian forms.

5.1   Croatian from Broz to Brozović

For the Croats, language issues gained prominence whenever they felt threatened by stronger or more numerous neighbors. In the middle of the nineteenth century the threat of Hungarian nationalism and moves towards Magyarization of Croatian culture spurred Croat linguists to advocate a Croat national revival through the Illyrian Movement and its pan-Slavic ideology. In the twentieth century, the Croats felt threatened by what they perceived to be hegemonistic tendencies radiating from Serbia. How were Serbs transformed from linguistic-cultural allies into enemies in such a short span of time? Did the Croat followers of Vuk and Daničić inadvertently provide the conditions for the future Serb/Croat language feuds? Is the issue of whether Croatian and Serbian are the same or different languages a political or linguistic matter? Croat linguists have addressed these questions almost obsessively since 1991 with the aim of creating a coherent narrative on the history of the Croatian language. Two periods in the recent history of Croatian have been essential for this narrative: (1) the formative years of the Štokavian-based Croatian standard language, terminating in the publication of Broz and Iveković's 1901 dictionary, and (2) the decisive years that gave impetus for the separate Croatian standard language, culminating in Brozović's "Ten Theses on the Croatian Standard Language" (circulated in 1971, and printed in Spalatin (1975)).

5.1.1   Contributions of the "Croat Vukovites": Traitors or Croat patriots?

Contemporary Croat linguists have been careful in their interpretations of the joint literary tradition in the late nineteenth century, referred to above as the period of "centrally monitored unity" (cf. 2.1.1). In the aftermath of the 1967 Resolution of the Zagreb Linguistic Circle, the Croat linguists were keen to distance the Croatian linguistic tradition from the Serbian one. In their interpretations, they suggest that in the nineteenth century the Croats "had discussions" with the Serbs, and signed a non-binding agreement with them, but that the Croat linguists of the nineteenth century contributed greatly to the development of a Croatian standard language, and not a joint Croato-Serbian/Serbo-Croatian language.

The approach put forth in Moguš (1995: 168) reflected this Croato-centric focus of the nineteenth-century Croat signatories to the 1850 Literary Agreement:

In discussions...with Vuk Karadžić and Daničić in Vienna during 1850, several well-known Croat literary figures (including Ivan Mažuranić, Dimitrije Demeter, and Ivan Kukuljević) considered that it would be good to base the future common [efforts in] building the standard language on the kind of stylization of Štokavian-ijekavian, which had developed among the Croats, and which Vuk Karadžić had formulated for the Serbs based on the texts of the folk literature.[5]

This statement implies that for the Croats, the Štokavian-ijekavian dialect had somehow developed naturally over time, whereas for the Serbs it had been brought about through the intervention of a single individual, who based it on a collection of folk literature he had uncovered. Moreover, although Vuk and Daničić may have influenced the decision on the choice of dialect, the Croats had made a "good" choice that brought maximal benefit to the Croat people. Moguš (ibid.) went on to minimize the importance of the Literary Agreement by claiming that the document signed in Vienna at the time was not referred to as an "agreement" ("dogovor"), but merely a "statement" ("izjava"), and was the opinion of only six signatories. Furthermore, he argued that

not one philological school in Croatian accepted such an agreement despite the stance of its signatories, since this would have meant the abandonment of the tradition of building a standard language on the basis of the Štokavian literary texts which already incorporated elements from old Štokavian and non-Štokavian writing styles.[6]

These elements included features from the Čakavian, Kajkavian, and older Štokavian-Slavonian literary traditions. Moguš and others have indicated that the Croats never intended to abandon these elements in order to create the unified language with the Serbs, despite the pressure from Daničić and some of the Croat Vukovites who collaborated with Daničić in Zagreb.

In assessing Daničić's role at the Zagreb Yugoslav Academy of Sciences and Arts after 1866, Croat linguists have focused on what they considered to be Daničić's agenda to prevent regional Croatian lexical items from infiltrating the literary standard. Since Daničić's primary responsibility was the preparation of the first volume of the *Dictionary of the Croatian or Serbian Language* (*Rječnik* 1880–1975), he wielded powerful influence in the initial stages of standardization. In 1975, this dictionary was hailed as one of several key factors of "primary importance" ("prvorazredna važnost") in the development of a Croatian national consciousness, and it was claimed that it demonstrated the "great antiquity of Croatian culture and the capability of the Croatian language to express everything that an

---

[5] "Raspravljajući...1850 godine u Beču s Vukom Karadžićem i Djurom Daničićem nekoliko je poznatih književnika (medju njima Ivan Mažuranić, Dimitrije Demeter i Ivan Kukuljević) smatralo da bi bilo dobro buduću zajedničku izgradnju standardnoga jezika temeljiti na onoj stilizaciji ijekavske štokavštine kakva se bila razvila u Hrvata i kakvu je za Srbe bio oblikovao Vuk Karadžić na osnovi tekstova narodne književnosti."

[6] "Ni jedna filološka škola u Hrvatskoj nije prihvatila takav dogovor unatoč ugledu potpisnika jer bi to značilo napustiti tradiciju da se standardni jezik izgradjuje na osnovi štokavskih književnih tekstova u kojima su već bili inkoporirani i elementi nenovoštokavskih i neštokavskih književnih stilizacija."

author... wished to express."[7] However, Daničić was seen as obstructing this mission through his refusal to include Kajkavian dialectal material in the 1880 volume he had prepared. He had not heeded the advice of some prominent Slavists of the time, including Sreznevskij, Weber, and Jagić, who had expressed their support for the inclusion of more contemporary Croatian elements in the dictionary.[8]

After Daničić's death in 1882, the prominent Croat Vukovites who took over the management of the dictionary project adhered closely to Daničić's intent. These Croat linguists, including Petar Budmani (from 1883 to 1907) and Tomislav Maretić (from 1907 to 1938), embraced Daničić's Štokavian-only policy regarding lexical items to be included in the Dictionary. The 1999 reference book on proper usage in Croatian, the *Hrvatski jezični savjetnik* (henceforth referred to as the *Savjetnik*), considered these Croat Vukovite linguists to be Štokavian purists. These linguists were responsible for directing the development of the Croatian standard lexicon in the late nineteenth and early twentieth centuries (Barić et al. 1999: 57). For the authors of the *Savjetnik*, such a movement represented an aberration in the development of the Croatian language, since

[t]he history of the Croatian standard language, as far as the lexicon is concerned, is characterized by a tri-dialectal interpenetration interrupted, to be sure, by the inflexible and the exclusive Štokavian purism of the Croat Vukovites... and it is completely normal and natural for the standard language to fill its lexicon and stylistic gaps with Kajkavian and Čakavian words (ibid.).[9]

Sensitive to the criticism heaped on the Croat Vukovites, Babić (1995: 172) attempted to explain their actions and demonstrated that they were not blindly following a Vukovian (Serbian) agenda. In his view,

Maretić's problem has been due to the fact that his descriptive grammar of a single dialect type, or if we desire to be more precise, of Vuk and Daničić's language, has been conceived of as a normative grammar of the Croatian literary language. But it is not, or rather it is [like that] only in those places where Maretić explicitly says that something is, or that something is a particular way, or something should be a particular way in the literary language, but it is chiefly a descriptive grammar written from a comparative-historical perspective.[10]

---

[7] *Rječnik* (1880–1975/23: 62): "[Rječnik] bi mogao pokazati veliku starinu hrvatske kulture i sposobnost hrvatskoga jezika da izrazi sve što je autor... želio izraziti."

[8] Ibid.: 66.

[9] "Povijest hrvatskoga standardnoga jezika obilježena je, što se leksika tiče, tronarječnim prožimanjem, prekinutim doduše krutim i isključivim štokavskim purizmom hrvatskih vukovaca... te je posve normalno i prirodno da standardni jezik svoje leksičke i stilske praznine popunjava kajkavskim i čakavskim riječima."

[10] "Nevolja za Maretića proizlazi odatle što je njegova opisna gramatika jednoga dijalekta ili ako želimo preciznije reći Karadžićeva i Daničićeva jezika shvaćena kao normativna gramatika hrvatskoga književnoga jezika, ali ona to nije, odnosno jest samo na mjestima gdje Maretić izričito kaže da tako jest ili da bi tako trebalo biti u književnom jeziku, ali je ona ipak svojom glavninom opisna gramatika s poredbeno-povijesnoga gledišta."

Babić stressed that under Communism and immediately following the Novi Sad Agreement, Maretić's grammar had been republished, and forced upon the Croats as the "complete codification" ("potpuna kodifikacija") of the "Croato-Serbian language" (ibid.).[11] Such a development revealed that the works of the Croat Vukovites had been exploited by those advocating a reaffirmation of the Serb/Croat linguistic union in Tito's Yugoslavia. Babić preferred to consider the work of the Croat Vukovites on their own merits in the context of the Croat young linguistic movement ("mladoslovničarski smjer"), which had embraced the idea of unity with the Serbs. For him, this movement lasted until the assassination of the Croat parliamentarian Stjepan Radić in 1928 (ibid.: 167).

Babić's moderate views on the Croat Vukovites are not shared by most linguists in Croatia. His careful approach is drowned by the rhetoric of ultra-nationalists, who have rejected all those who openly collaborated with Vuk and Daničić. Some nationalists have opted to distort the history of the joint language by ignoring the role of Vuk and Daničić in inspiring a generation of Croatian linguists. Others were persuaded that Vuk and Daničić were ill intentioned towards the Croats, and were guided by a Greater Serbian ideology.[12] Given Serb-Croat enmity in the 1990s, it is understandable why the Croats felt an aversion to any suggestions that Vuk and Daničić contributed to the development of the Croatian standard language. Katičić (1995: 18) addressed this matter emphatically, arguing that

for now it is more usual abroad to place Karadžić in the middle of what they consider should be Serbo-Croatian studies, and then they seek to include therein Croatian studies. It is necessary to state clearly that this is scientifically completely unacceptable. It is impossible for such a treatment to have any kind of scientific credibility.[13]

To summarize, contemporary Croat linguists of all political orientations have rejected Serbian claims that Vuk or Daničić helped create the Croatian language. While mostly lukewarm in their embrace of the work of the Croat Vukovites,

---

[11] Babić quoted from the grammar's foreword to the third edition published in 1963, some 25 years after Maretić's death.

[12] Two ultra-nationalistic viewpoints are found in the following sources: Tanocki's superficial sketch (1994) of the history of the Croatian language, in which the 1850 Literary Agreement was not mentioned, while the 1967 Declaration on the Name and Position of the Croatian Literary Language is prominently highlighted (1994: 11ff.); cf. also Kačić (1997), who devoted an entire monograph to correcting all "delusions and distortions" on the history of the Croatian language, dismissing any notions of a unified Serbo-Croatian language.

[13] "Za sada je u svijetu običnije da se Karadžić stavlja u središte onoga što bi, kako misle, trebala biti serbokroatistika i onda zahtijeva da time bude obuhvaćena i kroatistika. Treba jasno reći da je to znanosti potpuno neprihvatljivo. Na takvu se postupku ne može zasnivati nikakvo znanstveno dostojanstvo."

they have not dismissed their work outright. Rather, they have viewed them as misguided Štokavian purists, and overly zealous in their pan-South Slavic convictions. Nonetheless, for the most part, they have recognized their contributions to the standardization of the Neo-Štokavian ijekavian dialect in the Croatian lands.

5.1.2 Tito's Yugoslavia: Croatian and not Croato-Serbian

Many modern Croat linguists regard the first twenty years of Tito's Yugoslavia as a gloomy period stalling the development of a separate Croat linguistic identity. They felt that the Croatian people had been betrayed by the Communists, who, after their victory in 1945, reversed the 1944 decision of the Anti-fascist Committee for the National Liberation of Yugoslavia (AVNOJ) to recognize separate Serbian and Croatian languages.[14] Rather, language policy in the 1950s and early 1960s was decidedly in favor of maintaining a single Serbo-Croatian or Croato-Serbian language. Bašić (2001b: 88) called the Communist era a time when uneducated political commissars and party functionaries decided the fate of the Croatian language and its orthography. In her view, these ideologically driven individuals presided over a period of oppression, which lasted until the adoption by the Zagreb Linguistic Circle of its Declaration on the Name and Position of the Croatian Literary Language, and the dissemination of Brozović's "Ten Theses on the Croatian Standard Language" in 1971. After the breakup of Yugoslavia, many Croats began to view the period after 1966 as the decades in which the "battle" ("borba") for a Croatian language was being waged (Tanocki 1994: 6). Brozović, who was one of the leaders of this movement, has considered the whole Yugoslav period to be a constant struggle for Croat linguistic identity and freedom. He justified the Novi Sad compromises as being a necessary step toward the eventual goal of linguistic separation, describing the work of Croat linguists in the following manner:

These were difficult times. Temporary compromises had to be made, so that progress could be made according to the model: "one step backwards, two steps forward", but sometimes even the tactical compromises did not help, and many fighters for the Croatian language were suffering in various ways, and everybody was disregarded in every respect. Those who remained on the sidelines did not really have to make any kind of working compromises, but they did not contribute anything to the struggle—had everyone proceeded this way, after

---

[14] On 15 January 1944 AVNOJ declared Croatian, Serbian, Slovene, and Macedonian to be equal in the "entire territory of Yugoslavia." Cf. the opening of the volume edited by Pavletić (1969): "svi ovi jezici su ravnopravni na cijeloj teritoriji Jugoslavije."

almost a half-century, we would have been faced with many undesirable realities in the Croatian language, and freedom would have come too late.[15]

The 1967 "Declaration" has taken on special significance in post-Socialist Croatia. Several months after Tudjman was elected in Croatia, the Matica hrvatska proclaimed 13–17 March "The Days of the Croatian Language" ("Dani hrvatskoga jezika.") These dates in March commemorate the days in 1967 when the Declaration was first signed (13 March) and then published (17 March). The celebration of the "Days of the Croatian Language" was to occur annually. Brozović (1997: 88) complained that the Matica hrvatska was initially unsuccessful in promoting these celebrations, and was hopeful that the Croatian Parliament would formally recognize the annual commemorations. Indeed, the Parliament passed legislation regarding the "Days of the Croatian Language" in 1997. This legislation included a provision requiring that all schools devote one hour of instruction each March to the Declaration and its significance for the Croatian language.[16] The Parliament succeeded in passing the legislation in time for the thirtieth anniversary of the Declaration, and that year Matica hrvatska also published the third edition of a volume which included a reprint of the "Declaration," and of materials that were used in its preparation (cf. Hekman 1997). Brozović expressed his hope that the Croatian government would supply the school libraries with copies of the text of the "Declaration" so that future generations would remember the struggle that Croat linguists had waged for a separate Croatian language. Despite all this effort, Babić (2002: 39) lamented that even after the action of the Parliament, there was little local enthusiasm for the "Days of the Croatian Language," and felt embarrassed that the "Days of the German Language" held in Zagreb on 5–8 June 2001 had been better organized and better attended.[17]

For the Croatian language planners the "Declaration" has taken on legendary proportions, since it constituted the first instance in Tito's Yugoslavia when the Croats dared to call their language the "Croatian literary language." For the original drafters of the document, the Novi Sad Agreement, with its designation of the Western variant as "Croato-Serbian," represented an assault on a separate

---

[15] Cf. Brozović (1995: 26): "To su bila teška vremena. Morali su se praviti privremeni kompromisi kako bi se moglo napredovati po obrascu 'korak natrag, dva koraka naprijed', ali ponekad nisu pomagali ni taktički kompromisi i mnogi su borci za hrvatski jezik na razne načine stradavali, svi su bili zapostavljeni u svakom pogledu. Tko je bio po strani, nije morao doduše praviti nikakvih djelatnih kompromisa, ali nije ništa ni pridonosio borbi—da su svi postupali tako, nakon gotovo pol stoljeća imali bismo u hrvatskome jeziku mnoge svršene činove i sloboda bi došla prekasno."

[16] Ibid.: 89.

[17] According to Babić, "the Croatian Parliament adopted its decision on the holding of the Days of the Croatian Language, but nothing more than that" ("Hrvatski je sabor donio odluku o održavanju Dana hrvatskoga jezika, ali ništa više od toga").

Croat linguistic identity. The name had powerful symbolic meaning for the Croats, and raised their fears that the Serbs had renewed their hegemonic linguistic designs *vis-à-vis* the Croatian language. Brozović (1995: 26) unleashed harsh criticism against all those who silently stood by in Croatia while Croat linguists of the 1960s and 1970s fought for "Croatian linguistic individuality" ("hrvatska jezična individualnost"). He argued that many of those silent bystanders in the Yugoslav era were amateur linguists, who had since adopted an extreme anti-Yugoslav nationalist ideology which would deny the accomplishments of Croatian linguistics of the past fifty years (ibid.).

Ironically, contemporary Croat linguist have felt nostalgic for the days of the struggle for a separate name and status for the Croatian language. These feelings have been fueled by a disappointment in the discourse on the Croatian language in the post-1991 period. Both Brozović (1995) and Katičić (1999: 114) have complained that too often Croat linguists have been obsessive about the similarities or differences between Croatian and Serbian.[18] In 1999, the authors of the *Savjetnik* went so far as to claim that

judging by the number of language reference books (of this or that type), and handbooks of the differences [between Croatian and Serbian] (in the past ten years about ten of these have been published), the state of Croatian linguistic culture has never been worse.[19]

In a 1995 interview, Katičić rejected the practice among some Croat linguists, who had obsessively toiled to differentiate Croatian from Serbian. He concluded that

such a definition of the Croatian language in contrast to Serbian is the worst; moreover, it is completely false. After all, the Croatian language does not exist because it is different from Serbian; rather it exists on its own merits. We cannot discard words like *ruka* ['hand'], *nos* ['nose'], *voda* ['water'] because they are simultaneously also Serbian words. If we were to do so consistently, we would lose the Croatian language.[20]

[18] The differences between Serbian and Croatian have been treated in several Serbian–Croatian and Croatian–Serbian dictionaries, often called "razlikovnici" ("differentiating dictionaries"). They range in length from 107 pages (Pavuna 1993) to 632 pages (Brodnjak 1993). I even discovered a small dictionary specializing in the differences for construction terminology (Vazdar 1993). One such dictionary appeared in Serbia, entitled the *Serbo-Croatian Dictionary of the Variants* (Ćirilov 1989). The 180-page volume contained both Serbo-Croatian and Croato-Serbian sections, and presented the Serb view that the two variants constitute a single language.

[19] Cf. Barić et al. (1999:10): "Sudeći po broju jezičnih savjetnika (ove ili one vrste) i razlikovnika (u posljednjih deset godina objavljeno ih je desetak), stanje hrvatske jezične kulture nije nikada bilo lošije."

[20] This text was taken from an interview in *Globus* (no. 226) from 7 April 1995: "takva [je] definicija hrvatskoga jezika u razlici prema srpskome najlošija, što više: da je potpuno kriva. Pa ne postoji hrvatski jezik po tome što je različit od srpskoga nego po tome što jest to što jest. Ne možemo izbacivati riječi *ruka, nos, voda* zato što su ujedno i srpske. Kad bismo to dosljedno proveli, onda bismo izgubili hrvatski jezik."

Such statements reflected some of the disagreements that have arisen within Croatian linguistic circles over the past decade regarding the future directions of the Croatian language. As seen below (5.3), these disagreements were particularly heated in connection with the appearance of two rival orthographic manuals. However, before detailing these disagreements, I first discuss the corpus planning issues for the new Croatian standard.

5.2 The new Croatian

Many of the same linguists engaged in the struggles for a separate Croatian language during Socialist times were directing the course of the separate Croatian standard in the 1990s.[21] Several of them had written influential works at the time of the Declaration and its immediate aftermath (cf. Brozović 1970 and Težak and Babić 1973).[22] Some of the works at that time were so controversial that they were banned by Tito when he suppressed the Croatian Spring movement in 1971.

One of the best known of these works was an orthographic manual, *Hrvatski pravopis*, which was published in Zagreb in 1971, but quickly destroyed by the authorities. A copy of the manual was taken out of the country, and was published in London in 1972, and has been known as the Londonac 'the Londoner'.[23] The reissue of this manual in Croatia in 1994 exemplifies the linkage between the language planning activities of the 1960s and 1970s with those of present-day Croatian society (cf. 5.3.1).

Some of the principles that have guided current Croatian language planners can be found in the text of Brozović's "Ten Theses on the Croatian Language" from November 1971. The first three "theses" addressed issues of status planning, including a definition of the Croatian standard language, and the evolution of the Croatian standard or literary language from its earliest attestations. Points 4–6 have been significant for corpus planning, and are summarized as follows:

Point 4: "today,... the Croatian standard language remains open to the Kajkavian and Čakavian dialects and freely takes from them any linguistic element, if useful and appropriate, accommodating it to its own laws."

---

[21] In a similar fashion, the dominant group of linguists to emerge in Serbia—referred to in 3.2 as the status quo linguists—had also played leading roles in Socialist Yugoslavia.

[22] The volume by Težak and Babić was supposed to be published in Zagreb in 1973 under the controversial title of *Pregled gramatike hrvatskoga književnog jezika* ("Survey of the Grammar of the Croatian Literary Language"). The previous five editions had appeared under the title *Pregled gramatike hrvatskosrpskog jezika* ("Survey of the Grammar of the Croato-Serbian Language"). The eleventh edition was published simply as *Hrvatska gramatika* ("Croatian Grammar"), (cf. Težak and Babić 1996).

[23] Updated versions of this manual began appearing in Croatia after 1990, and its sixth edition was published in 2004, cf. Babić et al. 1971[2004].

Point 5: "The Croatian standard language developed its culturo-linguistic structure independently and in its own way...following the linguistic patterns established first by the Italian, German and Czech languages, assimilating with them and in a way similar to theirs, the ancient Latin and Greek heritage common to the whole of Europe."[24]
Point 6: "the Croatian standard language contains only the Western Neo-Štokavian features of the ijekavian and ikavian sub-dialects."[25]

These three points affirmed aspects of Croat linguistic purism, as described above (cf. 2.5.1). This purism is manifested in the tradition of incorporating vocabulary for the Croatian language from Croatian peripheral dialects, or what is typically called the Kajkavian and Čakavian "regional vernacular standards" (Point 4), and from other dialects marked as ethnically Croat, such as the Štokavian ikavian dialects of Central Dalmatia, Western Bosnia, and Western Herzegovina (Point 6). Such a puristic approach was consistent with that practiced by some German and Czech language reformers, who sought to infuse their languages with native words whenever possible, rather than with borrowings from other languages. When the reformers introduced foreign borrowings, they were normally modified to conform to the phonological structure of the receiving language (Point 5).

These principles have guided the language planners of the Croatian standard language since 1991, when Croat linguists accelerated the purification processes of the standard language. Some of the new words recently introduced were extracted from relatively obscure nineteenth-century dictionaries,[26] while others have been newly coined words with no antecedents in earlier Croatian linguistic history. While corpus planning for Croatian has included some aspects of Croatian phonology, morphology, and syntax,[27] the greatest innovations have been in the realm of vocabulary. In the following sections I will elaborate upon the increased insistence on use of words from the Kajkavian and Čakavian dialects (5.2.1), and the marked increase in native Croatian forms (5.2.2).

[24] In particular, the Czech language reformers during the late eighteenth and early nineteenth centuries influenced Gaj and his fellow Illyrians in Croatia.

[25] The translations have been taken from Spalatin (1975); I have made slight modifications in phraseology.

[26] Tanocki (1994: 30) argued that Croats should discard the word *avion* 'airplane', which had been used in Socialist Yugoslavia, and remains the standard Serbian form. He justified the use of the Croatian form, *zrakoplov*, since it was "native," having entered the language in the nineteenth century, as documented by its appearance in a German-Croatian dictionary from 1867.

[27] Many of the Croatian language handbooks have urged their readers to use the infinitive regularly, rather than *da* followed by the present tense (as in Serbian); cf. Kuljiš (1993: 34ff.) and Tanocki (1994: 21ff.). Some of the other non-lexical aspects have included the strict adherence to the distinctiveness of short and long adjectives, rules regarding the genitive endings *–oga* vs. *–og*, and rules for the use of the feminine clitic pronoun *ju* vs. *je*.

5.2.1   The Čakavian and Kajkavian lexical stock

For the Croats, the status of Kajkavian and Čakavian has continued to be a factor in determining the future identity of the Croatian standard language. Bašić (2001b: 91) synthesized the current thinking regarding the relationship of these two dialects to Croatia's standard Štokavian in the following manner:

The developmental patterns that are left for the Croatian language and orthography—the Neo-Štokavian ijekavian base enriched with Kajkavian and Čakavian material and a moderately phonological writing system—are good, and it is worth perfecting them.[28]

Katičić (1997: 183) was even more emphatic and unequivocal regarding the importance of the Kajkavian and Čakavian components in standard Croatian:

Only in the Croatian language, and in none other, do the Štokavian, the Kajkavian and the Čakavian dialects coexist in a specific flow of interconnected communication. It is the living contact between those who ask by saying *što*, those who do so by saying *ča* and those who do so by saying *kaj*, all meaning 'what?'—a contact taking place in quite common situations, as when the Štokavian mountaineers from neighbouring settlements descend to the Čakavian city of Senj on the coast in order to bring their products to the market, or when the Čakavian islanders from Korčula come with their boats to the port of Štokavian Dubrovnik, or when Čakavian people from the Littoral come up to nearby Kajkavian Fužina in the Mountain-District in order to run sawmills there and Štokavian villagers from neighbouring Lič come there to town, combining thus in spontaneous communication all three Croatian dialects—it is this contact taking place in various ways that has shaped the physiognomy of the Croatian language.

While this idealized picture of the development of a Croatian language enriched with its Kajkavian and Čakavian dialects originated with the leaders of the Illyrian Movement, Croat language planners have done little since the 1960s to increase these dialectal elements in their language. Only after 1991 has there been serious debate over introducing more of these elements into the new Croatian standard. The discussion or argument for Croatian as a true separate and different language from Serbian involved these elements. For instance, Katičić stated that

[t]he language of the Croats is both Kajkavian and Čakavian, of which the Serbs have not even a trace... [And] in Croatian the Štokavian dialect is in everyday and fundamental communication with Kajkavian and Čakavian, and bears many markers of the older Western Štokavian dialect; thus, a large portion of Bosnia does not say *štap* ['stick'], but *šćap* just like the Kajkavian and Čakavian speakers.[29]

---

[28] "Razvojni okviri koji su ostavljeni za hrvatski jezik i pravopis—novoštokavska jekavska osnovica obogaćena kajkavskom i čakavskom sastavnicom i umjereni fonološki pravopis—dobri su i valja ih usavršavati."

[29] This text was taken from Katičić's 1995 *Globus* interview (see note 20 above): "Jezik Hrvata jest i kajkavski i čakavski, čega kod Srba niti u tragovima nema.... [I] u hrvatskom je štokavski u bitnoj, u temeljnoj komunikaciji s kajkavskim i čakavskim, i nosi mnoge

Regardless of this "communication" between the Croatian Štokavian standard and the other Croatian dialects, the standard form remains *štap*, just as in Serbian. Thus, despite recent interventions, the Croatian standard has remained resistant to regional dialectisms. Such resistance is further seen in the use of the interrogative pronoun *što* vs. *kaj*. Hence, even though most natives of Zagreb use *kaj* for "what" rather than the standard form *što*, the form *kaj* is considered to be colloquial or dialectal. While Čakavian or Kajkavian dialectal forms are more likely to creep into standard Croatian than standard Serbian, the fact remains that very few dialectisms have actually entered Croatian from either of these two dialects. Moreover, distinctly Kajkavian and Čakavian phonological and morphological features are absent from the standard Croatian language. Even in the lexical domain, according to the *Savjetnik*, only a "certain number" ("odredjeni broj") of words from these dialects have been absorbed into the standard Croatian lexical stock, including: *hrdja* 'rust, corrosion', *imetak* 'property', *klesar* 'stone cutter, stone mason', *krstitke* 'baptismal party', *kukac* 'insect', *ladanje* 'farm/estate, country vacation', *podrobno* 'in detail', *pospan* 'sleepy, drowsy', *prah* 'powder, dust', *rubac* 'handkerchief', *rublje* 'laundry, linen', *skladatelj* 'composer', *spužva* 'sponge', *tjedan* 'week', *tlak* 'pressure' (Barić et al. 1999: 56). The authors of the *Savjetnik* confirmed that only in terms of lexicon can Croatian be simultaneously Štokavian, Čakavian, and Kajkavian, and that by contrast, in the realm of accentuation, the Croatian language is solely Neo-Štokavian in nature (ibid.: 70).

Clearly, these Čakavian and Kajkavian lexical items have become identified with the Croatian language, and would be considered non-native to Serbs, Bosniacs, and Montenegrins.[30] Nonetheless, after the Ottoman invasions in the Balkans, the Štokavian dialects spread across the Croatian lands at the expense of the Kajkavian and Čakavian dialects (Katičić 1984: 264–5). Despite their pronouncements, the Croats have sacrificed these dialects in the name of unity for the Croatian Štokavian standard. Today the Čakavian dialect continues to decline, while the Kajkavian dialect has remained vibrant as it affects the urban vernacular of Zagreb (cf. Magner 1966). This urban vernacular, however, has had little influence over the standard language. Croat linguists since 1991 seem more open than ever to increasing the role of the peripheral dialects, although this

biljege starijega zapadnoštokavskoga: tako velik dio Bosne ne govori *štap* nego *šćap*, kao kajkavci i čakavci." Some Štokavian speakers, especially Croat and Bosniac ikavian speakers, also would say *šćap*, alongside other forms in /šć/, which evolved from an original *sk + j* or *st + j*. In the dialectological literature, these types of dialects have been classified as "šćakavian" as opposed to a "štakavian" sub-group.

[30] Babić's list of Kajkavian and Čakavian words includes several additional items, such as: *hrvati* 'to wrestle', *hrzati* 'to neigh', and the prefix *protu-* 'anti-' (1997: 30). The relatively small number of lexical items from Kajkavian and Čakavian seem insignificant in comparison to the number of German, French, or Hungarian loanwords (cf. 2.5.3).

openness has not been matched by a noticeable increase in the Kajkavian and Čakavian components of the new Croatian standard.

5.2.2   Infusing the new standard with native Croatian forms

According to the Croatian *Savjetnik*, the most striking differences between Croatian and Serbian are lexical. These differences are found in some 20,000–25,000 words (Barić et al. 1999: 9). As discussed in 2.5.1, these differences have been partially attained through the Croatian linguistic practice of (re-)introducing native Croat forms and eliminating foreign borrowings. Moreover, the inventory of uniquely Croatian lexical items can be significantly increased through the inclusion of Croatian words that may have the same root as their Serbian counterparts, but differ from the Serbian forms in the types of prefixes (compare Croatian *poduzeće* vs. Serbian *preduzeće* 'enterprise'), grammatical and derivational suffixes (compare Croatian *osnovica* vs. Serbian *osnova* 'base, foundation', Croatian *regulirati* vs. Serbian *regulisati* 'regulate') and minor phonological differences (compare Croatian *uho* vs. Serbian *uvo* 'ear').

Since 1991, corpus planners in Croatia have formulated prescriptive rules concerning internationalisms and foreign borrowings. The first lexical rule given in the 1999 *Savjetnik* is that it is always better to replace foreign words with native Croatian ones, as in the example of the borrowed form *play-off*, for which the *Savjetnik* recommended the home-grown *doigravanje*.[31] The second rule introduces a hierarchy of three different kinds of foreign borrowings whenever a foreign word is unavoidable. This hierarchy consists of *tudjice* 'foreign-looking words', *prilagodjenice* 'foreign words adapted to look native', and *usvojenice* 'foreign words fully adapted to Croatian'.

Therefore, [i]f one must accept a word of foreign origin, it is better to accept a foreign word, fully adapted to Croatian, rather than a foreign word adapted to look native, and it is better to accept a foreign word adapted to look native, rather than a foreign-looking word.[32]

In such a hierarchy, a borrowing from English, such as *kompajler* 'compiler' would be classified as a *tudjica* 'foreign-looking word', since in its phonology, it violates the "natural" consonant-vowel structure of Croatian.[33] "The *Savjetnik* advised its readers to choose the *prilagodjenica* 'foreign word adapted to look native'

---

[31] The word *doigravanje* is a neologism, formed by the root *igra-* 'play' with a prefix *do-*. The form is a verbal substantive, conveying the meaning of "the process of playing to completion."

[32] Cf. Barić et al. (1999: 282): "Ako se već mora prihvatiti riječ stranoga podrijetla bolje je prihvatiti usvojenicu nego prilagodjenicu, a prilagodjenice je bolje prihvatiti nego tudjice."

[33] Presumably, the sequence *–jl–*, which is rare in Croatian, is felt to be an unnatural combination of consonants.

kompilator, which is viewed as exhibiting a consonant-vowel structure more typical of native Croatian words. Nevertheless, for the authors of the *Savjetnik* the very best choice would be the Croatian neologism, based on a native root, *prevodnik*.

Given such lexical preferences, the corpus planners for Croatian have displayed a bias against languages whose phonological system differs radically from their own. For this reason, they unequivocally stated that it is better to accept international terminology directly from the phonologically acceptable Greek or Latin source languages, rather than through the mediation of the phonologically problematic source languages, such as English, French, or German.[34] Even when the "mediated forms" may be equally melodious in Croatian, preference is given to the form that more closely resembles the Greek or Latin root, e.g., the Latin nouns terminating in *–alis*, for which the *Savjetnik* prescribes the Croatian adjectives *vizualan* 'visual' and *aktualan* 'current' as opposed to the forms mediated through French/German, i.e., *vizuelan, aktuelan*.[35] By contrast, computer and technical terminology from English, including *bajt* 'byte', *fajl* 'file', and *daunloudati* 'to download' were actively discouraged, and in some cases Croatian neologisms were recommended, including: *medjuspremnik* 'buffer', *preglednik/prebirnik* 'browser', *premosnica* 'bypass', *'uručak* 'handout', and *srčanik* 'pacemaker' (Barić et al. 1999: 288, 295).

Some of the Croatian corpus-planning choices have gone beyond merely the above-mentioned "phonological" compatibility. Thus, the authors of the *Savjetnik* have displayed tolerance towards borrowings from lending languages of nations for which the Croats have felt cultural affinity. Such tolerance is greater especially concerning borrowings from French, Italian, and Hungarian.[36] For example, Croatian is said to have adopted approximately 40 Hungarian words, and all these have become *usvojenice* 'integrated phonologically', i.e., native speakers of Croatian are unaware of their foreign origin, and inflect them all precisely as if they had been native words (e.g., *gulaš* 'goulash' and *lopta* 'ball'). Conversely, the Croats have been intolerant of borrowings from lending languages of peoples they have considered to be culturally alien. Thus, while some of the borrowings from Turkish have also been considered to be *usvojenice* (e.g., *rakija* 'brandy', *bubreg* 'kidney', and *limun* 'lemon'), the authors of the *Savjetnik* declared that all other Turkisms should be replaced by native Croatian forms (ibid.: 290). Even less tolerance is shown towards perceived Russianisms, which "whenever possible should be replaced by domestic words." The examples of Russian borrowings given include *učesnik* 'participant' and *saučešće* 'sympathy', for which the manual recommended the native Croatian forms *sudionik* and

[34] The example given is the form *tendencija* 'tendency', rather than *tendenca* (Barić et al. 1999: 282).

[35] Ibid.: 286. These latter forms are typical of Serbian.

[36] In addition, German loanwords are said to be frequent in colloquial and dialectal speech, but in the standard language they have mostly been "translated" into Croatian.

sućut, respectively. While they do not explicitly state this, the authors have rejected the Russian forms, since these are the very forms that have been adopted by the Serbs. The Croats, therefore, have rejected both Orthodox Slavic and oriental/Islamic elements from their language, thereby underscoring the place of the Croatian language within a Central European context, with the aim of imbuing the Croatian language with a distinctly European identity. In this way, they further differentiate their language from both Serbian, with its "Orthodox" influences, and Bosnian, with its strong Turkish/Arabic lexical components.

The final portion of the *Savjetnik*'s discussion on the Croatian lexicon included a list of neologisms ("novotvorenice"), and native Croatian words that were considered to be worthy of revival ("oživljenice"). The neologisms frequently constitute calques based on English or German models, ranging from *tjelogradnja* 'body-building' to *umjeritelj* 'moderator' (ibid.: 110).[37] Regarding the revived forms, the *Savjetnik* makes a spirited justification for their reintroduction into Croatian, cloaking the discourse in terms of the "human rights" of these lexical items:

We wanted to return to these words their dignity, which had been taken away, and to give them the right of citizenship, and to allow for those words not introduced by mandate a fair contest with their competitors.[38]

These types of lexical items have included "archaisms" and "historicisms." The authors of the *Savjetnik* offered several examples in these categories. Among the "historicisms" appear several words that had also been employed by the Croatian fascist state (NDH) during the Second World War, including the term *kuna* for the currency, and such puristic Croatian forms as *poglavarstvo* 'authority of a head-of-state' and *domovnica* 'document proving Croatian origin'. Nowhere in the text is the NDH mentioned, but the authors of the *Savjetnik* hint that the political or ideological credentials of a given word should not prevent the word from competing in the current standard language, paving the way for the return of some of the NDH-inspired lexical items.

The prescriptivist bias of the *Savjetnik* regarding foreign words, and the preference for native Croatian words, even those that appear to be archaic or testaments to discredited ideologically driven policies, remain in sharp contrast

---

[37] Literally, *tjelogradnja* is a compound consisting of the nouns *tijelo* 'body' and *gradnja* 'building' (in the meaning of 'constructing a building'). The form *umjeritelj* corresponds to the verb *umjeravati* 'to moderate' and the adverb *umjereno* 'moderately'. The *–telj* suffix is common in newly coined Croatian words to denote personal nouns deriving from verbs, e.g., *slušatelj* 'listener' and *gledatelj* 'viewer'. Here, too, the Croatian suffix differs from that of Serbian, where these same deverbal nouns acquired the suffix *-ac*, i.e., *slušalac, gledalac.*

[38] "Htjeli smo tim riječima vratiti oduzeto dostojanstvo, dati im pravo građanstva, a onima koje se ne uvode propisom omogućiti ravnopravnu utakmicu s njihovim konkurentima."

to the descriptive approach preferred by some Croat linguists. This debate between prescriptivists and descriptivists was particularly evident in the years immediately following Tudjman's death, when two rival orthographic manuals appeared in 2000–1.

5.3 Recent orthographic controversies

Some ten years after the break-up of Yugoslavia, an emotional debate erupted within Croatian linguistic circles regarding the future path of the Croatian language. As in Serbia in the mid-1990s, the controversy in Croatia was due to the appearance of two orthographic manuals in the course of one year (2000–1). The first manual was the fifth edition of the *Hrvatski pravopis* written by three prominent linguists at the Institute for the Croatian Language (cf. Babić et al. 1972[2000]), and the second manual was produced by two Zagreb University professors (cf. Anić and Silić 2001). The two manuals presented divergent visions of the degree to which lexical or orthographical variation should be tolerated in the new Croatian standard. These divergent visions reflected the attitudes of two groups of Croat linguists, the prescriptivist (5.3.1), and the descriptivist (5.3.2). When the nationalist Croatian Democratic Union headed the Croatian government in the 1990s, the prescriptivists often displayed nationalist credentials. Langston (1999) demonstrated that the Croat nationalist-oriented media tended to adhere to the prescribed "new" Croatian forms, while the opposition, often non-nationalist media outlets were more accepting of language variation. The pressure to eliminate lexical doublets was part of the campaign to eliminate perceived Serbian forms in the Croatian language, thereby strengthening the Croatian identity of the Croatian language. Katičić (1997: 189) called these two trends within Croatian linguistic circles "conservative" (nationalist) and "revolutionary" (non-nationalist). He concluded that an equilibrium would be found between these two trends, but that in the meantime the conservatives "have a strong case in the high degree of stability the Croatian standard usage has already reached. This has become irreversible." As seen below, the "conservatives" have become increasingly prescriptivist, and do not seem to be losing ground to the revolutionaries just yet.

5.3.1 *The prescriptivist* Pravopis

As discussed above (cf. 5.1.2) the *Hrvatski pravopis* (*HP*) (Babić et al. 1972 [2000]) represented a reissue of the manual written at the time of the Croatian Spring in the period leading up to 1971. The manual had constituted a direct rebuttal of the joint Matica srpska/Matica hrvatska *Pravopis* that had emerged from the 1954 Novi Sad Agreement. The *HP* symbolized Croat resistance to what was considered to be a unified language favoring the Belgrade/Eastern variant of the joint language; it endured despite the banning and destruction of copies of the manual by Yugoslav authorities in 1972. In 1990, while Croatia was still part of Yugoslavia, this manual was officially published and sanctioned in Croatia for the first time.

In the Preface to the fourth edition of the *HP* (1996: viii), the manual's authors affirmed the basic tenet guiding their orthographic decisions:

> As the deliberations of the relevant institutions and generally accepted practice have shown, the Croatian orthographic principles have been standardized as phonological within a single word, and morphophonological between words, and we are firmly convinced that in the future there will be no significant exceptions.[39]

This desire to reduce the number of exceptions reflected the need among the Croats to eliminate alternate spellings and flexible grammatical norms. It extended to all levels of the language, including phonology, morphology, and syntax. For instance, the language in the issues of the journal *Jezik* published after 1991 is striking for the degree of consistency with which authors adhere to the new prescriptive norms of the Croatian language. The following passage from Babić (2002: 39) illustrates this consistency especially with regard to the integrity of the grammatical endings –*oga* (masculine singular genitive for adjectives and pronouns), –*omu* (masculine dative singular for adjectives and pronouns), and –*ome* (locative singular for masculine adjectives and pronouns). Before 1991, the endings –*oga*/-*og*, –*omu*/-*ome*, and -*ome*/-*om* were in free variation.

Hrvatski je sabor donio odluku o održavanju Dana hrvatskoga jezika, ali ništa više od toga. Niti je on preuzeo brigu za njih niti ju je povjerio komu drugomu. Toga se zadatka prihvatila Matica hrvatska i ona je najviše napravila, ona još uvijek mnogo čini, ali to još nije dovoljno. Tražio sam da ona Dane uvrsti u svakogodišnji plan svoga djelovanja, ali ne znam je li to učinila iako ih potiče svake godine i polako u tome napreduju, ali osjećam da bi moglo biti i bolje. Unutrašnji dogadjaji u MH kao da utječu i na djelatnost na tome području.[40]

---

[39] "Kao što su pokazala mišljenja relevantnih ustanova i općeprihvaćena praksa, hrvatski se pravopis ustalio kao fonološki u okviru jedne riječi, a morfonološki medju riječima i čvrsto smo uvjereni da tu u budućnosti neće biti bitnih odstupanja."

[40] In this passage I underlined the words reflecting the effect of some of the new prescriptive norms. Most of the examples are for pronominal and adjectival endings. In addition, I highlighted the feminine pronominal form *ju*, which replaces *je* whenever the third person present tense form *je* appears in the same sentence. The forms with the root *djela*-'do/make' are highlighted because this root has become more frequent in Croatian since 1991. Here is a translation of this passage: "The Croatian Parliament made a decision on the celebration of the 'Days of the Croatian Language'" but nothing more than that. It neither accepted the responsibility for them, nor did it entrust the responsibility to

The move towards limiting variation can be seen when comparing the prefaces of *HP*'s 1996 (fourth) and 2000 (fifth) editions. In the 2000 edition several examples of spelling variations permitted in 1996 are eliminated. These variations included the writing of plural forms for masculine nouns terminating in *-dac*, *-tac*, *-dak*, *-tak*. Prior to 1996, the plural of *mladac* 'young man' could be written in three ways: morphophonologically as *mladci*, phonologically as *mlatci*, or phonetically as *mlaci*. The 1996 edition eliminated the form *mlaci*, which is typical of Serbian. Seeking to avoid all doublets ("dvostrukost"), the authors in 2000 have insisted on the morphophonological spelling only—*mladci*. Similarly, in the writing of the negative particle *ne* with the future short form clitics, the 2000 edition advised its readers to move away from the practice of writing these two forms as a single word, e.g., *neću* 'I won't', suggesting instead the writing of two separate words, i.e., *ne ću*. This form is said to be the manner of writing preferred prior to the 1954 Novi Sad Agreement (p. viii). Such recommendations have helped create the perception that Croatian prescriptivist practices have been part of the state agenda; the Bosnian newspaper *Dani* (2000) made the following observation, under the heading "Jezička politika" ("language policy"): "Croatian state-forming linguistic practices have no mercy, nor do they leave anything to chance."[41] Among the items reflecting this type of language policy, the article lists the "Days of the Croatian Language," active Croatian support of the use of the Croatian language in Bosnia-Herzegovina, segments of radio and television programs, and newspaper columns on the Croatianness of specific words.

Furthermore, the *HP* has incorporated many of the most recent prescriptivist-oriented changes relating to the lexicon of the Croatian language. For entries such as *avion* 'airplane', *ambasada* 'embassy', *sport* 'sports', *učesnik* 'participant', *učešće* 'participation', *saučešće* 'sympathy', *Evropa* 'Europe', and *hiljada* 'thousand', the *HP indicated* to the readers that these words have been replaced with the proper Croatian ones, i.e., *zrakoplov*, *veleposlanstvo*, *šport*,[42] *sudionik*, *sudioništvo*, *sućut*, *Europa*, and *tisuća*.

Upon the publication of the second edition of the *HP* in 1994, not all elements in Croatian society were pleased with the updated manual. Babić, the manual's

somebody else. The Matica hrvatska has taken on this task, and it has achieved the most, and it is still doing a lot, but it is still not enough. I requested that it implement the 'Days' in the annual plan of its activities, but I do not know if it did so, although it marks the 'Days' every year, and slowly is progressing in this, but I sense that it could be better. Internal matters within Matica hrvatska seem to influence the activities in this area."

[41] Cf. the *Dani* website, **www.bhdani.com/arhiva/146/t1466.htm**: "hrvatska državotvorna jezikoslovesnost nema milosti niti išta prepušta slučaju."

[42] The form *šport* indicates that this item is a German borrowing. In a *Glas Hrvatske* ("Voice of Croatia") radio program I heard on 18 March 2002, the announcer introduced a segment on the competing Croatian orthographic manuals by asking whether or not it is correct to say *sport* or *šport* in the Croatian language.

co-author, defended the *HP* in the pages of the journal *Jezik*, especially in reaction to a review of the *HP* by the Zagreb University professor, Ivo Pranjković. Pranjković, in the magazine *Republika*, stated about the HP that it contains

orthographic rules which are either illogical, poorly formulated, inconsistent, incomplete, excessive, too 'flexible', such that they destabilize the evolved norms, while in the orthographic dictionary there are too many elements that do not in any way belong to it.[43]

In his view, one of these unnatural elements was an excessive use of ijekavian reflexes of *jat*.[44] Babić (1995: 57) reacted sharply to Pranjković's criticisms, claiming that Pranjković "spoke out in newspapers that did not care in the least to solve the problems, but used the sensational aspects of the orthographic issue to extract as much money as possible from the pockets of consumers,"[45] i.e., as a ploy to sell more newspapers. He disputed Pranjković's complaint regarding excessive ijekaviainism in the *HP*. Pranjković had rejected hyper-ijekavianisms in such forms as *pogrješno* 'mistakenly', which in his view should have been rendered by *pogrešno*. Babić's rebuttal was uncompromising, stating that the /-rje-/ sequences were characteristic of the literary works of sixteenth-century Dubrovnik, and *pogrješka* 'mistake' and *strjelica* 'arrow' were consistent with the manner in which people have spoken and written. While Babić admitted that ekavian-like forms with /-re-/ developed "later," he still felt justified in insisting on the older forms in the *HP* (ibid.: 59). Such an orthographic choice was consistent with the *HP*'s overall emphasis on reviving older Croatian words, and discovering characteristics of the Croatian language that could be considered authentically Croatian. Pranjković's negative opinions of the *HP* were a precursor to new emotional debates between the prescriptivist and descriptivist linguists over orthographic rules. These debates were sparked by the publication of the *Pravopis hrvatskoga jezika* (*PHJ*) by two of Pranjković's colleagues at Zagreb University, Vladimir Anić and Josip Silić.[46]

5.3.2   The descriptivist Pravopis

The authors of the *PHJ* manual were not newcomers to the craft of producing an orthographic manual. Their first collaboration was on a 1986 manual, when

---

[43] This citation was taken from www.aimpress.org/dyn/pubs/archive/data/199601/ 60115-001-pubs-zag.htm: "[—pravopisnih] pravila koja su ili nelogična, ili loše formulirana, ili nedosljedna, ili nepotpuna, ili suvišna, ili previše 'rastezljiva', pa nepotrebno destabiliziraju ustaljenu normu, a u pravopisnom rječniku ima previše elemenata koji mu ni po čemu ne pripadaju."

[44] As seen in 4.3.2, the issue of expanding ijekavianisms has also arisen in the debate over the nature of the separate Montenegrin language. Providing justifications similar to those put forward by Babić, Nikčević strongly advocated for these "hyper-ijekavianisms."

[45] "[Pranjković je] razglasio u noevinama kojima nimalo nije stalo da probleme riješe, nego da pravopisnom problematikom kao senzacijom izvuku iz džepa potrošača koju kunu više."

[46] Cf. Anić and Silić 2001.

Yugoslav linguistics had not yet fully given up on a unified literary language for Serbs and Croats. This manual did not have the association with the rebellious spirit of Croatian linguists of the late 1960s, and therefore from its very inception was more of a reflection on the Yugoslav realities that had influenced usage within Croatia. In the Preface to their 2001 manual, Anić and Silić stressed the need to have an orthographic manual that "maximally" reflected the actual manner in which the modern Croatian language is pronounced, while simultaneously incorporating the trends of "newer Croatian literature" ("novije hrvatske književnosti"). Such an approach was in stark contrast to that taken by the authors of the *HP*, who justified forms such as *pogrješno* based on literary traditions dating back to sixteenth-century Dubrovnik literary works.

While not directly mentioning the *HP*, Anić and Silić stated their intentions to produce a non-prescriptive orthographic manual, written in a spirit of tolerance. They sought "to avoid rigidity and exclusivity in rules, to avoid dualities not accepted in the spoken variety of the living language, but to tolerate those dualities that have come into practice in recent times." Underscoring this tolerance, they further asserted that:

An orthographic manual that is open to a multiplicity of forms precludes neither the choice of these multiple forms, nor the possibility of establishing their stylistic status. Wherever it has been possible, that is, wherever it has been within its competence, the PHJ has used multiple grammatical and lexical options, as well as multiple options in the realm of orthography (p. 3).[47]

Thus, by contrast to the *HP* with its goal of minimizing linguistic variation, the *PHJ* opted to embrace language choices in an attempt to describe fully the stylistic nuances and variations within contemporary standard Croatian. Hence, when the *HP* recommended a preferred, often post-1991 Croatian form, the *PHJ* tolerated lexical variation, and often admitted the pre-1991 lexical item alongside the "new Croatian" variant. Examples of acceptable doublets in the *PHJ* include: *avion/zrakoplov* 'airplane', *ambasada/veleposlanstvo* 'embassy', and *hiljada/tisuća* 'thousand'. Some of the new prescribed forms in the *HP* are completely absent from the *PHJ*. These forms include *šport* 'sports', *tlak* 'pressure', and *pogrješan* 'mistaken'. The *PHJ* includes both *evropejizam* and *europejizam* 'Europeanism', and three possible spellings for the plural of nouns terminating in -*dac*/-*dak*, e.g., *mladci*, *mlatci*, and *mlaci* 'young men' (pp. 134–5).

According to Bašić (2001*a*:43), the publication of the *PHJ* has placed Croatian linguistics in an absurd situation, in which the public will be confused as to what is the correct manner of spelling and pronouncing the language. She noted that

---

[47] "Pravopis koji je otvoren prema višestrukostima ne priječi izbor tih višestrukosti, pa onda ni mogućnost utvrdjivanja njihova stilističkog statusa. Gdjegod je to bilo moguće, tj. gdjegod je to bilo u njegovoj kompetenciji, *Pravopis hrvatskoga jezika* iskoristio je gramatičke i leksičke višestrukosti, pa onda i pravopisne višestrukosti."

despite this chaotic situation, the Croatian Ministry of Education and Sports had stood by its decision of endorsing the fourth edition (1996) of the *HP*. In a subsequent article (2001*b*), she proceeded to lambast the authors of the *PHJ* and their supporters, who in her view considered the *PHJ* to be a necessary transitional orthographic system on the way towards "an Orthography without unnaturalness" ("pravopis bez neprirodnosti"). The following excerpt, directed most notably at the publisher Slavko Goldstein, is particularly revealing regarding the emotional political subtext of this orthographic controversy:

Using the thesis of the "modern and tolerant" Croatian language, that which is presumably characterized in the *PHJ*, as opposed to the "archaic and unnatural" *HP*, which "nobody in Croatia speaks", Goldstein tries to dismiss the officially legitimized *HP*, and to direct the development of the Croatian language and orthography down a different path. In order to make room for the future "correct" Croatian orthography... and through it by means of the once again revived political and linguistic projects about the indivisibility of the Štokavian speech territory, which is at the core of the freeing of Croatian from its own identity, and from its linguistic-orthographic heritage, he has drawn upon the mean-spirited disqualification of the *HP*, connecting its provisions with the alleged rehabilitation of the NDH etymological writing system under the protection of the Tudjman regime (p. 88).[48]

Bašić went on to accuse Goldstein of using "all the characteristics of his worn-out Bolshevik hammer" ("sa svim obilježima njegova potrošena boljševičkoga malja," p. 87) in order to return the Croatian language to the days of the language union, where all Štokavian speakers, i.e., Serbs, Croats, Bosniacs, and Montenegrins, had no choice but to embrace a single language. In her view, Goldstein and the *PHJ* represented a reaffirmation of the 1954 Novi Sad arrangements, and ignored 11 centuries of Croatian orthographic traditions. She rejected any claims that the prescriptive norms of the *HP* were developed in accordance with any of the practices found in the etymological orthography published by the Ustasha regime in 1942 and 1944. Rather, she suggested (2001*a*:44) that the Tudjman regime had interfered little in the development of the new Croatian, and that

[a]fter a long time, the Croats, along with other free peoples, have found themselves in the situation where they can independently decide on the standardizing actions in their own

---

[48] "Tezom o 'modernome i tolerantnome' hrvatskome jeziku, kakav je tobože zabilježen u Anić–Silićevu pravopisu, nasuprot 'arhaičnom i neprirodnom' Babić–Finka–Moguševu, kojim 'nitko u Hrvatskoj ne govori', Goldstein pokušava ukloniti službeno legitimiran Hrvatski pravopis S. Babića, B. Finke i M. Moguša i usmjeriti razvitak hrvatskoga jezika i pravopisa drugačijim putem. Da bi oslobodio prostor budućemu 'pravomu' hrvatskomu' pravopisu ... a i preko njega ponovno oživjeli političkim i jezikoslovnim zamislima o nedjelivosti štokavskoga govornoga područja, kojima je i podlozi oslobadjanje hrvatskoga od vlastitoga identitetam i jezično-pravopisne baštine, poslužio s politikanskom diskvalifikacijom, aludirajući u dijelu rješenja Babić–Finka–Moguševa Hrvatskoga pravopisa na tobožnju obnovu endehazijskoga korijenskoga pravopisanja pod zaštitom Tudjmanova režima."

language and orthography. Seasoned by the experience of the past totalitarian regimes, democratic Croatia has rejected the model of managing language policy through a state-sponsored language bureau and already during the time of the so-called Tudjman regime it allowed scholars to organize independently and lay the foundation of language policy in order to safeguard the free development of the Croatian language and its orthography in the future.[49]

While the Tudjman regime did not ultimately establish a state-run institution to oversee language planning, members of Tudjman's Croatian Democratic Union (CDU) did make several attempts to interfere in language matters. These attempts included a proposed Law on the Defense of the Croatian Language, which aroused much controversy because some nationalists reportedly sought to levy fines for linguistic transgressions. Vice Vukojević, who introduced such a law during both the first and second CDU parliamentary mandates, argued that even the Croatian language that had been used by the Parliament of Socialist Yugoslavia was "purer" ("čišći") than that used by the post-1991 Croatian Parliament. Daria Sito-Sučić (1996) described Vukojević's initiatives in the following manner:

In August 1995, four years after Croatia proclaimed its independence, Vice Vukojević, a parliamentary deputy from the ruling Croatian Democratic... [Union], proposed two draft bills on language. In the first, Vukojević proposed that the phonetic alphabet be replaced by an etymological one and that 30,000 of the existing 60,000 to 80,000 words be purged from the Croatian language as non-Croatian... The other draft bill was aimed at establishing a Government Office for Croatian Language, which would have a police function. Anyone found breaking the new language rules would be fined or even imprisoned, depending on how serious the violation was. Both draft bills were rejected by the parliament, while the independent media and some of the top Croatian linguists regarded the proposals as outrageous.[50]

Another government attempt to legislate language matters was the establishment of the "Council for the Norms of the Croatian Language" ("Vijeće za normu hrvatskoga jezika"), which began work in 1997. This Council was largely inactive until 2005 when it was reconvened and has since ruled on some questions relating to the standardization of Croatian.

---

[49] "Nakon duga vremena i Hrvati su se, poput drugih slobodnih naroda, našli u prilici da samostalno odlučuju o standardizacijskim postupcima u vlastitome jeziku i pravopisu. Poučena iskustvom prošlih totalitarnih režima demokratska je Hrvatska odbacila model nadzora jezične politike institucijom državnoga ureda za jezik i već za tz. Tudjmanova režima prepustila struci da se samostalno organizira i postavi temelje jezične politike, koja bi jamčila u budućnosti slobodan razvitak hrvatskoga jezika i pravopisa."

[50] Cf. Zlatko Šešerin, "Hrvatski jezik-danas" (January 1998), in a Croatian émigré publication from Sweden, *Hrvatski glasnik,* available at **www.algonet.se/~bevanda/ 19814.htm**. The sub-heading for this article is "Will People in Croatia be Fined for Linguistic Impurity?" ("Hoće li se i u Hrvatskoj kažnjavati za jezičnu nečistoću?").

While overt government intervention was absent or unsuccessful in the 1990s, the debate surrounding the two competing orthographic manuals after 2001 pitted nationalist supporters of the *HP* against the non-nationalist authors of the *PHJ*. For instance, Bašić wrote that the *PHJ* manual denied the accomplishments of the Croat linguists who had fully supported the separateness and distinctive identity of the Croatian language. For her, the *PHJ*'s tolerance of language variation represented a return to the Yugoslav system, in which language variation was accepted in the Novi Sad formula of a single language with two equal and official variants. She considered the authors and defenders of the *PHJ* to be "Yugo-nostalgics," and warned that acceptance of this manual would result in the loss of Croatian identity. By contrast, Goldstein objected to the *HP*'s excessive purism and prescriptivism, which for him conjured up images of the fascist-inspired etymological spelling system forced on the Croatian people by the Ustasha government during the Second World War.

5.4   Conclusions

As seen in the above discussion, until the publication of the *PHJ* in 2001, the standard Croatian language had been developing rapidly and unmistakably as a language separate from the other Serbo-Croatian successor languages. While I have focused especially on the rival orthographic manuals, other works, including the *Savjetnik*, new dictionaries, and grammars,[51] have also advanced the separateness of the Croatian language, increasingly transforming it into a language less mutually intelligible with Bosnian, Montenegrin, or Serbian. The nationalist-leaning Croat language planners have had to abandon what Brozović had called the rights of closely related or nearly identical languages to have their own separate standards, as described in Point 9 of his 1971 "Ten Theses on the Croatian Literary Language":

The rights of the Croatian standard language are determined by the functions it performs for the Croatian nation, and not by the degree of similarity or dissimilarity it may have with other languages. The fact that, after being adopted by the Croatians, the New-Štokavian dialect . . . was adopted as the basis for a standard language also by other nations that speak the dialects of the Croat-Serbian diasystem, does not permit us to speak, not even from the strictly linguistic point of view, of a concrete Croato-Serbian standard language. Not only because the choices were made independently and at different times, and not only because their dialectal bases are not identical, but because for every standard

---

[51] For the grammars, cf. Barić et al. (1995) and Težak and Babić (1996). For dictionaries, cf. those specifically written to differentiate Croatian from Serbian (Brodnjak 1993) and Pavuna (1993), and the conventional ones, such as Anić (1991) and the new comprehensive Croatian–English Dictionary (Bujas 1999).

language as such the culture-linguistic superstructure is of essential importance... The rights of a certain language cannot be determined by the fact that it is more or less similar, completely dissimilar or very similar to some other language. That would be just as senseless and unacceptable as if in human society we would deny civil rights to fraternal or identical twins.[52]

Through prescriptive spelling rules, the revival of archaisms and historicisms, and the coining of neologisms, mainstream Croat linguists—under the influence of resurgent Croat nationalism—could no longer feel comfortable with the notion of "standard twin languages." Language planners have recognized that in order to achieve a new Croatian linguistic identity, they needed to focus on changes in the written language, since it is easier to change the way people write than to change the manner in which they speak. For this reason, much attention was devoted to the correct spelling, punctuation, and orthographic rules prescribed in the orthographic manuals. These manuals were designed to educate a new generation of Croats in the realm of the new Croatian standard. Babić (1997: 29) expressed confidence that through an insistence on and strict adherence to the new literary norms found in the *HP* and the Težak/Babić grammar, Croats both in Croatia and in Bosnia-Herzegovina were likely to modify their spoken language. In this manner, over time they would develop a more complete Croat linguistic identity.[53] During the Tudjman years, the government-controlled media was also instrumental in promulgating the new Croatian, and potentially affecting the speech of the citizens of Croatia. As Langston (1999) demonstrated, however, the media in Croatia did not universally adopt the prescriptive norms, and it would be naïve to assume that average citizens would consciously and consistently acquire the new Croatian language in their speech. The true "battle" for the new Croatian now rests in the hands of educators of the next generation of Croatian pupils, and the extent to which the school grammars, orthographic manuals, and dictionaries reflect the usage recommended by the nationalist-oriented linguists. Thus far, the school textbooks have incorporated many of the prescriptive rules of the *Savjetnik* and *HP,* and it is possible that this trend will continue.

Following Tudjman's death in 1999, and his party's loss of power, dissenting voices could be heard on the future of the Croatian language. This debate was dominated by the prescriptivist-nationalists on the one hand, and the descriptivist-more tolerant faction on the other. Katičić noted that similar debates erupted in Yugoslavia after 1971:

---

[52] This translation of Brozović's text was published by Spalatin (1975: 15).

[53] Babić praised the effectiveness of Croatian-language publications in Bosnia-Herzegovina, such as *Hrvatska riječ* and *Branimir,* which in his view have ensured that the Bosnian Croats acquire knowledge of the new Croatian language, and maintain a strong sense of Croat identity.

"We all know that there is a Croatian language of our own!" said the Croat from my audience. This is true, everybody who really lives with this language experiences it. All Croats know it. Most valuable witnesses in this respect are those Croats who for whatever reasons did not want to admit it and tried to promote "Serbo-Croatian" linguistic unity. While exposing their views and "fighting linguistic nationalism", as their activity was called in communist Yugoslavia, they always used the "purest" Croatian language, absolutely flawless, without the slightest trait of what could have been recognized as Serbian. They knew all too well that they had to do so because otherwise they would have no chance to reach a Croatian audience with their message and their arguments. Otherwise they would invariably repel instead of attract, any chance to convince would be lost. It is another thing that even so the results of their efforts were rather poor. So, while advocating the existence of any relevant difference between the Croatian and the Serbian language, they were compelled to take into account the very real existence of such differences, important enough to influence in a decisive manner their pragmatic choice of means of linguistic expression.[54]

This observation reveals the peculiar nature of group identity. In such an atmosphere, often when individuals would speak, others made judgments regarding their ethnic affiliation; therefore, even those individuals who did not adhere to the ideology of a separate Croatian language and identity often had to conform to the new linguistic realities, rather than risk the criticism of their interlocutors. Since even the voices of dissent would be spoken in the purist possible Croatian, it seems unlikely that there would be any return to a unified language with the other peoples/nations of the former Yugoslavia. Nevertheless, as relations between Croatia and Serbia return to normality, those intellectuals and linguists advocating a more tolerant and descriptive approach may be poised to make serious inroads in the Croatian linguistic scene.

[54] Katičić (1997: 181).

6

Bosnian: A three-humped camel?

The Vukovian linguistic norm was the basis of the first [attempts at] language standardization in Bosnia and Herzegovina. However, language of Bosnia-Herzegovinian writers, especially of the Bosniac ones, is based not on rural dialects, but rather on the urban ones which constitute the foundation of the Bosnian linguistic standard.

(Muhamed Šator 1999: 107)[1]

6.0 Introduction

The Sarajevo suburb of Ilidža was the site of a conference organized in 1991 by the Democratic Party of Serbia. Bringing together legislators from the six republics of Yugoslavia, the organizers hoped to halt the war in Croatia, and prevent the conflict from spreading to Bosnia-Herzegovina. However, the conference quickly deteriorated, as Glenny recounted:

The intention of the participants was to achieve what the leaders of the six republics had failed to do so abysmally: to unearth the road to peace. Mićunović made this plain in a tactful and encouraging opening speech. He finished by saying that simultaneous translation of the proceedings into Slovene and Macedonian would be provided. This harmless remark was the signal for the remaining guests to inject a lethal dose of Balkan absurdity into the proceedings, which would demolish any marginal hopes that the conference might have produced anything of value. Neven Jurica, the leader of the Croatian Democratic Union delegation and an uncompromising Croat nationalist, raised his hand on a point of order. "I was pleased to hear that Slovene and Macedonian translations will be provided but there are other languages as well to be translated . . . I would also like to request a simultaneous translation of the proceedings into Croatian". Jurica's request provoked uproar and laughter. An avalanche of fists thumped the table, one delegate walked out in disgust never to return, the assembled observers had tears of laughter in their eyes but there was more to come as one of the delegates from Sarajevo

---

[1] "Vukovska jezička norma bila je temelj prvih standardizacija jezika u Bosni i Hercegovini, ali jezik bosanskohercegovačkih pisaca, posebno Bošnjaka, nije zasnovan na seoskim nego na gradskim govorima, koji su temelj bosanskog jezičkog standarda."

stood up and screamed above the commotion in all seriousness, "I demand a translation into Bosnian!" . . . This farcical beginning was at the same time the nail in the conference's coffin.[2]

Demands for translators for Croatian and Bosnian may have seemed outrageous in 1991, but in 1995 at the Dayton peace talks, each party requested translators at the talks. The Serbs, Croats, and Bosniacs suddenly could no longer understand each other. Such was the state of affairs even before the first Bosnian language books appeared; the first *Pravopis* for Bosnian was published only a year after Dayton (cf. Halilović 1996), and the first modern Bosnian grammar appeared some five years after Dayton (cf. Halilović, Jahić, and Palić 2000). With the publication of the Dayton Peace Accords in Bosnian, along with Croatian, Serbian, and English, observers have concluded that the Dayton process gave the Bosnian language legitimacy and international recognition.[3]

The processes leading to the emergence of the new Bosnian language clearly have not followed the script of other European standard languages. Thus, while Slavic standard languages, such as Czech, Slovene, or Polish developed over several centuries, the Bosnian language erupted suddenly and unexpectedly in the context of the 1992–5 war in Bosnia-Herzegovina. The birth of a new Bosniac identity coincided with the proclamation of the language in 1992. Moreover, of the three peoples/nations of post-Dayton Bosnia-Herzegovina, only the Bosniacs have truly embraced the name "Bosnian language." The Croats and Serbs have mostly rejected this term, preferring instead to identify their language as Croatian or Serbian, respectively. Hence, the task of establishing a new Bosnian language has been particularly arduous, since it has also involved the dispelling of the common perception that Bosnian is merely a cross between Croatian and Serbian. The Croats and Serbs could claim that their languages emerged out of the Western and Eastern variants of Serbo-Croatian, respectively; the Bosniacs had no clearly defined antecedent language to build upon. As seen in this chapter, Bosniac linguists have toiled to provide evidence that a Bosnian language should exist (6.1), and that this language should be known as "Bosnian" rather than "Bosniac" (6.2). Thereafter, status planning of the dialectal base of the new language took place (6.3.1), and issues of corpus planning, especially in the area of lexicon, were negotiated (6.3.2). However, approaches to standardization have not been uniform, as manifested at the Symposium on the Bosnian Language held in Bihać in 1998 (6.4). Given continued opposition of the Serbs and Croats to the term "Bosnian language," the Bosniacs have closed ranks in support of their new standard with the publication of the "Charter on the Bosnian Language" in 2002 (6.5).

---

[2] Glenny (1996: 144–5).

[3] The Serbs, through a decision of the Committee for the Standardization of the Serbian Language, suggested that the international recognition of the Bosnian language occurred with the signing of the Dayton Accords (cf. Brborić 2001: 334).

6.1 History is on our side: The origins of the Bosnian language

The codifiers of the new language have argued that a separate Bosnian language had been evolving since the Ottoman occupation. In particular, they have hearkened back to the literary activities of Bosnian Muslim writers, who used modified Arabic script between the seventeenth and early twentieth centuries in the so-called Alhamijado literary tradition.[4] One of these writers was the poet and traveler Jusuf Livnjak who wrote an account of his pilgrimage to Mecca in 1615. Another poet, Muhamed Uskufi, published a Bosnian–Turkish dictionary in 1631.[5] Barring this dictionary, there were no grammars or handbooks for the Bosnian language until 1890, when the Austro-Hungarian administrator Benjamin Kallay sought to counteract Serbian nationalism in Bosnia-Herzegovina by promoting a Bosnian identity by establishing a Bosnian language. To this end, Frane Vuletić, a high school teacher from Sarajevo, was asked to write a Bosnian grammar, which appeared in 1890.[6] Vuletić himself opposed the term "Bosnian," and had preferred calling the language "Serbo-Croatian," "Croato-Serbian," "Croatian or Serbian," or "Serbian or Croatian." When the Austro-Hungarian authorities rejected all these names, he agreed to write the "Grammar of the Bosnian Language" ("Gramatika bosanskoga jezika"), provided it be published anonymously (Ford 2001: 64).[7] The language elaborated upon in this grammar bears little resemblance to that advanced by the current codifiers of the Bosnian language. As Ford pointed out, one of these codifiers, Dževad Jahić, dismissed this grammar as "some kind of multiconfessional, 'compromise' grammar," written in the spirit of the now defunct unified Serbo-Croatian language (p. 88). Others, however, have affirmed that this grammar provided the historical

---

[4] During Ottoman times, the Islamicized Slavic writers in the territory of Bosnia-Herzegovina also wrote in Turkish, Persian, and Arabic; according to Katičić (1984: 237) these works were more prestigious than those written in the Slavic vernacular.

[5] Bosniacs frequently mention this dictionary when justifying their naming of the language "Bosnian." On one website, this dictionary was called one of the "oldest in the Balkans," pre-dating Vuk's dictionary by 197 years (cf. Daniel Toljaga, "Projekat poznati Bošnjaci" at www.geocities.com/famous_bosniaks).

[6] According to Salihović (1999: 161), the writing of this grammar was to be overseen by the government and a "Commission for Language" ("Komisija za jezik") consisting of members of all three of Bosnia-Herzegovina's "confessional" (ethnic) communities.

[7] The grammar was reissued in 1908 as *Gramatika srpsko-hrvatskog jezika* ("Grammar of the Serbo-Croatian Language"). The original 1890 version was reprinted in 1994 by the publisher Bosanska riječ in Wuppertal, Germany.

precedence for the (re-)emergence of a new Bosnian language. Thus, Salihović (1999: 161) maintained that:

This book is a valuable document about the conditions of the struggle for the right of Bosniacs to their own language, to the preservation and affirmation of the culture and tradition of Bosnia and Herzegovina.[8]

Even if the linguistic merits of the 1890 grammar remain in dispute, the supporters of a separate Bosnian language have nodded approvingly at Kallay's attempts to introduce the Bosnian language. Accordingly, Jahić (1999a: 29) contended that "[t]he Bosnian language (as was demonstrated during Kallay's times) is not a political invention; rather it is a significant cultural current, which has been part of Bosnia throughout [its] history."[9] The history Jahić referred to here is exclusively that of the Muslim Slavic population, since nearly all those who identified their native language as Bosnian were Islamicized Slavs. Jahić viewed this group as representing a bridge between the pre-Islamic—mostly Franciscan and Bogomil—language traditions, and modern Bosniac literary culture. He outlined the following 16 points to prove "the scientific foundation of the Bosnian language" (ibid.: 28–9):

(1) The Bosnian language is not a hybrid consisting of Serbian and Croatian elements; rather it descended directly from a Common Slavic proto-language.

(2) The ancestors of the speakers of the Bosnian language arrived in the Central Balkans in the seventh century, AD and used a Central Štokavian dialect.

(3) The Bogomils spoke the Central Štokavian dialect, but modified it with some of their own features.

(4) The medieval Bosnian "state" affected the distinctly "Bosnian" developments in the language.

(5) The Islamicized populations of Bosnia-Herzegovina remained geographically stable, therefore maintaining the special language features they had inherited.

(6) Islamic culture brought more changes to the language especially in phonology and lexicon.

(7) The term "Bosnian language" was first used in the Middle Ages, thereby proving that it is not a recent invention.

(8) After Islamicization the uniquely Bosnian Alhamijado literary tradition developed.

(9) The Muslim Slavs in some portions of Bosnia maintained a special writing system first developed by the Franciscans; this system, known as bosančica, was used between the sixteenth and eighteenth centuries.

(10) Uskufi's Bosnian–Turkish dictionary appeared in 1631.

(11) The specificities of Bosnian speech were taken into consideration by Vuk Karadžić when he reformed the Serbian language and created the unified language with the Croats.

[8] "Ova knjiga je vredan dokument o uslovima borbe za pravo Bošnjaka na vlastiti jezik, čuvanje i afirmaciju kulture i tradicije Bosne i Hercegovine."

[9] "Bosanski jezik (što se pokazalo u Kalajevo vrijeme) nije politička izmišljotina već značajna kulturna tekovina koja prati Bosnu kroz historiju."

(12) In the late nineteenth century, publications oriented towards the Muslim Slavs appeared, and the Bosnian Latin and Arabic writing systems were modified.[10]

(13) The support given to the Bosnian language by the Austro-Hungarian authorities between 1878 and 1908 was significant in the development of a Bosnian linguistic consciousness.

(14) The rich oral tradition among Muslim Slavs, including oral poetry and ballads, contribute to the separate cultural-linguistic identity.

(15) The Muslim Slavs developed a newer distinctly Bosnian literature after the middle of the nineteenth century.

(16) Each nation/people should have the right to call its language by the name it deems appropriate.

Eleven of these 16 points relate directly to the Muslim Slav/Bosniac culture, and would not apply to the other inhabitants of Bosnia-Herzegovina—the Orthodox Serbs and the Catholic Croats. Of the five remaining points, four relate to the pre-Islamic period in Bosnia-Herzegovina; however, point (3) on the Bogomils is difficult to prove, and point (4) on the medieval Bosnian state has questionable relevance to a Bosnian language. The Bosnian influences on Vuk alluded to in point (11) include his acceptance of the fricative-velar consonant *h* and Turkish/Arabic loanwords. However, the velar fricative can be found also in Croatian Štokavian dialects, while Turkish words were also common in Serbian and Croatian Štokavian dialects. As seen below (6.3), Jahić and other Bosniac linguists have attempted to prove that these two features are more salient for the Bosnian language than for either Croatian or Serbian, and therefore constitute the primary linguistic markers for this new standard.

Jahić's 16 points have been condensed into the seven points of the "Charter on the Bosnian Language" ("Povelja o bosanskom jeziku"), which was signed by 61 leading Bosniac intellectuals on 21 March 2002.[11] This "Charter" will be discussed in 6.5, below, after an analysis of the developments in the new Bosnian standard during the years 1992–2002.

6.2   It's all in the name: Bosnian or Bosniac

Controversies over a name are not new to the peoples of the former Yugoslavia. The signatories of the Vienna Literary Agreement could not agree on a name for the joint literary language in 1850, and the Croats rejected the terms "Serbo-Croatian" and "Croato-Serbian" as agreed upon in the 1954 Novi Sad Agreement. While Serbs and Croats have now accepted their respective terms for their new

---

[10]   In this context Jahić referred to the work of Mehmedbeg Kapitanović Ljubušak, who founded the first national newspaper *Bošnjak* ("Bosniac") in 1891.

[11]   The complete text of the "Charter" is available at **www.bosnianlanguage.com**.

separate standards, both groups have expressed opposition to the insistence of the Bosniacs on calling their language "Bosnian," rather than "Bosniac." While the controversy over the name has not undermined the post-Dayton arrangements in Bosnia-Herzegovina, it has proven to be an obstacle to ethnic harmony and reconciliation. In this section, after a discussion of the two rival terms "Bosnian language" and "Bosniac language", the arguments for and against both terms are provided. Since cooperation among Bosnia's three main ethnic groups on language issues is virtually non-existent, it is unlikely that a compromise regarding the name "Bosnian language" can be reached in the near future.

The two names for the Bosnian language both derive from the toponym Bosna, the name of a spring near Sarajevo.[12] On a purely linguistic level, the two adjectives differ in their derivation. Thus, while *bosanski* derives directly from the toponym *Bosna*, and strictly speaking is the neutral adjectival form for Bosnia,[13] the adjective *bošnjački* is derived from the noun *Bošnjak* 'Bosniac', denoting a native of Bosnia.[14] The term preferred by Bosniac linguists, *bosanski jezik* is best rendered in English by "Bosnian language," while the term *bošnjački jezik* is usually translated into English as "Bosniac language." Both terms can be traced back several centuries. According to Halilović (1991: 18–19), the term *bošnjak* originated in the fifteenth century, and on the basis of this term, the Ottoman Turkish occupiers coined the phrase *bošnakca* 'Bosniac language'. With the rise of a national consciousness among the Southern Slavs in the nineteenth century the terms *Bošnjak/bošnjački* were revived to denote a Muslim Slav identity. This identity extended beyond Bosnia's boundaries to include Štokavian-speaking Muslim Slavs in the territory of the former Ottoman Empire, including the Sandžak, Montenegro, Kosovo, Macedonia, and Turkey (cf. Halilović 1991: 28 and Jahić 1991: 14). However, this term was not used widely to derive the name of the language. Rather, the term *bosanski jezik*, which had been used by the writers in the Alhamijado literary tradition since the seventeenth century, became the official name of the language of Bosnia-Herzegovina after 1878 under Austro-Hungarian rule. The newspaper *Bošnjak*, which first

---

[12] Halilović (1991: 28) considered the term Bosna to be "pre-Slavic" and possibly even "pre-Indo-European." Such statements on the ancient origin of a name bring to mind Fishman's notion (1972: 7) of "stressed authenticity," whereby ancient terms provide the necessary trappings of legitimacy to a linguistic revival.

[13] Only this form of the adjective is used for place names (e.g., Bosanski Brod, Bosanski Novi), and in the compound forms *bosanskohercegovački* 'Bosnia-Herzegovinian'.

[14] *Bošnjak* is itself derived from *Bosna*, i.e., from *Bosna* + *-jak*. The suffix *-jak* occurs in South Slavic to denote the inhabitants of a place, but is not as common as other suffixes, including *-anin* and *-ac/-ec*. Two of the most common examples are for individuals connected closely to the land, e.g., (Central South Slavic) *seljak* 'villager' and *zemljak* 'farmer'.

appeared in 1891, contributed to the construction of a new Bosniac identity. According to Jahić (1991: 28), this publication was

the first Muslim paper published in the Latin script, in which the powerful Bosniac tendencies would be expressed, and would also propagate the name Bosnian language for the native language of the Muslims in the context of Kalláy's policy of the Bosnian nation.[15]

A century later, the language codifiers of the new Bosnian language insist that the majority of Bosniacs consider their language to be best rendered by the term "Bosnian," rather than by the ethnic term "Bosniac," which replaced the Yugoslav ethnic designation "Muslim."[16] In the introduction to his Bosnian *Pravopis*, Halilović (1996: 6) claimed that the Bosniacs "consider their entire cultural milieu" ("obuhvaćaju svoju ukupnu kulturnu okomicu") in terms of the "Bosnian language." As proof of this statement, he noted that in the final Yugoslav census of 1991, 90 per cent of the Bosniacs claimed their language to be "Bosnian," and acknowledged that non-Bosniacs who consider the Bosnian language to be "their own" have the right to embrace this language. Only three years later, Jahić (1999: 26) stated that the Bosnian language should be the appropriate name for the language of the Bosniac people alone, and that the

[r]egional, and not the ethnic name of the Bosnian language properly confirms the extent to which the Bosniac people connect their origins and fate to Bosnia, as their most relevant geophysical and geographical setting, and the extent to which the very language of that people is marked by the [very fact of] belonging to Bosnia.[17]

Such a statement implies that had Bosniacs called their language by the "ethnic name" (Bosniac language), rather than the "regional term" (Bosnian language), they would have weakened their link to Bosnia, their geographical and spiritual homeland. However, it ignores Bosnia-Herzegovina's Serb and Croat communities, who might share with the Bosniacs a spiritual affinity for the region of Bosnia, but disagree that because of such an affinity they should call their own language Bosnian as well.

For this reason, Serb and Croat linguists have rejected the term "*Bosnian language*." Dalibor Brozović (1999: 13), who was born in Bosnia-Herzegovina, stated that:

Every people has the right to name its language the way it wants. Thus, the Bosniacs have the right to call their own language Bosnian if for whatever reason it so suits them. But we

---

[15] "[Bošnjak je] prvi muslimanski list štampan latinicom, u kojem će se ispoljiti snažne bošnjačke tendencije i za maternji jezik muslimana propagirati naziv bosanski jezik, u kontekstu Kalajeve politike bosanske nacije."

[16] In Tito's Yugoslavia, *Muslimani* written with an upper-case letter was used as the name for the Muslim Slav "nation" ("narod") of Yugoslavia, while the same form written with a lower-case letter was used to designate adherents to the Muslim religion.

[17] "'Regionalni' a ne nacionalni naziv bosanskog jezika upravo potvrdjuje koliko bošnjački narod svoje porijeklo i sudbinu vezuje za Bosnu, kao svoju najbitniju geofizičku i geografsku odrednicu i koliko je i sam jezik tog naroda obilježen tom bosanskom pripadnošću."

[Croats] have ourselves the right not to accept in our social and scholarly practice such a name for a concept we know by another name . . . However, if they call the language Bosnian and not Bosniac, then it is accordingly the local, home-grown language, while Croatian and Serbian are imported, and the Bosnia-Herzegovinian Croats and the Bosnia-Herzegovinian Serbs would actually have to accept the Bosniac language under the Bosnian name as their own, and as the common language for Bosnia and Herzegovina. That this is pretentious is absolutely clear.[18]

The members of the Committee for the Serbian Language were even blunter in their decision of 13 February 1998, when they refrained from recognizing the Bosnian language as a separate language, preferring to call it "an idiom" (*"izraz"*): "Only the attribute *bošnjački* (Bosniac) can be recommended in the naming of that idiom in the Serbian linguistic standard."[19] The Serbs have maintained that the Bosniac insistence on naming their language "Bosnian" has reflected the drive among Bosniacs to establish a unitary Bosnia-Herzegovina, in which the only official language would be named Bosnian, thereby denying the Bosnian Serbs the right to call their language Serbian.

As this discussion demonstrates, the name "Bosnian" has emerged as the official name of a Bosniac-oriented standard language. This name has been acknowledged by the international community, but has been snubbed by both the Croats and Serbs living inside and outside the boundaries of Bosnia-Herzegovina. The specific features of the Bosnian language were mostly taken from the speech of the Bosniac community, and this fact has further alienated the Bosnian Serbs and Bosnian Croats.

6.3   The peculiarities of the new Bosnian standard

The Seattle-based company Multilingual Books has the following advertisement on its website for its *Concise Bosnian–English/English–Bosnian Dictionary*:

This is the only dictionary reflecting the daily use of language in modern-day Bosnia and Herzegovina, with phonetic pronunciation guides for both languages. Bosnians,

---

[18] "Svaki narod ujedno ima pravo da svoj jezik naziva kako hoće. Prema tome Bošnjaci imaju pravo nazivati svoj jezik bosanskim ako im to iz bilo kakva razloga odgovara. Ali mi imamo pravo da mi sami u svojoj društvenoj i znanstvenoj praksi ne prihvatimo takav naziv za objekt koji inače priznajemo. . .Ali ako taj jezik nazovu ne bošnjačkim nego bosanskim, onda iz toga proizlazi da je to domaći, zemaljski jezik, a hrvatski i srpski da su uvozni i da bi bosanskohercegovački Hrvati i bosanskohercegovački Srbi zapravo trebali prihvatiti bošnjački jezik pod bosanskim imenom kao svoj i kao opći jezik za Bosnu i Hercegovinu. Ta je pretenzija savršeno jasna."

[19] Cf. Brborić (2001: 334): "U srpskome jezičkom standardu, za imenovanje tog idioma može se preporučiti samo atribut bošnjački (Bosniac)."

Serbs, and Croats who are learning the English language as well as English-speaking travelers or business people can use this dictionary. The author is a native of Sarajevo.[20]

It is doubtful that Croats or Serbs would be caught carrying around a Bosnian–English dictionary. Moreover, this advertisement would mislead would-be travelers to Bosnia-Herzegovina by implying that the citizens of Sarajevo would be exemplary native speakers of the new Bosnian language.[21] As seen below, the codifiers of the new Bosnian language have infused some elements more typical of rural Bosniac dialects than of the capital city (6.3.1); they have blended these elements with their Central Štokavian lexicon, walking a tightrope between words perceived as "Croatian" and those considered to be "Serbian" (6.3.2).

6.3.1   The dialectal base

The new Bosnian standard is based on the Neo-Štokavian/ijekavian dialect. This is the same dialect that Vuk Karadžić and the Croat Illyrians embraced in the 1850 Literary Agreement. With its system of four tones, long unstressed vowels, and ijekavian reflexes of *jat*, this dialect is pervasive in Bosnia-Herzegovina, stretching from Eastern Herzegovina to Eastern and Northern Bosnia. The codifiers of the new Bosnian standard have modified this dialect by adding some linguistic features typical of the Bosniac population.

Prior to the massive population shifts in Bosnia-Herzegovina caused by the war between 1992 and 1995, the Serbs, Croats, and Bosniacs lived in ethnically mixed cities, towns, and villages. The dominant dialect was the Neo-Štokavian/ ijekavian dialect, which was used extensively in the urban areas, in Eastern Herzegovina, Central and Northern Bosnia, and portions of Western Bosnia. Otherwise, in Western Herzegovina and Western/Northwestern Bosnia, the ijekavian dialects were mixed with Štokavian/ikavian ones. The ikavian speakers were mostly Croats and Bosniacs. Historically, the Islamicized Slavs resided in urban areas, while the Catholic Croats and the Orthodox Serbs lived in rural communities. During the twentieth century, rural inhabitants frequently migrated to the cities, and as a result the cities increasingly became ethnically diverse and multicultural. In these urban centers—such as Sarajevo or Tuzla—Serbs, Croats, and Muslim Slavs intermingled and often intermarried, and the ethnic differences among these groups were often blurred. In Socialist Yugoslavia, the ethnic blurring was reflected in the "Yugoslav" identity, and a relatively high percentage of citizens

---

[20] This text is available at **www.multilingualbooks.com/bosnian.html**.

[21] The advertisement also reveals the common perception in the United States that the term "Bosnian" is equivalent to the term "Bosnian Muslim," or the preferred ethnic term, "Bosniac."

of Bosnia-Herzegovina declared themselves to be Yugoslavs.[22] By contrast, inhabitants in rural towns and villages retained their linguistic, ethnic, and confessional identities. Thus, while language could unify urban dwellers in Bosnia-Herzegovina, it served to mark differences within the rural populations, where specific ethnic dialect features could still be distinguished.

The dialectological materials from Bosnia-Herzegovina suggested that two linguistic features have pervaded the speech of the Bosniacs, as opposed to their Serb and Croat neighbors.[23] These features included: (1) the greater frequency of the velar-fricative *h*, and (2) the greater number of Turkish/Arabic loanwords. For the Bosnian-born linguist, Asim Peco (1975: 72), these features were so frequent among the Bosnian Muslims of Western Bosnia that they represented primary markers for Bosnian Muslim speakers well beyond that region, and were characteristic of Muslims of all social classes and levels of education. He argued that:

Dialectal features, once established, are hard to relinquish; this is especially difficult to achieve in cases where the speaker is marked in a well-known fashion, in our case nationally marked. And that is the reason why our Bosnia-Herzegovinian Muslims, no matter what their social standing or place of residence, preserve in their speech the velar fricative *h* and numerous Turkish borrowings.[24]

Indeed, such ethnic marking also applied to the Bosniac populations of Eastern Bosnia. Before the outbreak of war in 1992 the Serbs and Bosniacs in that region spoke similar Štokavian/ijekavian dialects. The differences were manifested mostly in the accentual patterns, and in the use of the phoneme /h/. Thus, while the Serbs displayed the Neo-Štokavian accentuation typical of the dialect of their ancestral homeland in Eastern Herzegovina and Northwestern Montenegro, and lost *h* in most positions, their Bosniac neighbors had a more archaic accent pattern, and frequently preserved the *h*.[25] Senahid Halilović, one of the primary codifiers of the new Bosnian standard, was a native of Eastern Bosnia, and would have been keenly aware of the differences between the speech of Serbs and that of

---

[22] According to the 1981 Census, 7.9 per cent (or approximately 326,000) of Bosnia-Herzegovina's population declared themselves to be Yugoslavs; cf. Greenberg (2001: 25).

[23] For an analysis of the speech characteristics of the Bosniacs, Croats, and Serbs of northwestern and western Bosnia, cf. Peco (1975), Dešić (1976), and Greenberg (1996: 410–12). For a contrasting analysis of the Serb and Bosniac dialects of Eastern Bosnia, cf. Greenberg (2001c).

[24] "Jednom ustaljene govorne osobine teško se napuštaju, posebno je to teško postići u onim slučajevima gdje je govorna osobina na izvjestan način markirana, u našem slučaju nacionalno markirana. To i jest razlog zašto i naš bosanskohercegovački Musliman bez obzira na socijalnu pripadnost i mjesto življenja, još uvijek čuva u svom fonetizmu zadnjonepčani konstriktiv *h* i brojne turcizme."

[25] For a classification of the South Slavic dialects based on types of accentual types, cf. Alexander (1993).

Bosniacs in that region. Coincidentally, the prominent Serb dialectologist, Slo-bodan Remetić, was also a native of Eastern Bosnia. He wrote a short study of the Serb dialects of Kladanj (1970), while Halilović (1990) treated the Muslim dialects of Tuholj. Both authors firmly believe that the Serbs of Kladanj have a distinctly different dialect from that of the Muslim Slavs in neighboring Tuholj, even though many of the villages around Tuholj and Kladanj were ethnically mixed. Remetić's 1970 study was one of the first articles on an ethnic Serb dialect of Bosnia to appear in Serbia. Halilović's study was published in 1990, when the Bosnian Muslims openly were discussing their separate ethno-linguistic identity, and elaborating on a new Bosniac identity. Remetić's study reflected the tumultuous times when Serbs and Croats first talked openly of linguistic separation in Tito's Yugoslavia; Hali-lović's study appeared on the very eve of Yugoslavia's collapse, and shortly before the ultimate break-up of the Serbo-Croatian unified language.

Both Halilović and Remetić underscored that the Muslims and Serbs differ pri-marily in the frequency in which the phoneme *h* is preserved in the respective ethnic speech communities. Thus, whereas the Muslims preserved *h* in all positions, and even expanded its use by pronouncing *h* in etymologically unjustified environments (cf. Halilović 1990: 281), the Serbs tended to lose *h* in most positions, especially final, intervocalic, and initial positions. This phoneme characteristic of the ethnic Bosniac dialects has been included as a key feature in the new Bosnian standard. However, not all speech features of the Bosniacs of Eastern Bosnia were incorporated into the new Bosnian standard. According to Remetić (1970: 105) the majority of Bosniacs near and around the Eastern Bosnian towns of Kladanj and Tuholj also merge the palatals č/ć and dj/dž; this feature is frequently cited as a Bosniac speech characteristic, but too radical an innovation for the new Bosnian standard (cf. Jahić 1999*a*: 28).

The Bosniac dialectal data on the phoneme /h/ motivated the codifiers of the new Bosnian language both to preserve and to expand the use of the phoneme *h* beyond what was accepted in the previous Serbo-Croatian standard. The new Bosnian grammars and dictionaries now admit such forms as: (1) *lahko* 'easy', *mehko* 'softly', where *h* is etymologically justified; (2) *hudovica* 'widow', *hlopta* 'ball', where *h* is not justified etymologically; and (3) *sahat* 'hour', *halat* 'tool', *havaz* 'voice' where *h* is found or added in words of Turkish origin. In this manner, the Bosnian language could boast forms different from the corres-ponding Serbian and Croatian forms, e.g., *lako, meko, udovica, lopta, sat*. Not all the recent handbooks of the Bosnian language are consistent in their inclusion of these forms with *h*. For instance, the school edition of the Bosnian *Pravopis* listed forms with *h* for *lahko* and *sahat*, but did not include *hlopta* (Halilović 1999*b*: 23).[26] It is possible that such inconsistencies may depend on the dialect of the authors of a given work. Thus, Halilović may have favored the vocabulary from his own native dialect of Tuholj, where *hlopta* was unattested.

---

[26] As Ford (2001: 116) pointed out, *hlopta* is cited by Jahić (1999*b*), but is absent from Halilović et al. (2000).

To recapitulate, the phoneme /h/ has taken on symbolic importance, as a shibboleth marking the speech of Bosniacs, bringing the phonological system of Bosnian closer to the Arabic sounds, with its guttural consonants, and a step farther from Serbian, which often loses *h*.[27] The numbers of lexemes that have acquired *h* in the new Bosnian standard would not in itself seem to warrant the establishment of a separate standard. As seen in the next section, broader issues regarding the vocabulary of the new standard have required the attention of the language planners in Bosnia-Herzegovina.

6.3.2   Is Bosnian a mixture of Serbian and Croatian?

A distinctive variety of South Slavic began emerging in Bosnia-Herzegovina with the adoption of a "Bosnia-Herzegovinian standard linguistic idiom" through the 1974 Constitution of the Socialist Republic of Bosnia-Herzegovina. This idiom represented a republican norm of the unified Serbo-Croatian language. Naylor (1978: 460) characterized this idiom, based on the Sarajevo dialect, as "western [i.e., Croatian] in phonology but closer to the eastern variant [i.e., Serbian] in morphology and vocabulary." He made no mention of specifically Bosniac features in this "standard idiom." Similarly, Vujičić (1984: 383ff.) affirmed that the Bosnia-Herzegovinian standard linguistic idiom was not based on the speech of any single "people" ("narod") in Bosnia-Herzegovina. In his view it was intended to be a standard variety acceptable to the republic's Serb, Croat, and Muslim Slav communities.[28]

Karadža (1999: 35) suggested that the standard linguistic idiom in Bosnia-Herzegovina underwent dramatic changes after 1992, when its development was "powerfully hastened by the events of the war, the political situation, the breakdown in communication, and especially the fracturing of the media."[29] Halilović (1999a: 97) took this analysis one step farther, asserting that the Bosnian language has had two stages in its development: (1) the period up to

---

[27] As seen above (2.2.1), in Vuk's first edition of the *Srpski rječnik* (1818), the Cyrillic grapheme /x/, corresponding to the phoneme /h/, was not even included in the inventory of Serbian letters. Salihović (1999: 162) estimated that in the second edition of Vuk's dictionary (1852) there were about 3,500 words of Turkish origin; this number is much lower than the 8,442 words of Turkish origin found in Škaljić's 1973 dictionary of Turkisms in the Serbo-Croatian unified language.

[28] One of my colleagues, a native of Foča in Bosnia-Herzegovina, reported to me that in the 1970s and 1980s Bosnian Muslim linguistic features were absent in the speech of newscasters on Sarajevo television or radio.

[29] "[Razvoj standardnojezički izraz je bio] snažno ubrzan ratnim zbivanjima, političkom situacijom, prekidom komunikacije, naročito raslojavanjem medija."

1992 when Bosnian evolved in the framework of "standard Neo-Štokavian" (i.e., with outside interference from non-Bosniacs); and (2) the period since 1992, when Bosnian has broken from the joint language tradition, and moved ahead on its own terms ("vlastitim putem"). He argued (1996: 6) that the Bosnia-Herzegovinian standard linguistic idiom under the rubric of the Serbo-Croatian language had been flawed, since its manuals "did not respect the peculiarities of the Bosniac linguistic reality" ("nisu uvalžavali osobenosti bošnjačkogž jezičkog bića"). Such a Bosniac reality included the rural dialect features discussed in 6.3.1, which were also frequent in many of the works of Muslim Slav literary figures since the seventeenth century.

For Halilović and his colleagues, the task of breaking away from the Serbo-Croatian unified language has involved delicate corpus planning for the new Bosnian standard. On the one hand, the language planners have had to explain the uniquely "Bosnian" nature of their inherited Slavic lexical stock; on the other hand, they have had to introduce new words of Turkish/Arabic origin that might not be used by many of the members of the Bosniac community. They have frequently rejected the notion that the Bosnian language merely constitutes a mixture of Serbian and Croatian elements. Thus, Jahić (1999*a*: 27) complained: "for years it was argued that words from the Western and Eastern variants 'intersect' in the Bosnia-Herzegovinian linguistic idiom,"[30] but the history of the Bosnian lexicon is a reflection of "an original development" ("radi se o iskonskom razvoju"), which coincided with what Jahić considered to be the "thousand-year" Bosnian state.[31]

Nevertheless, the core vocabulary of the Bosnian language is of Slavic origin, and is found in both Serbian and Croatian. For example, the language used in the papers from the 1998 Symposium on the Bosnian Language held in Bihać included many examples of doublets that had traditionally been considered "Croatian" or "Serbian." Individual writers represented at the symposium were Bosniacs, who have adhered to either "Serbian" lexical items or "Croatian" lexical items. The latter included *točno* 'exactly', *slavenski* 'Slavic', *klasificirati* 'classify', while the former included the forms *tačno, slovenski, and klasifikovati*. Since Orthodox, Catholic, and Muslim Slavs interacted and lived together for centuries, it should be of no surprise that several synonymous forms would be in active use within Bosnia-Herzegovina. Moreover, despite the rhetoric to the contrary, the authors of the first dictionary (Isaković 1995) and *Pravopis* (Halilović 1996) for the new Bosnian standard language were liberal in accepting lexical variation. In these

---

[30] "Tumačilo se godinama da se riječi iz istočne i zapadne varijante u bosansko-hercegovačkom standardnojezičkom izrazu 'ukrštaju.'"

[31] Jahić's reference to a thousand-year-old Bosnian tradition parallels similar claims among the Croats about the thousand-year history of the Croatian literary language; cf. Babić (1991), who edited a volume entitled *Tisućljetni jezik naš hrvatski* ("Our Thousand-Year-old Croatian Language").

works many lexical doublets were listed without any additional commentary, and there was no consistency between these two works on this issue. For instance, Halilović provided both the native Croatian and the internationalist Serbian names for the months of the year in his *Pravopis*, while Isaković listed only the Croatian forms. Other lexical doublets included *pozorište/kazalište* 'theater', *hljeb/ kruh* 'bread', and *centar/središte* 'center'. On some occasions, Halilović implied an acceptance of the "Serbian" form, by cross-referencing the "Croatian" variant, as in the entries for *vlak* 'train' and *točka* 'period' (Croatian), which referred the reader to the forms preferred by the author: *voz* and *tačka* (Serbian). When a uniquely Bosnian form was given, it was usually a Turkish/Arabic borrowing, such as *selamiti* 'greet' (cf. Serbian/Croatian *pozdravljati*).

Otherwise, unique Bosnian forms were derived through the addition of *h*, and when doublet forms with or without h were possible, the *codifiers of the Bosnian language tended* to favor the variant forms containing *h*. The norm in Halilović's 1996 *Pravopis* avoided overt prescriptivism on the issue, particularly with regard to words of Slavic origin. His preference for forms with *h* was expressed subtly, mostly through cross-referencing. Hence, while both *lahko* and *lako* 'easy' are listed, the reader looking up *lako* is told to see what the author perceives as the correct form, *lahko*. Halilović's preference for this form is underscored by its use several times in his 1998 presentation at the Symposium on the Bosnian Language.[32] When *h* occurs intervocalically in words of Slavic origin, Halilović has consistently favoured the forms preserving the original *h*. This preference is consistent with the practices found among the codifiers of standard Croatian, and further distances Bosnian from Serbian. Thus, in the 1996 *Pravopis* for the entries *duvan* 'tobacco' and *uvo* 'ear', the reader was directed to look up the "correct forms:" *duhan* and *uho*. Even in the rendition of the internationalism equivalent to (English) *history* and (French) *histoire*, the codifiers of the Bosnian language have prescribed a form with an initial velar-fricative *h*, i.e., (Bosnian) *historija*, in contrast to the Serbian form *istorija*.[33]

Both Halilović and Jahić, the two primary advocates of a distinctive Bosnian language, have in their own writing styles shown a preference for "Croatian" forms including some of the puristic forms introduced after 1991 into Croatian. Thus, Halilović (1999*a*) used the marked "Croatian" forms: *stoljeće* 'century', *uopće* 'at all', *bit će* 'it will be', *prošlome* '(dat.) past', *bosanskoga* '(gen.) Bosnian' (cf. the Eastern variant forms *vek*, *uopšte*, *biće*), *prošlom*, *bosanskog(a)*. This choice may be a pragmatic one, since the Bosniacs and Croats have been joined together in a Federation in post-Dayton Bosnia-Herzegovina. This

[32] Cf. Halilović 1999*a*: 97–8, where *lahko* and *lahak* are used.

[33] The Croats have long used a native Croatian form, *povijest*. In ethnically mixed Bosnia-Herzegovina, however, even some Croats may have used the internationalism (*h*)*istorija*. In most other examples, the Bosnian/Croatian/Serbian velar fricative *h* corresponds to the English velar aspirate *h* found in internationalisms, such as *humanist(a)* 'humanist', *horoskop* 'horoscope'.

conscious decision to favor Croatian forms may also be a political hint of the anti-Serbian feelings among the Bosniac population.

To summarize, Halilović (1999*a*: 100) dismissed any attempts to call the Bosnian lexicon a hybrid of Serbian and Croatian vocabulary. He stressed the crucial importance of the attitude [within Bosnian linguistic circles] towards

[t]he lexicon, which during the twentieth century emphasized the nationally marked variants (i.e), in accordance with the predominant binary, two-variant treatment of standard Neo-Štokavian; [now] we would have to view it as our own lexicon, which is simultaneously both Bosniac and Serbian, or Bosniac and Croatian. We need not be concerned later on should someone adhering to a greater Serbian or greater Croatian ideological concept see in this the alleged tendency of the "neutralization of variants".[34]

Halilović emphasized that any features the Bosniacs share with Serbs and Croats are legitimately "Bosniac" in nature. This notion is consistent with his view that the presence or absence of major differences between the Bosnian standard and its Croatian and Serbian rivals is irrelevant in any determination on the legitimacy of a separate Bosnian standard. He further argued that very few features may be truly considered to be "nationally marked" as exclusively Serbian, Croatian, or Montenegrin, and that even these features can remain in Bosnian as stylistic variants.

In the first years of the new Bosnian standard, Bosniac linguists refrained from a full-fledged campaign of linguistic engineering whereby the Bosnian language would be cleansed of perceived Serbian or Croatian elements.[35] However, towards the end of the 1990s, Bosniac linguists felt pressure to increase their intervention in the codification of the Bosnian language. These pressures resulted from the outright rejection of the Bosnian language by Bosnia's Serb and Croat communities, and dissatisfaction within the Bosniac community on the implementation of a new Bosnian standard. The language planners addressed these issues at the Symposium for the Bosnian Language in 1998, which Ford (2002) considered to be the first Congress on the Bosnian language.

---

[34] "Naročito je važno pitanje odnosa prema leksici koja je tokom *dvadesetog stoljeća* sukladno preovladjujećem bipolarnom, dvovarijantskom pogledu na standardnu novoštokavštinu—oglašavana varijantski, odnosno nacionalno obilježenom (tj. srpskom ili hrvatskom): na nju bi trebalo gledati kao na svoju leksiku, koja je ujedno bošnjacka i srpska ili i bošnjačka i hrvatska. Ne treba se osvrtati na to što će neko, eventualno, slijedeći velikosrpski ili velikohrvatski ideologijski koncept, u tome vidjeti tendenciju nazvanu 'neutralizacijom varijanata'."

[35] At the Bihać Symposium Halilović supported the notion that the Bosnian language could still be written in either Latin or Cyrillic (1999*a*: 100). However, since the signing of the Dayton Accords, Cyrillic has all but disappeared in the Croat-Bosniac Federation.

6.4   The first Symposium on the Bosnian language

The "Symposium on the Bosnian Language" was held on 7–8 September 1998 in Bihać. Organized by the Sarajevo Institute for Language, the federal Ministry of Education Culture, and Sport, and the local government of the Unsko-Sanski Canton, the Symposium brought together linguists, philosophers, journalists, pedagogues, and policymakers to discuss the status of the Bosnian language and its future. The 28 papers presented at the conference were published in 1999 by the Institut za jezik in Sarajevo, under the editorship of Ibrahim Ćedić, the Institute's director. Ćedić (1999*a*: 7ff.) asserted that the Symposium's presenters shared certain suppositions, especially regarding the notion and legitimacy of a separate Bosnian language. In his view, the three literary standards are all official within Bosnia-Herzegovina, which does not preclude the possibility of a future super-national Bosnian language. This language would include Bosniac, Croat, and Serb elements, and could serve as the official language in the entire territory of Bosnia-Herzegovina.

Most of the papers at the Symposium treated sociolinguistic topics. As Ford (2002) suggested, the linguists were split between two distinct groups, prescriptivists and descriptivists. The former included Dževad Jahić and Senahid Halilović, who espoused a more activist approach to corpus planning, while the latter included Josip Baotić and Ibrahim Ćedić, who favored a more tolerant approach which would avoid rigorous differentiation of Bosnian from either Serbian or Croatian.

Jahić's and Halilović's presentations were concerned with justifying a separate Bosnian standard, rather than with specific decisions affecting the future standardization of Bosnian. Their prescriptivist approach was reflected in their assertions that the Bosniac elements of the Bosnian language, especially regarding the phoneme /h/ and the Bosniac-specific vocabulary, are indispensable. Jahić's primary goal was to expound upon his 16 principles, which provided an outline of the historical context justifying the emergence of the new Bosnian standard (cf. 6.1). Halilović's presentation, while similarly meager in specific proposals for new norms, presented a call for new resources to support the process of standardization. He complained that the neighboring peoples (Serbs and Croats) had made "large strides forward" ("krupnim koracima odmiču naprijed"), while the Bosniacs had been left behind, and were "running in place" ("tapkaju na mjestu").[36] While conceding that the Bosniacs faced major challenges, from the high rates of illiteracy to the massive displacement of persons during the war, he cited the following three main reasons for the slow progress in the standardization of Bosnian: (1) the Bosniac linguists were not active enough; (2) lack of funding from the government for the completion of

---

[36] Cf. Halilović 1999*a*: 101.

the protracted and expensive task of standardization; and (3) too few experts have been trained in "bosniacistica" ("Bosniac studies").[37] Halilović used the Symposium as a forum to urge the government to allocate resources for training new experts, and to publish the necessary dictionaries and grammars that would stabilize the norms of the new Bosnian standard. He rejected what he viewed as the excessive purism practiced by Croat linguists engaged in the standardization of the new Croatian language, and proposed that new borrowings into Bosnian be monitored by the Bosniac language planners (1999a: 100).

In their rhetoric, both Jahić and Halilović displayed nationalist credentials. Jahić's statements were reminiscent of Herderian concepts on the powerful link between language and national/cultural identity, or as Fishman (1972: 45) put it, the view that "language was also the surest way for individuals to safeguard (or recover) the authenticity they had inherited from their ancestors as well as to hand it on to generations yet unborn." Thus, according to Jahić (1999a: 25),

[i]nsofar as language is above all a means of communication, it is equally well an aspect of national identification. In it are the whole culture, history, and consciousness of a given people... [or] better put, [language is a people's] collective subconsciousness about its past, its present, and perhaps even its future.[38]

He further asserted that the Bosnian language had been suppressed for years, and this policy was part of a pattern of denying the Bosniacs their legitimate status as a separate nation and people. Halilović (1999a: 97) was particularly critical of the Serbs for what he considered to be their attempts to stifle the Bosnian language, from the days of "V. S. Karadžić [(Vuk)] to D. Ćupić."[39] He explicitly mentioned the work of the ultra-nationalist Serbs, who have revived the Vukovian notion that all Štokavian speakers are Serbs (cf. 3.2). Simultaneously, he noted that Croat linguists are also opposed to the Bosnian language, and suggested that the sociolinguistic "fact" ("činjenica") that Bosnian exists as a separate language can no longer be denied. Moreover, Halilović envisaged a bright future for the Bosnian language in which, unlike its Serbian and "especially Croatian" counterparts, "programmed impoverishment" ("programirano osiromašivanje") would not be needed, and purism and overly zealous prescriptivism would not predominate (ibid.: 102).

---

[37] In Yugoslav linguistic circles, the field of Serbo-Croatian studies was often called "serbo-croatistica." Since 1991, with the emergence of the new languages, the terms "croatistica" and "serbistica" have been used instead. The reference to "bosniacistica" reflects the emergence of this burgeoning field, and may become a frequent term in Bosniac academic circles.

[38] "Koliko god je jezik prije svega sredstvo komunikacije, on je jednako i vid nacionalne identifikacije. U njemu je čitava kultura, historija i svijest jednog naroda...[ili] bolje reći [jezik je] kolektivna podsvijest [jednog naroda] o svojoj prošlosti i sadašnjosti, pa možda i budućnosti."

[39] The Montenegrin-born linguist Drago Ćupić was the director of the Institute for the Serbo-Croatian language in Belgrade in the turbulent 1980s and early 1990s.

Other linguists at the Symposium either (1) were mildly critical of the standardization process since 1992; or (2) advocated a pluricentric unity model for the Bosnian language. Muhammad Šator criticized the standardization of Bosnian since 1992, while advocates of a pluricentric-unity model for Bosnian were Ibrahim Ćedić and Josip Baotić.

Šator (1999: 113) went so far as to point out the flaws in the standardization process, which he considered was being conducted without broad consensus.[40] In his view,

[i]t is possible to speak of a kind of sub-standardization, which is advanced by some of the media, or certain intellectuals, who, relying on the Serbian, and more recently the Croatian linguistic standard, create within [the framework of] the Bosnian language completely different directions [of development], which are often very distant from the native idiom. This is completely anachronistic and detracting for the process of standardization of our language.[41]

Šator explained the reference to anachronism as a tendency among the would-be codifiers of the Bosnian language to incorporate many Turkish borrowings frequent in the writings of nineteenth-century Bosniac writers. He opposed the uncritical acceptance of their outdated lexicon, complaining that currently

[a] certain number of Bosnian—especially Bosniac—writers in an attempt to prove their linguistic patriotism have gone so far that they have, in order to write in a "more Bosnian" manner, adopted a vocabulary so archaic that the average educated reader has difficulty understanding.[42]

Šator's strongest criticism, however, concerned the frequency of several post-1991 Croatian vocabulary words, which have become popular in "public use" among Bosniacs. Warning that the Bosniacs must be vigilant in preserving their "cultural and linguistic tradition," he suggested that new Croatian words—such as *izviješće* 'report', *samovrtjelica* 'mixer', and *pjesmotvor* 'poet'—are non-native to citizens of Bosnia-Herzegovina.[43] Šator did not propose any alter-

---

[40] Šator made no explicit mention of Halilović and Jahić in his presentation, and despite his criticism, he displayed a strong pro-Bosniac agenda, and enthusiastic support for a Bosnian language.

[41] "Može-govoriti o jednoj vrsti supstandardizacije koju nameću neki mediji ili pojedini intelektualci koji, oslanjajući se na srpski, u posljednje vrijeme na hrvatski jezički standard, prave unutar bosanskog jezika potpuno divergentne tokove, često veoma udaljene od matičnog idioma, što je sasvim anahrono i pogubno za standardizaciju našeg jezika."

[42] Šator 1999: 110: "Jedan [je] broj bosanskih, a naročito bošnjačkih autora, u dokazivanju svog jezičkog patriotizma otišao dotle da su neki posegli za tako arhaiziranom leksikom da bi pisali 'bosanskije' da je prosječno obrazovanom čitaocu teško razumjeti."

[43] The threat of Croatization of the Bosnian language was also reflected in the name given to the language of the Federation in some public spheres. Thus, Karadža (1999: 35) cited a job announcement for teachers of "Bosno-Croatian" in an August 1998 issue of the Sarajevo daily *Oslobodjenje*.

native to the current processes of standardization. Rather, he suggested (p. 112) that the Bosniacs need to "safeguard our Bosnian language" from external (Serb/ Croat) and internal (Bosniac) forces.

Both Ibrahim Ćedić and Josip Baotić opposed an interventionist approach to the standardization of the Bosnian language. They suggested that the language needed to develop organically. Baotić, the only Bosnian Croat linguist at the Symposium, asserted that on the level of the "organic idiom," Bosnian, Serbian, Croatian, and Montenegrin represent a single language, and that extra-linguistic factors have caused the break-up into separate standard languages. In his view, the Bosnian language must only be construed as the "Bosnian literary language" or "Bosnian standard language." While not explicitly opposing a separate Bosnian language, he argued that a sensible language policy is one where

[l]anguage should not serve the aims that are contrary to its very nature—the hindrance and impediment of communication . . . but could be useful in deepening the consciousness regarding linguistic communality in the past, present, and . . . future of all three of the Bosnian nations.[44]

Baotić's opposition to prescriptivism was based on his perception that forced changes to the organic idiom are unnatural and serve to deepen the ethnic divisions in Bosnia-Herzegovina, especially through the establishment of separate school curricula. He lamented the absurdities that have resulted from the break-up of the unified language, noting that

[w]hen foreigners come to our country . . . they mention that in Zagreb they are told that they speak Croatian excellently, in Belgrade that they speak Serbian excellently, and in Sarajevo that they speak Bosnian excellently, but they always speak the same way. Yet, how will the assertion be acceptable to a Croat, say, from the Posavina region, that he and some resident of Dalmatia, or even of the Zagorje area, speak the same Croatian language, while he and his Bosniac or Serbian neighbor, with whom he communicates every day, do not speak the same language, but rather different languages[?][45]

Baotić was in the minority regarding language planning in Bosnia-Herzegovina. In his view, the language adopted in the republic should be inclusive of the

---

[44] "[j]ezik ne bi služio ciljevima suprotnim svojoj prirodi, onemogućavanju ili otežavanju komuniciranja, . . . a mogao bi biti iskorišten za produbljivanje svijesti o jezičkom zajedništvu u prošlosti, sadašnjosti, pa i . . . u budućnosti sva tri bosanska naroda."

[45] "[s]tranci kada dodju u našu zemlju. . .ističu kako im u Zagrebu kažu da odlično govore hrvatski, u Beogradu da odlično govore srpski, a u Sarajevu da odlično govore bosanski, a oni uvijek govore isto. No kako će i jednom stanovniku, recimo, s Posavine, recimo, Hrvatu biti prihvatljiva tvrdnja da on i neki Dalmatinac, da ne kažem i Zagorac govore istim hrvatskim jezikom, a da on i njegov komšija Bošnjak ili Srbin s kojim on svakodnevno komunicira ne govore istim, nego različitim jezicima."

largest possible number of citizens. Only academics such as Ibrahim Ćedić and Mevlida Karadža echoed this ideology. Ćedić (1999b: 121) espoused tolerance of lexical variation in the Bosnian language, noting that the more nationalist media has consistently rejected certain lexical doublets,[46] and therefore "it is necessary to affirm that the variations represent a highly developed feature in the literary expression of the Bosniacs" ("nužno konstatovati da su varijacije vrlo razvijena osobina u književnom izrazu Bošnjaka"). Karadža (1999: 34ff.) believed that the Bosnian language had reached a critical crossroads, and that the politicians needed to decide whether the Bosnian language would become the new unified language for all of the ethnic groups, a kind of successor to the Serbo-Croatian language, or would continue to develop as a separate standard, even though in her view the dialects of Bosniacs, Serbs, and Croats of Bosnia-Herzegovina display only "superficial" distinctions (p. 36).

The participants at the Symposium made seven recommendations regarding the future of the Bosnian language. The most important of these proposals included: (1) the strengthening of the Institute for Language in Sarajevo, which was to be renamed the Institute for the Bosnian language;[47] (2) the initiation of short-term and long-term projects, including a comprehensive Bosnian dictionary, a one-volume Bosnian dictionary, grammars and orthographic manuals for schools, and other language manuals for the wider public; and (3) cooperation with the Ministry of Education to improve the quality of Bosnian language studies in the schools. The conclusions contained no words on the future of Bosnian language standardization, nor did they indicate any inadequacies with the dictionaries and manuals already produced. Halilović and Jahić have continued to author most of the post-Symposium materials, including a *Pravopis* for the schools (Halilović 1999b), and the first post-1992 grammar of the Bosnian language (Halilović, Jahić, and Palić 2000). Soon after, Refik Bulić (2001) published a new *Pravopis* for elementary and high school pupils. This manual purported to be based on the work of Halilović and Jahić, and is noticeably more prescriptivist than previous works. The first few pages dedicated to rules of punctuation provide a lengthy explanation of the correct way of writing the nouns *Bog* 'God' and *Allah* 'Allah' and their adjectival derivatives in Bosnian. The author insisted that these nouns and adjectival forms should always be written with capital letters, and that *Allah* be written with double *l* (pp. 11–12).[48] The discussion of the Muslim deity continues for several more pages (13–16), when

---

[46] Ćedić cited a study by the Institute for Language in Sarajevo. In this study, the relative frequency of doublets in nationalist Bosniac newspapers and non-nationalist publications was compared. The doublets included such traditionally "Croatian" vs. "Serbian" forms as *općina/opština* 'county', *nositelj/nosilac* 'bearer', *juče r/juče* 'yesterday', *organizirati/organizovati* 'to organize'.

[47] When I visited the Institute in the summer of 1998, I was told that the number of experts employed there had fallen from 25 before the war to seven after the war.

[48] Such spelling is in contrast to the phonetic spelling in Serbian with a single *l*.

the author advises the readers that all 99 ways of referring to Allah should also be capitalized, e.g., *Tvorac* 'Creator', *Svjetlo* 'Light', and *Vladar* 'Ruler'. Readers of such a *Pravopis* would quickly understand that the author of this manual believes that the Bosnian language belongs exclusively to the Bosniacs.

Given their leading role at the University of Sarajevo, it is likely that Halilović and Jahić will continue to dictate language planning and language policy issues among the Bosniacs. Their dominance was reaffirmed in the 2002 "Charter on the Bosnian Language," which encapsulated their Bosniac nationalist agenda in their defense of the Bosnian language.

6.5   Closing ranks: A new charter for a new century

On 21 March 2002, several of the participants from the Bihać Symposium—including Halilović, Jahić, and Ćedić—joined with dozens of Bosniac intellectuals to sign the "Charter on the Bosnian Language." This document consisted of the following seven main points:

(1)   The Bosnian language is the language of the Bosniacs and all others who consider their language to be "Bosnian".

(2)   The name "Bosnian language" is legitimate, since it is the term Bosniacs have used for their language since the Middle Ages.

(3)   Despite the divergences and convergences in the diasystem of the Central South Slavic speech territory, the Bosniacs have the right to call their language Bosnian, just as Serbs can call their language Serbian, and Croats Croatian.

(4)   The Bosniac people have the right to call themselves Bosniacs and to call their language Bosnian, despite all the political manipulations of these terms in the past.

(5)   The Bosniac people have no intentions of threatening the rights of any other people in Bosnia through the use of the term "Bosnian language," nor does this term indicate any Bosniac designs for unification and unitarism on the territory of Bosnia-Herzegovina.

(6)   Any attempt to deny the Bosniacs the right to use the term "Bosnian language" reflects Serb and Croat "paternalism" as manifested in their negation of Bosniac national distinctiveness.

(7)   By using the historical and popularly rooted name of their language, the Bosniacs have the same rights as the other peoples of Bosnia-Herzegovina.

These points illustrate that a decade after the beginning of the Bosnian war the controversies surrounding the term "Bosnian language" had not subsided. This recurrent theme came to the fore in 2002, when international intermediaries and the Office of the High Representative under the leadership of Wolfgang Petrich sought to guarantee equality of the three nations in Bosnia-Herzegovina in both its entities. These efforts were supported by a decision of Bosnia's Constitutional Court in January 2000. The language issue proved to be particularly contentious, as nationalist politicians in Republika Srpska and the Federation opposed the equality of Bosnian, Croatian, and Serbian in their respective entities.[49] Furthermore, the Bosnian Serbs refused to make references to the "Bosnian language" in their Constitution, since they never had recognized this designation for the language. The High Representative to Bosnia-Herzegovina, Wolfgang Petrich, intervened in Republika Srpska on 19 April 2002, by imposing the constitutional amendments. The amendment on language avoided the use of the disputed "ethnic" terms for the languages, stating:

The official languages of the Republika Srpska are: the language of the Serb people, the language of the Bosniak people and the language of the Croat people. The official scripts are Cyrillic and Latin.[50]

This provision replaced paragraph 1 of Article 7 of the Republika Srpska Constitution, which had declared Serbian to be the official language of the entity.

Wrangling over the name of the language may have brought together many Bosniacs in support of their preferred name "Bosnian language." However, the emotional debates over the name have detracted from their laborious tasks of codifying the Bosnian language, and guaranteeing its viability in a country with two other more well-defined standards, Serbian and Croatian, which have historically received much more attention from linguists and language planners.

6.6   Conclusions

In Bosnia-Herzegovina the emergence of the new standards has proven to be a barrier to reintegrating the country's ethnic groups into a viable and cohesive nation that would function independent of the United Nations, the Organization for Security and Cooperation in Europe (OSCE), and the Office of the High Representative (OHR).

The Serbian language continues to predominate in Republika Srpska. The Bosnian language has primacy in Federation cantons with a Bosniac majority, while Croatian is preferred in regions with a Croat majority. The internationally mediated constitutional changes in 2002 formally equated Bosnian with the language of the Bosniac people, and this development is likely to serve the

---

[49] Cf. the Institute for War and Peace Reporting, "Balkan Crisis Report," no. 328 of 5 April 2002 at **www.iwpr.net**.

[50] Cf. Amendment LXXI, found at **www.ohr.int/decisions/statemattersdec/default.asp**.

political agendas of the language planners favoring a Bosniac-oriented standard for the Bosnian language. This constitutional formulation obliterates any aspirations of the non-nationalist linguists, who had proposed the adoption of the Bosnian language by all the citizens of Bosnia-Herzegovina at the 1998 Bihać Symposium.

The fate of the Bosnian language within Bosnia-Herzegovina will continue to depend on the developments within the Serbian and Croatian languages. Whereas Croatian and Serbian will continue to develop largely independent of one another, the Bosnian language will continue to be influenced by the Serbian and Croatian spoken within its midst. The Bosniac linguists will be under much pressure to continue justifying the need and legitimacy of their separate standard, and some linguists may continue to resist perceived Serb or Croat influences. While the spoken Bosnian vernacular heard in Sarajevo or Tuzla may continue to be what many linguists have called the mixture of Serb and Croat linguistic features, the literary language will probably continue to stress Bosniac linguistic features, especially the Turkish/Arabic borrowings and the phoneme *h*. The Bosnian language will look to the Islamic East for its specialized vocabulary, but essentially retain the grammatical structure, phonology, and core vocabulary of the Neo-Štokavian dialect on which it is based.

The drafters of the Dayton Accords indicated that Bosnia-Herzegovina had to abide by the 1992 European Charter for Regional or Minority Languages, designed to ensure that citizens are not discriminated against because of their language. There have been difficulties in implementing the Charter in Bosnia-Herzegovina, because the issue of "majority" vs. "minority" languages is not straightforward. While Serbian, Croatian, and Bosnian are all purported to be "official languages," and therefore ostensibly do not require the protection of a Charter on minority languages, in practice speakers of these three languages are de facto minorities within specific regions.[51] Thus, Bosniacs and Croats are in the minority in Republika Srpska, Serbs and Croats are in the minority in several cantons of the Croat-Bosniac Federation, including Sarajevo, and in Croat majority areas Bosniacs and Serbs constitute the minority populations. It will be difficult to enforce a realignment of majority/minority relationships on populations still reluctant to live in an ethnically diverse society. This difficulty has been especially evident in education. Pašalić-Kreso (1999) blamed nationalist policies for creating "national schools" in Bosnia-Herzegovina, in which the

---

[51] According to the Charter, a minority language cannot be an official language of a state, nor a dialect of that language: "'regional or minority languages' means languages that are: traditionally used within a given territory of a State by nationals of that State who form a group numerically smaller than the rest of the State's population; and ... [are] different from the official language(s) of that State;...[they do] not include either dialects of the official language(s) of the State or the languages of migrants." The text of the Charter is available at **conventions.coe.int/Treaty/EN/Treaties/Html/148.htm.**

majority population has tried to assimilate the minorities, while the minorities have fought "for full educational and schooling autonomy" (p. 4). The OSCE and the OHR have been leading efforts to reform the educational system in Bosnia-Herzegovina. In May 2001, the OHR published its educational policy for Bosnia-Herzegovina, and asserted that,

[b]ased on the Swiss model, each constituent people will develop curricular modules with regards to culture, language and literature that will be integrated into the curricula of the other constituent peoples. Both alphabets and the linguistic/literary heritage of the three communities will be taught throughout BiH, in a balanced and meaningful way.[52]

As discussed in 2.4.1, however, under Tito many Croats had never truly learned the Cyrillic alphabet, even though the study of Cyrillic was compulsory in Croatian elementary schools. It seems unlikely that in Bosnia-Herzegovina in the aftermath of the war, citizens would embrace such a multicultural school curriculum. Would Bosniac parents sincerely hope that their children would learn Cyrillic or Croatian neologisms in school? Would Serb parents encourage their children to master the Turkish and Arabic loanwords infused into the new Bosnian standard? The complex language situation in Bosnia-Herzegovina is unwieldy for a country of four million, as the competition among the three standards becomes a marker of language apartheid, rather than language diversity.

[52] The text is available at **www.ohr.int/ohr-dept/hr-rol/thedept/education/default.asp**.

7

Conclusion

7.0   The Serbo-Croatian successor languages: Shared obstacles and divergent solutions

The above discussion demonstrates the paramount importance of language in creating some of Europe's newest states. Language has functioned as a means to exert control and influence over societies torn apart by ethnic conflicts. The citizens of these societies are discovering that the language you speak defines your place in a society and marks your ethnic identity and even your political orientation. The accent you display lands you a job, or brands you a traitor. These harsh realities afflict many societies, but as this work demonstrates, in the former Yugoslavia the power of language has at times reached absurd proportions.

The language situation in the former Yugoslavia was irrevocably transformed after the break-up of the unified Yugoslav Federation in 1991. The joint Serbo-Croatian language, with its unstable foundation, did not survive the cataclysmic political events. The displacement of people and the search for new national identities contributed to the disintegration of the language. The official demise of the Serbo-Croatian language occurred through a series of unilateral decisions taken in the successor states of the former Yugoslavia. Thus, even before the Federation broke apart, the Croats amended the article in their republican Constitution, renaming their language Croatian. The Serbs and Montenegrins followed suit in 1992, by declaring the language of the Federal Republic of Yugoslavia to be Serbian. Simultaneously, once Bosnia-Herzegovina attained international recognition in April 1992, the Bosniac language planners began elaborating on a separate Bosnian language, which gained legitimacy through the Dayton Accords and the post-Dayton arrangements in Bosnia-Herzegovina. As discussed in Chapter 4, however, the processes of language birth in the Balkans have not abated, this advocates of a separate Montenegrin language attained official status for a Montenegrin standard language through the 2007 Constitution of the newly independent Montenegrin state. All four of the "successor languages" to Serbo-Croatian have been chosen from similar

Neo-Štokavian dialects. Official pronunciation of the new Bosnian, Croatian, Montenegrin, and one of the two Serbian standards originate in the Neo-Što-kavian-ijekavian dialect spoken in the southwest of the former Yugoslavia (southern Dalmatia, eastern Herzegovina, western Serbia, and northwestern Montenegro). The emergence of four standards from a single dialect area is unprecedented in the sociolinguistic literature.

The codifiers of the new standard languages have endeavored to create new linguistic identities despite the similarities in the dialectal base for their respective languages. For the Croat and Serb language planners, this task has been simpler, since these two ethnic groups could hearken back to the works of their ethnic kin, beginning with the nineteenth century. The Croats have claimed that the nineteenth-century dictionaries and grammars produced in Zagreb for the joint language are the source as well for the development of their new Croatian language. Similarly, the Serbs have traced the evolution of the separate Serbian standard to the work of Vuk Karadžić and his devoted follower, Djura Daničić. Moreover, the emergence of separate Croatian and Serbian languages was foreshadowed in 1954 with the binary distinction within Serbo-Croatian of Western and Eastern variants formalized in the Novi Sad Agreement. Superficially Serbian was viewed as a continuant of the former Eastern variant, while Croatian has succeeded the Western one. Chapter 2 demonstrated that this categorization of the splintering of the unified language in Tito's Yugoslavia was more complex. New discrete varieties emerged after 1974 in the Republics of Bosnia-Herzegovina and Montenegro, ones that did not allow for ethnic divisions within the Republics' speech territories. The 1990s have been more challenging for the codifiers of the new Bosnian and Montenegrin standards. Unlike their Serb and Croat counterparts, these language planners have not been able to rely on long philological and linguistic traditions. They have had to construct much of the new linguistic identity only after the break-up of Yugoslavia, drawing upon literary traditions of the nineteenth century and some ethnically marked dialectal features. Serbian language planners have completely rejected the newly constructed Montenegrin standard, and together with the Croats have objected to the decision by the Bosniacs to call their language "Bosnian." The victory of nationalist-oriented parties in the elections of 5 October 2002 in Bosnia-Herzegovina suggests that the ruling Bosnian Serb and Bosnian Croat nationalist parties will continue to oppose the term "Bosnian language" in the coming years. Similarly, after Montenegro's independence in 2006 Serbs and pro-Serbian Montenegrins continue to reject the very notion of a separate Montenegrin language, and the issue of designating Montenegrin as an official language of the country has evoked much heated debate.

Table 5 provides a summary of the main developments of the new Bosnian, Croatian, Montenegrin, and Serbian standards since 1991. As the table reveals, internal squabbles on orthographic matters have erupted in both Serbian and Croatian linguistic circles. In Serbia they were solved through government intervention and the establishment of a centrally monitored model for preserving the unity of the Serbian language (Chapter 3). Some Montenegrins,

TABLE 5. Developments within new Bosnian, Croatian, Montenegrin, and Serbian standards since 1991

Year	Development
1990	Croatian Constitution changes, ensuring that the official language would be Croatian.
1991	Halilović's *Bosanski jezik* appears, claiming the right of Bosnian Muslims to call their language "Bosnian."
1992	The FRY is formed, and Serbian is designated official language in Serbia and Montenegro.
	War breaks out in Bosnia-Herzegovina, Bosnian language planning begins in earnest.
1993	Bosnian Serbs decide to impose Belgrade-ekavian pronunciation, sending shock waves through Serbian linguistic circles.
	Montenegrin linguistic separatists produced their first language manual (Nikčević 1993).
1994	Revised Croatian and Serbian orthographic manuals appear.
	Orthographic controversies flare in Serbia and Montenegro as two manuals vie for official backing.
1995	The Dayton Accords provide for de facto recognition of Bosnian, Croatian, and Serbian as official languages in Bosnia-Herzegovina.
	Publication of the first Bosnian language dictionary (Isaković 1995).
	Second attempt to pass law on the "Defense of the Croatian language" failed in Croatian Parliament.
1996	Publication of the first orthographic manual of the Bosnian language (Halilović 1996).
	Republika Srpska enacts a law regulating the use of language and scripts in the entity, giving preference to Serbian-ekavian.
1997	Matica crnogorska proclaims its support of a separate Montenegrin language; Nikčević's orthographic manual and history of Montenegrin appear.
	The Committee for the Standardization of the Serbian Language is formed in order to monitor the codification of Serbian.
	The Serbian government endorses one of two rival orthographic manuals; the Montenegrin government does not follow suit.
1998	The Symposium on the Bosnian Language is held in Bihać.
1999	Radmilo Marojević is dismissed as dean of Belgrade University's Philology Faculty after publicly espousing nationalist notions regarding Serbian language and identity.
2000	The Croatian "prescriptivist" orthographic manual is reissued.
	The Constitutional Court in Bosnia-Herzegovina mandates Bosnian, Croatian, and Serbian to become official languages in all of Bosnia-Herzegovina.
2001	Croatia experiences "orthographic chaos" as a new descriptivist *Pravopis* appears, rivaling the reissued 2000 prescriptivist manual.
2002	61 Bosniac intellectuals sign the "Charter on the Bosnian Language," staunchly defending their decision to call their language "Bosnian."
2003	The establishment of the state of Serbia-Montenegro triggers calls for replacing the term "Serbian" as the name for Montenegro's official language.
2006–7	In the aftermath of the establishment of an independent Montenegrin state, controversy flared regarding the designation of Montenegro's official language(s)—Montenegrin and/or Serbian—in a new Montenegrin Constitution.

however, interpreted these moves as evidence of Serbian aims to absorb the Montenegrin language and identity, and became more determined than ever to win legitimacy for the Montenegrin language (Chapter 4). Simultaneously, the Croatian debates over orthography also remain unresolved, and have implications for the future directions of the Croatian language. The new descriptivist manual that appeared in 2001 threatens to reverse a long-standing tendency within Croatian linguistic circles to favor pure and authentic Croatian words (Chapter 5). Table 5 further illustrates the link between politics and language. In Croatia, for instance, after the nationalist-leaning Croatian Democratic Union lost power in 1999, dissenting voices on language policies were heard. In the FRY, once Milo Djukanović was elected president of Montenegro in 1997, the pro-independence movement swelled, and consequently the forces advocating a separate Montenegrin language became bolder and more active. In Bosnia-Herzegovina, the international community has toiled to reduce nationalist policies in Bosnia's two entities. On the language issue, the OHR has been committed to allowing the languages of Serbs, Croats, and Bosniacs to be in official use throughout the country. This goal is difficult to achieve without true ethnic reconciliation in the country, and a significant increase in the numbers of displaced persons returning to their former homes. Bosnia-Herzegovina struggles with three similar standard languages, and there are few signs that the country's language apartheid can be removed in the near future.

The successor languages are still shaping their identities and destinies. The following discussion uses four of Friedman's (1998) five categories to show the status of recent controversies surrounding the implementation of the four successor languages.[1]

(1) Recurring issues:
  (a) *Naming of the languages*: Disputes on what to call the unified language lasted from its inception at the time of the 1850 Literary Agreement through the break-up of Serbo-Croatian in 1991. These disputes continue over the naming of the Bosnian language, and the controversy over whether Montenegrins speak "Serbian" or "Montenegrin."
  (b) *Can a standard have two official pronunciations?* This issue became salient in the first two Yugoslav states; the 1954 Novi Sad Agreement created

---

[1] Friedman (1998: 34) called the four categories: recurring, remissive, resolved, and new issues. He defined them as follows: recurring issues are those that have surfaced repeatedly over time; remissive issues are those that were once raised, and "subsequently ceased to be the object of dispute only to be raised again in the most recent phase"; resolved issues were the subject of debate at an earlier time, but no longer discussed; and new issues are those that have "only recently acquired salience." Friedman's fifth category is that of "non-salient" issues, which include features that could have been a source of dispute but were not. This category is useful in his discussion of the implementation of Macedonian, but less applicable to the current analysis.

a pluricentric-unity model, and the Serbian successor language has continued this duality of official pronunciations.

(c) *Should peripheral dialects contribute to the standard language?* This issue first arose regarding the status of Kajkavian and Čakavian in the nineteenth century, and continues to be debated in Croatia.

(d) *Tolerance for lexical variation:* As the unified language developed, lexical variants in Serbo-Croatian were tolerated. Since 1991, the degree of lexical variation has been hotly disputed among Croat and Bosniac language planners, who have viewed the tolerance as a lack of a true identity.

(2) Remissive issues:

(a) *Etymological vs. phonological orthography:* Vuk waged a battle with the Vojvodina Serbs over this issue in the middle of the nineteenth century. Still, the issue that seemed to have been solved, resurfaced in the post-1991 period in Croatia and Serbia.

(b) *Vuk's Cyrillic script:* Vuk faced fierce opposition to his decision to reform the Serbian Cyrillic alphabet, especially because of his introduction of the Latin grapheme *j* and elimination of the *jat'* grapheme in his alphabet. These issues recurred in the first decade of the new Serbian standard.

(c) *Turkish borrowings:* Vuk included several thousand Turkish loanwords in his dictionary; after 1991, Turkish borrowings were stressed for Bosnian, and restricted in Croatian.

(d) *The velar-fricative* h: Vuk reinstated *h* after signing the 1850 Literary Agreement; in the 1990s, this phoneme was claimed to be a primary marker to distinguish Bosnian from both Serbian and Croatian.

(3) Resolved issues:

The Neo-Štokavian dialect is the basis for the Central South Slavic standards: this dialect was chosen in 1850 for the joint language, and language planners for all four successor languages use similar varieties of this dialect, characterized by the distinctive newer Štokavian accentual patterns, for their standards. It is unlikely that any of the new languages would adopt another dialect base.

(4) New issues:

New phonemes: The pro-independence Montenegrins introduced three new phonemes to distinguish Montenegrin from Serbian.

Most of the issues, which have continued to arise in the Central South Slavic speech territory, have been either recurring or remissive. The one resolved issue—the status planning one on choice of dialect—has continued to reverberate in the writings of some extremists. Typically, a Serb nationalist would accuse the Croats of "stealing" a dialect, while Croat extremists would claim that it was never a Serbian dialect in the first place. All these discussions inevitably bring up alleged Serbian hegemonistic designs on all Štokavian-speaking Croats, and notions of Croatian ungratefulness for the work of Vuk and Daničić in creating a Croatian standard.

7.1   My language, my land

The coalescence of language and ethnic affiliation in the Central South Slavic speech territory has been accelerated by both the nationalist discourse and the events of the wars between 1991 and 1995. Anticipating the demise of Yugoslavia, a majority of Muslim Slavs in Bosnia-Herzegovina identified their language as Bosnian. Many Croats had called their language Croatian since the 1960s, while the Serbs and Montenegrins, the two groups hoping to preserve Yugoslavia, continued to consider their language to be Serbo-Croatian up until the break-up of the Yugoslav federation. Through the policies of ethnic cleansing, the nationalist leaders in Croatia, Bosnia-Herzegovina, and Serbia sought to create new states in which language, ethnic affiliation, religion, and territory would all correspond. To this aim, language has been used as a tool for unifying a territory. As Ramet (1997: 147) pointed out, "Within six months of seizing power, Milošević pushed through a bill declaring Serbo-Croatian the official language of Kosovo, thereby disallowing the use of Albanian for official business." Such language legislation underscored Serbian claims to Kosovo, just as Radovan Karadžić's 1993 decree to implement Serbian in Serb-held territories of Bosnia-Herzegovina demonstrated his intentions to join those territories to Serbia. Such policies represented a reversal of the tolerance for minority languages enshrined in the 1974 Yugoslav Constitution, as language policies turned from tolerant to intolerant.[2]

In the Yugoslav successor states the contentious issue of minority language rights has had a destabilizing effect. For example, language rights issues were central to the demands of Albanians in Macedonia, and the subject of protracted negotiations to end the 2001 conflict in that former Yugoslav republic. Prior to the break-up of Yugoslavia, the joint Serbo-Croatian language had functioned as the language of broader communication (*lingua communis*) for the Yugoslav Albanians and other minority groups (cf. Naylor 1978). In Macedonia, the Serbo-Croatian language was taught in all elementary schools, and the republic's citizens often acquired proficiency in the language. Macedonia's ethnic Albanian community had to learn both Serbo-Croatian and Macedonian. For them, fluency in Serbo-Croatian often proved to be essential for economic advancement, and took precedence over the study of Macedonian. With the establishment of

---

[2] Cf. Hayden (1999) for a comprehensive analysis of "constitutional nationalism" in the former Yugoslav republics.

an independent Macedonia on 8 September 1991, the language situation for Macedonia's Albanians changed radically. Serbo-Croatian was completely removed from the elementary school curriculum, and the 1992 Macedonian Constitution declared the Macedonian language and Cyrillic script to be in official use. The new state protected the language rights of the minorities, but the Macedonian Albanians rejected their classification as a minority, challenging the legitimacy of the Macedonian nation-state, and seeking to achieve a co-national status with the ethnic Macedonian majority. The ethnic Albanians resisted the sudden change in their *lingua communis* from Serbo-Croatian to Macedonian. Through some of their actions, such as the demand for a state-sponsored Albanian language university, the ethnic Macedonians felt the Albanian community was bent on undermining the status of the Macedonian language, and the Macedonian state. Hence, the 1990s in Macedonia were characterized by Macedonian–Albanian tensions surrounding the language rights issue. Ethnic Macedonians often considered the Albanian demands for more language rights to be a pretext for gaining enhanced privileges, leading to their secession from the state. The link between language and territory became transparent in 2001, when the Albanian paramilitary National Liberation Army (NLA) took control of villages in the Tetovo and Kumanovo regions. Declaring these villages "liberated territories," the leaders of the NLA claimed that they had taken up arms in order to improve the status of the ethnic Albanians, including their right to use the Albanian language for all official matters in Macedonia. As armed conflicts continued in Albanian-majority areas, the Macedonian press highlighted the appearance of a new Albanian-language orthographic manual, with a politically charged headline, "The First Step towards Unification of the Albanian Nation" ("Prvi čekor za obedinuvanje na albanskata nacija"), claiming:

It is expected that the orthographic manual will be used in 80 elementary schools in Albania, and in ethnic Albanian schools in Kosovo, Macedonia, and Montenegro. One of the members of the committee that prepared the orthographic manual, Agim Vinca, reportedly announced: "this textbook represents the first step towards the unification of the Albanian nation".[3]

During the negotiations to end the Albanian insurgency in the summer of 2001, the language issue proved to be one of the final sticking points, which almost derailed the Ohrid peace agreement. The Macedonians feared that a compromise allowing Albanian to be co-official with Macedonian would be tantamount to giving up the concept of a Macedonian nation-state. Under the pressure of the

---

[3] The article appeared in the daily newspaper *Dnevnik* on 4 May 2001: "Predvideno e pravopisot da se upotrebuva vo 80 osnovni učilišta vo Albanija i vo učilištata za etnički Albanci vo Kosovo, Makedonija i vo Crna Gora. Eden od členovite na Odborot što go pogotvil pravopisot, Agim Vinca izjavil deka 'Ovoj učebnik pretstavuva prv čekor za obedinuvanje na albanskata nacija.'" As discussed above (1.3), the first moves towards such a language unity of Albanian occurred in 1968, when the Kosovo Albanians accepted a Tosk standard.

international mediators, both sides had to compromise. This compromise involved amendment to the Macedonian Constitution eliminating the traditional formulations of "nation" ("narod") and "national minorities" inherited from Tito's Yugoslavia. Macedonia became a state of "its citizens," and communities constituting more than 20 per cent of the population (i.e., the Albanians) gained new rights, including enhanced language rights.[4]

This compromise came one year before the international community changed the article relating to the official languages in the Constitution of Republika Srpska. Thus, in the post-conflict Balkans, the international community has for the first time intervened in resolving disputes over language. It seems that in the future language grievances of the former Yugoslavia may be mediated through European institutions, such as the European Court for Human Rights or the OSCE. However, several sensitive language policies will be determined by politicians and language planners in the successor states of the former Yugoslavia, including the status of a separate Montenegrin language and the language rights of "new" minorities, such as Serbs in Croatia or Croats in Serbia.

For individuals in ex-Yugoslavia, the demise of the unified Serbo-Croatian language has changed many language attitudes. Within Croatia, citizens have felt pressure to adopt the new Croatian in order to prove their patriotic beliefs. The Bosniac intellectual elite has attempted to spread an appreciation for the Islamic roots of Bosniacs by infusing the language with new words and expressions from Turkish and Arabic. The message to average citizens was transmitted at times in not so subtle ways, such as when Sarajevo television began opening its newscasts with the Arabic phrase *selam aleikum* 'peace be with you', rather than the traditional *dobro veče* 'good evening'. It is unlikely that a Sarajevo Serb or Croat would consider these language changes to be a sign of linguistic diversity worthy of celebration. Rather, the former majority populations have been transformed into the minorities, and their native languages have become minority languages virtually overnight.

Writing in the final year of the Bosnian war, Hammel observed that:

> What is perhaps most curious is the situation in Bosnia, where persons distinguished by religion and ethnicity (Catholic Croats, Orthodox Serbs, and Muslim Slavs) speak virtually indistinguishable [i]jekavian dialects but use written standards that reflect their ethnic and religious differences. Bosnian Serbs, Croats, and Muslims all write in [i]jekavian, although there is said now to be some pressure for Bosnian Serbs to write in ekavian, and the Muslims have a higher proportion of Arabo-Turkic words in their vocabulary.[5]

Indeed, Bosnia-Herzegovina is where three of the four new standards are forced to coexist, and where the linguistic differences have been used to keep ethnic

---

[4] For an analysis of the constitutional changes relating to language rights issues, cf. Belamarić (2003).

[5] Cf. Eugene Hammel's "Backward through the Looking Glass: the Yugoslav Labyrinth in Perspective," posted at **www.demog.berkeley.edu/~gene/looking.glass.html**. (2000).

groups apart, rather than bring them together. Bosnia-Herzegovina's three official languages are currently on a path towards divergence, but the possibility remains that at some future point, when ethnic reconciliation is possible, language convergence would once again be in order. For now, however, language planners are bent on reducing mutual intelligibility as much as possible. The separating function of language has reached nearly absurd proportions, but in the near term this policy seems irreversible. Perhaps after the next generation of Croats, Bosniacs, Serbs, and Montenegrins assume positions of power, they will have a much more difficult time communicating with one another in their native language(s).

8

Postscript: Developments
since 2004

8.0   Observations four years later

Many of the premises and conclusions of the first edition of this book have withstood the test of recent times. Scholars and other observers from outside the former Yugoslavia now speak of three or four languages, when prior to 1991 these same individuals considered Serbo-Croatian to be a single language, albeit fractured. Within the former Yugoslavia, linguists have continued to define and shape the new languages. They have worked to solidify the new linguistic standards while simultaneously striving to convince local speakers of the new norms and rules for these languages. The new languages may exist on paper but it remains unclear to what extent the citizens are incorporating these norms into their everyday written and oral communications.

In this chapter, I provide updates on corpus and status planning issues affecting the development of Bosnian, Croatian, Montenegrin, and Serbian. In particular, I focus on the most recent publications and scholarly efforts that define similarities and differences among the languages that used to be subsumed under "Serbo-Croatian" (8.1). I then respond to the acrimonious debate this book's translation sparked in Croatia (8.2). The next section focuses on recent trends in the development of the Bosnian standard language (8.3), and I then move to the still unresolved status of Montenegrin (8.4). I conclude with some perspectives from Serbia (8.5), and a few final observations and suggestions for future research (8.6).

8.1   Scholarly attitudes towards the new language realities in ex-Yugoslavia

One of the key challenges to those of us who used to teach "Serbo-Croatian" before 1991 or "Croatian/Serbian" in the 1990s or "Bosnian/Croatian/Serbian" since the middle or late 1990s was the lack of textbooks that accurately could take into account the new language situation in the former Yugoslavia. Most universities in the United States and other countries outside of the Balkans have resisted offering separate courses for each of the new languages. The politically correct designation for the former Serbo-Croatian has become Bosnian, Croatian, Serbian or "BCS," where the three languages are listed alphabetically and treated in a single language course at U.S. universities.

Recently, Ronelle Alexander and Ellen Elias-Bursac published a textbook with that same title, *Bosnian, Croatian, Serbian,* to fill the void left by the new language realities.[1] Their work is an impressive effort to provide pedagogical materials, a grammar, and exercises for students interested in learning Bosnian, Croatian, and Serbian. A companion volume by Ronelle Alexander provides a more thorough analysis of grammar and valuable sociolinguistic commentary. The two volumes contain much useful information, and are particularly effective for motivated students. Several departments in the United States have adopted these materials for the first-year language course. Students at the University of California Berkeley, Princeton University, and the University of Chicago are now able to pick and choose sections of the two books that might relate to their particular language of interest.

For instance, a student planning to conduct dissertation research in Croatia can learn to read and write using the Latin alphabet, and has an option to study the Cyrillic alphabet in order to access source materials published during the times of Socialist Yugoslavia. The student whose parents emigrated from Montenegro can learn to read and write using the Cyrillic alphabet, and is likely to use only ijekavian forms and to avoid distinctly Croatian vocabulary items. However, it is still unclear how these volumes will be viewed by those insisting on separate language textbooks for each of the "successor" languages.

While Alexander acknowledges the new realities in the titles of the books and throughout the text, the work grows out of a tradition of viewing Bosnian, Croatian, and Serbian as a single linguistic system where mutual intelligibility is still preserved. No scholar can predict the future state of affairs, and whether in 50 or 100 years separate courses and separate textbooks for Bosnian, Croatian, and Serbian would be a necessity, as the languages potentially drift further and further apart.

An important scholarly effort designed to carry out a systematic analysis documenting precisely how the languages are becoming increasingly differentiated has emerged at the University of Graz. A team of scholars at the University's Institute for Slavic Studies ("Institut für Slawistik"), under the

---

[1] I taught from this textbook in a pre-publication version at Yale University in 2005, and I thank Ronelle Alexander and her co-author on one of the two volumes, Ellen Elias-Bursac, for allowing me to use the materials. See Alexander (2006) and Alexander/Elias-Bursac (2006).

leadership of Prof. Branko Tošović, assembled an international team of experts in a three-year research project entitled "The Differences among Bosnian/Bosniac, Croatian, and Serbian." In 2006, the project received financial support from the Austrian Fund for Science and additional support from Austrian regional and local governments.

The first scholarly Symposium was held in Graz on 12–14 April 2007, with discussions centering on orthographic, orthoepic, phonetic, and phonological differences among the languages. Selected papers were scheduled for publication later in 2007, and additional Symposia were planned for 2008 and 2009. All correspondence from the organizers is written in German and "Bosnian/Bosniac, Croatian, and Serbian" (BCS). The BCS version is written typically with alternative forms separated by slashes or with alternate suffixes in parentheses. For instance, the most recent correspondence I received began in the following manner; I inserted the letters in brackets to show the correspondence between the forms and the languages (B = Bosnian, C = Croatian, and S = Serbian):

Poštovana kolegi(ni [BS])ce [BC]!
Poštovani kolega!
Želio [BCS]/Želeo [S] bih da Vam se još jednom iskreno zahvalim na aktivnom učešću [BS]/sudjelovanju [C] u radu 1. simpozij(um [C])a [BS], koji je protekao u tolerantnom duhu. Po mojoj oc(j [BCS])eni [S], diskusije su bile argumentovane [BS]/argumentirane [BC], korektne i odm(j [BCS])erene [S].[2]

In all the messages I received since joining this project in 2006, I do not recall seeing a single form with three possible variants listed between slashes, i.e., with one distinct "Bosnian/Bosniac," "Croatian," and "Serbian" form. Moreover, in many instances I would still be hard-pressed to declare with any degree of certainty which of the two forms listed in their frequent messages is truly the best Bosnian form—do the codifiers of Bosnian prefer the feminine form *koleginica* as in Serbia or *kolegica* as in Croatia? If both are admitted, which is more frequent among speakers in Bosnia's entities, cantons, towns, and villages? The same question applies to the infinitive forms in -*irati* (Croatian) vs. -*ovati* (Serbian). Clearly, these and other similar issues are to be studied and discussed among the many eminent scholars invited to participate in this project from the former Yugoslavia, Europe, and North America.

The Graz project's organizers have also been politically correct in listing the two competing names—"Bosnian" and "Bosniac"—for what I have opted to call "Bosnian language" in this work (see 6.1). Since this volume's first appearance in

---

[2] The translation of this text is as follows: "Dear Colleague [female]! Dear Colleague [male]! I would like once again to thank you sincerely for [your] active participation in the first Symposium which was conducted in a tolerant spirit. In my estimation, the discussions were reasoned, respectful, and measured."

2004, I have continued to refer to the language as "Bosnian," since this is the name that the linguists in Bosnia-Herzegovina have preferred.[3]

The Graz project is unique in that it has brought together ex-Yugoslav and international linguists. It is one of the few venues where specialists, mostly from University faculties, from Croatia, Serbia, and Bosnia-Herzegovina can discuss the language situation in the former Yugoslavia. Noticeably absent from the roster of specialists are the individuals espousing nationalist-oriented language policies.

These scholarly efforts for a new textbook and sound analysis of language differences are contrasted by the continuing politically motivated efforts to differentiate the languages within the former Yugoslav republics. As I discuss in the next sections, advocates for separate Croatian, Bosnian, and Montenegrin languages remain vocal and determined to press forward with their national language agendas.

8.2   Croatia: A roundtable controversy

I was very pleased when my colleague, Anita Peti-Stantić of the University of Zagreb contacted me to ask if she could translate this book into Croatian. The volume was published by Srednja Europa in November 2005, and became the subject of a roundtable discussion at the Matica hrvatska on 2 February 2006. Unfortunately, I was unable to attend the event; however, Anita Peti-Stantić sent me several of the texts read by academicians and scholars who presented, and described the day's events in detail to me. Prior to the event, the translated book had been sent to leading Croatian scholars, including Radoslav Katičić, Stjepan Babić, Dalibor Brozović, Milorad Pupovac, Ivo Pranjković, Dubravko Škiljan, Damir Kalogjera, and others. The main auditorium at the Matica hrvatska was filled to capacity, extra chairs had to be brought in, and

---

[3] I wish to propose a distinction in the English language between the terms "Bosniak" and "Bosniac." Currently, these two spellings are used in English as a translation of both the noun designating the ethnic group *Bošnjak*, and for the adjectival form bošnjački. My proposal would be to use the form "Bosniak" for the noun designating the ethnic group, and "Bosniac" for the adjectival form (with the adjectival ending -iac corresponding to several other adjectives in English, such as "cardiac," or "demoniac"). Such a regularization of English spellings would help disambiguate a sentence such as "As both a Bosniac and a Bosnian, I consider Bosniac to be the improper name of my language" to read, "As a Bosniak [= a member of the ethnic group] and a Bosnian [= a citizen of Bosnia-Herzegovina], I consider Bosniac [= adjective from "Bosniak"] to be the improper name of my language." Both English spellings are found extensively on the web, although it appears that there is a growing preference for the use of the form "Bosniak." A definitive ruling on the proper English spelling is long overdue.

more than fifty individuals had to stand throughout the five-hour-long roundtable discussion. The leading academicians long involved in the drive for establishing a separate Croatian language were adamant in their criticisms of the book's main theses, particularly regarding the tradition of the joint Serbo-Croatian language and the significance of the Literary Agreement and the Novi Sad Agreement. They were especially disturbed by my assertion that the external identity of the joint language had ceased to exist in 1991 with the disintegration of Yugoslavia, and inaccurately believed that I had argued that Croatian only began to exist after 1991. They further objected to the very title of the book, especially the use of the geographical term "Balkans" (with its negative political connotations), and the use of the term "Serbo-Croatian," a language most Croats never believed truly existed.

My response to the flurry of criticisms and accusations was published in *Jutarnji list* in early March 2006. Here is an abridged version of that response:

I welcome the debate that my book has opened within Croatian linguistic circles. I hope that my critics can move beyond their personal attacks and come to terms with how others may view the Croatian language. It is time to consider Croatian language identity in a broader European context and in the context of the vast literature on language and national identity. This area of scholarship should prove fruitful for future scholars in Croatia, and will allow for a more level-headed understanding of the country's own language issues. It is not merely a matter of whether or not a separate Croatian language has always existed and should have been recognized as such. Politics, historical circumstances, and the work of individuals play a significant role in the emergence of all major standard languages. In the United States, Noah Webster believed that an "American English" language was necessary and he worked hard to create a new standard for the United States. During his lifetime politicians criticized him and objected to his inclusion of "vulgar Americanisms" in the English language. And yet, Noah Webster's reforms endured, and there is a separate American standard. In the past, some politicians in the U.S. tried to change the name of our language to "American," and in the State of Illinois in the 1920s the State Legislature actually passed a law declaring the official language of the State of Illinois to be the American language. However, this movement did not spread throughout the country, and in the United States we still consider our own language to be English, not American. We still believe in an overarching unity of English, and I call this kind of unity "pluricentric" in my book. The Linguistics Society of America addressed the issue of "dialect" vs. "language" in its well-known resolution on the status of African American Vernacular English from January 1997: "different varieties of Chinese are popularly regarded as 'dialects', though their speakers cannot understand each other, but speakers of Swedish and Norwegian, which are regarded as separate 'languages', generally understand each other." Most of my colleagues from the former Yugoslavia seem to understand each other quite well, even when one colleague may speak Croatian and another Serbian. Some observers may consider the language a single language with a "pluricentric unity" (more than one standard form), while others will insist that the languages are separate. Even Prof. Pranjković suggested that the Croatian and Serbian languages are a single language, and Academician Brozović had admitted in his writings that the two standards are part of the same "diasystem." My book also clearly stated that the internal identity was always weak, but that the external identity of the joint language was strong. In institutions of higher learning in the United States, the language courses were always called "Elementary Serbo-Croatian," or "Intermediate Serbo-Croatian." The instructors may have been trained in Croatia or Serbia, and may not have always felt comfortable with forms that were absent in their native speech, but students could learn about both variants. In addition, all our scholars who worked on the area wrote about the Serbo-Croatian language (some still do). This was the situation because foreign scholars have not experienced the issue of social and personal identity which seems to be predominant in the writings on the Croatian language by Croatian linguists. My book was written for an English-speaking audience, one which regarded Socialist Yugoslavia as having a single Serbo-Croatian language. It is this external identity which is finally shattered in 1991, and this external perception of unity that has ended. For many Croats, the unity either never existed or was so fractured that they simply never truly believed in it. However, for many others in the former Yugoslavia (especially in Bosnia-Herzegovina, Serbia, and Montenegro), the language unity was real [and they embraced this unity]...

[My effort was to offer a scholarly perspective and not] judge... one nationalist stance [or another]... Even today, some scholars assert that Bosnian, Croatian, and Serbian are merely national names for the same unified language, but my book counters that argument and recognizes that these are now autonomous and separate languages, embarking on divergent paths of codification. Of course, I am talking about the standard language, which should not be confused with vernaculars or dialects. Some of my critics claim that they have always spoken only Croatian, and they are certain that the joint language did not exist.... However, when reading about the 1850 Literary Agreement and when studying the numerous grammars and dictionaries produced at the Yugoslav Academy of Sciences and Arts between 1867 and 1899, it quickly becomes apparent that there was a group of solid linguists of Croat and Serb origin who were busy codifying a single standard or literary language.... I hope that my book also encourages more scholarship in Croatia on the neighboring languages—Bosnian, Serbian, and Montenegrin. If Croats had felt a strong sense of linguistic distinctiveness over the past centuries, then... did the Bosniaks [and Montenegrins] also always consider their language to have been a separate language?... Did these other peoples always consider Croatian to be a separate language? Is not the history of Croatian—like it or not—bound up with the history of the other languages that are based on the Štokavian dialect?...

My critics at the roundtable seemed also keen on denying the validity of the book's many arguments simply based on the title, which includes two words that raised eyebrows in Croatia: Balkans and Serbo-Croatian. Again, this book was written for an English-speaking audience. The... [aim was to adopt] a title that would be searchable and meaningful to its readers. Here again, perceptions differ inside and outside of Croatia: where does Central Europe end and the Balkans begin? Is Dubrovnik on the geographic Balkan peninsula, but Pula is not? Should the term "Balkan" be expunged from the literature because of all its negative connotations? These terms, "Balkans" and "Serbo-Croatian" are frequently used in the American scholarly tradition (e.g., "Serbo-Croatian prosody," "Balkan Slavic," "Balkan Sprachbund," "Balkanisms"), and in using these conventional terms there was no intention of insulting Croatian sensibilities....

Ultimately it is my hope that we can expand our horizons and begin a real debate. When we compare the language situation in ex-Yugoslavia with that in Scandinavia, or on the Indian subcontinent (Hindi/Urdu), or in China, we can contribute to our understanding of the link between language and identity. I urge my colleagues in Croatia to move beyond arguments about the past, on whether or to what degree the language was unified or separated, and look towards the future—what will be the nature of the Croatian language, and what will be its future relationship with the other languages based on the Štokavian dialect?

Finally, my book attempts to be a comprehensive study of the language–identity link in the former Yugoslavia for all Štokavian speakers. It relies primarily on written sources: new grammars, dictionaries, statements by contemporary linguists, and media reports. Future research should expand this analysis to social attitudes within each independent state and how each society perceives the past, the present, and the future of their respective languages. One of my students from Sarajevo made a presentation in which she lamented what she considered the fracturing of the "Serbo-Croatian" language. Her view was that the local linguistic varieties of what she considers to be a single language added great richness to the language, and commented how her High School diploma had in the early 1990s five different names for the same language: "Serbo-Croatian," "Mother tongue," "Bosnian," "Serbian," and "Croatian," even though she never changed the way she speaks. My American students were aghast that such inconsistencies in naming the standard language were even possible. The Croatian census questionnaires from 2001 included the languages "Croatian," "Serbian," "Serbo-Croatian," and "Croato-Serbian." How is an average American going to understand such a variety of names of these languages? My conclusions are based on what linguists themselves have written or said, and why language issues have been such a source of controversy and debate in the former Yugoslavia. These issues are so close to the heart of my Croatian readers, but very difficult to comprehend in an English-speaking world, where regional and national variants have more or less stabilized.[4]

This response seemed to quiet the storm the book's publication had caused in Croatia. In 2007, a more reasoned assessment of the book was written by Daniel Bunčić in *Književna republika*, the journal of the Croatian Writers' Society. Bunčić recognized that this volume was meant to be a comprehensive and comparative analysis of all of the territory that had been traditionally subsumed under "Serbo-Croatian." It does not represent an attack on any one of the successor languages and their bona fide or would-be codifiers. For instance, he welcomed the analysis in Chapter 4 that critiques several of Vojislav Nikčević's assertions regarding the origins of the Montenegrin people, and sees the value of many of the conclusions of this volume as those of an objective outsider's view of the situation.

The planned publication of the papers from the Matica hrvatska roundtable event may inspire a more nuanced debate over the direction of the Croatian language, and the nature of the relationship between Croatian and the other successor languages.

---

[4] The entire text in its Croatian translation is available at **www.jutarnji.hr/ ispis_clanka.jl?artid=14673**.

8.3   Bosnia-Herzegovina: Two new dictionaries on their way

In Chapter 6, I discussed many of the challenges faced by the codifiers of a new Bosnian standard language. These codifiers have had to justify the legitimacy of Bosnian in relation to the two more established neighboring languages—Croatian and Serbian. As seen in 6.4, two different approaches to language standardization emerged at the first Symposium on the Bosnian language in 1998. The prescriptivist-leaning linguists, led by Senahid Halilović, published new orthographic manuals, grammars, and dictionaries. Recently, the descriptivist-oriented linguists have actively worked on their own instruments of codification for the new standard. Currently, the political situation in Bosnia-Herzegovina has impeded the creation of a coherent Bosnian language policy or language-planning process. The Republic of Bosnia-Herzegovina, with its two entities, FBiH and RS, has remained a weak state still largely under the control of foreign officials and institutions. In the FBiH entity, where the Bosnian language has been promoted, the federal structure, with its ten cantons and ten cantonal governments, lacks a central authority or ministry that can support a clearly defined Bosnian standard language. Simultaneously, in the RS entity, with its centralized structures, the Serbian language has continued to be promoted, albeit the RS government has moved away from its initial insistence on the ekavian pronunciation within the entity.

Senahid Halilović and his colleagues at the University of Sarajevo have concentrated their efforts on the publication of a new comprehensive dictionary of the Bosnian language which, according to the publisher's website, was scheduled to appear in spring 2007. The site proclaims that

this is the first descriptive-normative dictionary in the history of the Bosnian language. It is the result of many years of team work on the part of associates of the Sarajevo Faculty of Philosophy. The Dictionary contains more than 100,000 entries on over 1,000 pages.[5]

For Halilović and his collaborators, this dictionary represents the crowning achievement in the standardization process of the language. The authors of the dictionary's official website proclaim that

[t]he last ten years in the history of the Bosnian language will be considered the period in which the language was standardized. In this decade the standard Bosnian language joined the community of Slavic, European, and world standard languages.[6]

---

[5] See www.rbj.ba: "[o]vo je prvi opisno-normativni rječnik u historiji bosanskoga jezika. Plod je višegodišnjeg timskog rada saradnika Filozofskog fakulteta u Sarajevu. Sadrži oko 100.000 riječi na više od 1.000 stranica."

[6] Ibid. "[p]osljednjih desetak godina u historiji bosanskoga jezika bit će označene kao period u kome je taj jezik normiran. U ovoj deceniji standardni bosanski jezik pridružuje se slavenskoj, evropskoj i svjetskoj zajednici standardnih jezika."

Once the volume is available, it will be possible to evaluate whether this assertion is true and whether Halilović and others at the Sarajevo Faculty of Philosophy have remained keen on limiting flexibility within the Bosnian standard. The discussions from the Bihać meeting in 1998 had called for the appearance of a new authoritative dictionary; however, by contrast to the multi-volume Croatian Academy and Serbian Academy dictionaries, this volume is relatively modest. Its contents will reveal the degree of prescriptivism championed by Halilović and his co-authors, especially the level of acceptance of neologisms from Croatian, and the extent Bosnian may be purged of perceived Serbianisms.

The assertion that the process of standardization of the Bosnian language is now complete is not shared by all linguists in Bosnia-Herzegovina. Just as Halilović et al. were completing their work on the new Bosnian dictionary, a group of linguists at Sarajevo's Institute for Language, led by Ibrahim Ćedić, were preparing a rival dictionary of the Bosnian language.[7] Without having the chance to compare the two volumes, I am reluctant to draw definitive conclusions regarding the differences in approach. However, based on an article in the Sarajevo daily *Oslobođenje* from 1 August 2007, it appears that the Ćedić et al. volume advocates for a flexible norm for the Bosnian language. The article attributed the following statement to Ćedić:

[o]ne of the special dimensions within the Bosnian language is the existence of expressions [rendered by] doublet forms or multiple forms. The Bosnian language is so rich lexically...that...we can express certain things in different ways. It is precisely for this reason that the Bosnian language is also unique and all its doublet forms and multiple forms must be present in the final inventory of its lexicon, so that users of the language could have freedom to choose [from among] linguistic tools. The populations of Bihać and Sarajevo do not use the same lexicon and for this reason there must be freedom of choice.[8]

This approach appears not to be "normative" and attempts to appeal to a broad spectrum of the population. Ćedić, in a veiled reference to the work of the more prescriptivist Bosnian linguists, claims that he and his colleagues from the

---

[7] In Bosnian the two books have nearly identical titles. Halilović et al. is called *Rječnik bosanskoga jezika*, while the Ćedić et al. volume is called *Rječnik bosanskog jezika*. The longer genitive singular masculine adjectival ending *-oga* is found mostly in the written language, while *-og* is more frequent in the spoken language.

[8] The article can be found at **http://www.oslobodjenje.ba/index.php?option= com_content&task=view&id=51083&Itemid=50**: "[j]edan od posebnih slojeva u bosanskom jeziku jeste postojanje izraza dvostrukosti i višestrukosti. Bosanski jezik je toliko bogat leksikom da...određene stvari možemo izreći na različite načine. Upravo zbog toga je bosanski jezik i specifičan i u konačnom sastavu njegove leksike moraju postojati sve dvostrukosti i višestrukosti kako bi korisnici jezika mogli imati slobodu izbora jezičkih sredstava. Istu leksiku ne upotrebljava stanovništvo Bihaća i Sarajeva i zbog toga mora postojati sloboda izbora."

Institute for Language do not believe in "a return to the past" ("vraćanje u prošlost"), and that therefore the Bosnian language should contain words that are commonly used in contemporary society, and not found in the writings from the past as advocated by Bosniac nationalist linguists.[9]

Thus, as was seen in Croatian and Serbian linguistic circles in previous chapters, discord has also emerged among Bosnian linguists. The divergent philosophies noted at the Bihać Symposium have blossomed into two different dictionaries that are likely to espouse contradictory standardizations of the Bosnian language. Without the cooperation of the two main groups of linguists—Halilović's circle at Sarajevo University and Ćedić's team based at Sarajevo's Institute for Language—a viable single Bosnian standard language may elude us for some time.

8.4   Montenegro: The pains of language separation

The final status of the joint state of Serbia and Montenegro was decided in a May 2006 referendum. Soon after the necessary majority of Montenegro's eligible voters cast their ballots in favor of an independent Montenegro, the newest European state was born. However, the politicians in newly independent Montenegro had a difficult time agreeing upon a new Constitution for Montenegro, and one of the key controversial issues was that of the designation of the country's official language(s). Proposals included (1) Montenegrin; (2) Montenegrin and Serbian; and (3) Serbo-Montenegrin.

Simultaneously, a significant number of Montenegro's scholars and academicians have been skeptical regarding the existence of a separate Montenegrin language; as seen in Chapter 4, the strongest advocates of a separate Montenegrin language remain a group of writers and intellectuals, few of whom have a background in linguistics. Across the new international boundary in Serbia, Serb linguists continue to assert that a separate Montenegrin language does not exist. While the Montenegrin language gained symbolic recognition as an official language in a compromise formula for the country's Constitution, it remains unclear whether efforts to standardize the language will gain true credibility among linguists in Montenegro and abroad.

On 24 April 2007, the Montenegrin daily *Pobjeda* published one of many articles on the debate surrounding the language(s) to be declared as official in the new Constitution. In this article, Dr. Jelica Stojanović, a Professor of the

---

[9] Compare also the criticisms that Muhamed Šator made at the Bihać Symposium of the drive to include archaic words from Bosnia's literary past in the standardization of a new Bosnian language (section 6.4).

history of the Serbian language and contemporary Serbian at the Faculty of Philosophy in Nikšić, argued that Montenegro's sole official language should be the Serbian language. In her view, the language of Montenegro is "genetically and structurally" the Serbian language, and the political boundaries of Montenegro in no way correspond to the linguistic boundaries. She considered Montenegro's dialects to be part of the broader Serbian speech territory, and she believed that this notion can be proven scientifically. Even on the sociolinguistic level, Stojanović cited the fact that 63 percent of Montenegro's population claimed their language to be Serbian in the census of 2003. She rejected any name compromises for Montenegro's language, asserting that debates surrounding the official designation of Montenegro's language are merely a political game and that

[t]he game surrounding the renaming of the language has not stopped. Following the changing of the name from Serbian to mother tongue, our language, this language . . ., and thereafter the replacements of the name Serbian language with four names among which is introduced "Montenegrin," an empty designation for a language lacking any content. Yet another absurd decision has been reached—the Serbian language should be called Serbo-Montenegrin, Serbian or Montenegrin . . .[10]

New designations for the former joint Serbo-Croatian language, such as "mother tongue" were proposed in Montenegro after the establishment of the loosely federated state of Serbia and Montenegro in 2003.[11] Several alternatives to the designation "Serbo-Montenegrin" were suggested for the official language in a new Montenegrin constitution. In May 2007 the media reported that a compromise had been reached between Montenegro's ruling coalition and one of the opposition parties (the Movement for Changes). According to this compromise, the new constitutional names for the language would be either

---

[10] See **http://www.pobjeda.co.yu/naslovna.phtml?akcija = vijest&id = 116928**: "[i]gra oko imena jezika ne prestaje. Nakon preimenovanja srpskog u maternji, naš, ovaj . . ., zatim zamjene imena srpskog jezika sa četiri imena među koje se uvodi puki naziv jezika bez ikakvog sadržaja—"crnogorski", došlo se do još jednog apsurdnog rješenja – srpski jezik treba da se nazove srpsko-crnogorski, srpski ili crnogorski . . ."

[11] See an article from *Nezavisna svetlost* which appeared on 5 February 2005 entitled "Bosanski jezik u Srbiji." The article makes reference to the moves in Montenegro to change the name of the subject "Serbian language" in the schools to "mother tongue," allowing students the choice of calling their language whatever they please—"Bosnian," "Croatian," "Montenegrin," or "Serbian." The author of the article asserts that new challenges to the status of the Serbian language have also spread to the Republic of Serbia itself, where "Croatian" was officially recognized as a minority language in Vojvodina, and "Bosnian" gained official sanctioning as a minority language in the Sandžak region. See **http://www.svetlost.co.yu/arhiva/2005/489/489-3.htm** and 8.5 below.

"Montenegrin-Serbian" or "Montenegrin, Serbian."[12] These optimistic reports, however, were premature since the main nationalist parties, including the Montenegrin-oriented Liberal Party and the Serbian-oriented groups (the Serbian List, the Democratic Serbian Party, the People's Party, and the Socialist People's Party) vehemently opposed such solutions. In a joint platform, the pro-Serbian opposition parties agreed in September 2007 to conduct negotiations through "transparent democratic dialogue." However, in this same platform they declare that it would be unacceptable for the Constitution to specify only a Montenegrin language.[13]

In another interview published in *Pobjeda*, the Montenegrin academician, Branislav Ostojić, one of the leading pro-Serbian Montenegrin linguists, declared that all those who deny the existence of a joint Serbo-Croatian language still continue to speak this language. In this view, the linguistic facts remain clear: linguistically all four "successor languages" are still the same language, and the division into separate national languages has been merely motivated by political considerations. Therefore, any Montenegrin Constitution should not "prescribe the name of the language" ("ne propisuje ime jezika"), but should take into consideration the true linguistic situation.[14]

Some similar opinions were expressed at a scholarly conference organized on 25 May 2007 in Podgorica at the Montenegrin Academy of Sciences and Arts. The conference, entitled "The Language Situation in Montenegro: Norm and Standardization," was co-sponsored by the Montenegrin Petar II Petrović Njegoš Institute for Language and Literature and the University of Oslo's Institute for East European and Oriental Studies with funding provided by the Norwegian government.[15] The sub-headline in the daily *Pobjeda* from 25 May 2007 proclaimed "Language Norms are Made Inside the State" ("Jezik normirati unutra države"), referring to statements by Sven Milensfeld regarding the opportunity for Montenegrins in their newly independent state to unite in deciding on the

---

[12] See Bojana Stanišić's "Compromise Unlikely to Silence Row over Montenegro's Language" (15 May 2007) on the website of the Balkan Investigative Reporting Network at **http://www.birn.eu.com/en/1/190/2950/?tpid = 7**.

[13] See a news report from the Balkan Investigative Reporting Network from 17 September 2007 at **http://www.birn.eu.com/en/103/15/4393**.

[14] See the article "Javna rasprava o Nacrtu ustava: Akademik Branislav Ostojić, prof. emeritus" from 23 April 2007 available at **http://www.pobjeda.co.yu/naslovna.phtml? akcija = vijest&id = 116849**.

[15] According to press reports, the participants at the conference included Branislav Ostojić, Snježana Kordić, Božo Ćorić, Branko Tošović, Per Jakobsen, Sven Menesland, Sven Gustavson, Radojica Jovićević, Ljiljana Subotić, Mihailo Šćepanović, Drago Ćupić, Miodrag Jovanović, Ana Janjušević, Sanja Šubarić, and Milena Djurić. I thank Snježana Kordić for sending me information on this conference and for the links to several articles reporting on the meeting. One such link includes a commentary on the conference published in *Nin* available at **http://www.nin.co.yu/pages/article.php?id = 31692**.

nature and character of a new Montenegrin standard.[16] However, there seemed to be little evidence of new initiatives on the part of the Montenegrin and Serb participants in the conference to organize a new standardization process for the language of Montenegro.

Ultimately, the Montenegrin Parliament adopted a compromise formula for the designation of the country's official language(s) in a stormy debate held on 19 October 2007. Article 13 of the Constitution declares that "The official language in Montenegro" ("službeni jezik u Crnoj Gori") is the Montenegrin language, that the Cyrillic and Latin scripts are both equally valid, and that other languages in official use are Serbian, Bosnian, Albanian, and Croatian.[16]

Thus, though Montenegrin was finally named an official language of a new state, the nature of this language remains mired in controversy and confusion. The pro-Nikčević Montenegrin nationalists continue to push for their own version of a separate Montenegrin standard, and the majority of linguists remain content to retain a linguistic unity of Montenegrin and Serbian. Simultaneously, citizens of Montenegro have not felt pressure to change the way they speak despite the efforts of Nikčević and his followers. While the political separation is now final, it is much more difficult to achieve a cultural and linguistic divorce between the Serbian and Montenegrin peoples.

8.5   Serbia: Recent perspectives

The breakup of the state of Serbia-Montenegro in 2006 has had little effect on the official support for bidialectalism among Serb linguists, who continue to maintain that the Serbian language has two official pronunciations—ekavian and ijekavian. Given the large number of ijekavian-speaking Serbs who reside in Bosnia-Herzegovina, Montenegro, and Western Serbia, it is unlikely for that policy to change. Official state language policy, however, has evolved since Serbia-Montenegro joined the Council of Europe in 2003 and adopted the European Charter on Regional and Minority Languages, which the joint state of Serbia-Montenegro ratified on 15 February 2006. In this process, the Serbian government granted official minority language status to both Bosnian and Croatian.[18]

---

[16] See "Naučni skup 'Jezička situacija u Crnoj Gori: norma i standardizacija' počeo juče u CANU" from *Pobjeda* (25 May 2007), p. 15.

[17] The text of the new Constitution is available at www.snp.cg.yu/strana.asp?kat=1& id=1278.

[18] The other regional and minority languages recognized are Albanian, Bulgarian, Hungarian, Romani, Romanian, Rusyn, Slovak, and Ukrainian. See **http://www.coe.int/t/e/ legal_affairs/local_and_regional_democracy/regional_or_minority_languages/2_monito ring/2.2_States_Reports/Serbia_report1.pdf**.

While many in Serbia may have regarded such a move as a blow to the status of Serbian within the Republic of Serbia, it represents a final demise of any official attitude that the breakup of the former joint Serbo-Croatian language did not occur or that the joint language could be reconstituted. Thus, at least on the official state level, all parties in the former Yugoslavia have recognized Bosnian, Croatian, and Serbian as new national languages. Montenegrin remains controversial; while Serbian was declared an official language in Montenegro, it is unlikely for the foreseeable future that Montenegrin would become an eleventh minority language in Serbia.

8.6 Final remarks and future research

As seen here, the language/identity issues in the former Yugoslav republics have remained of key social and political concern. Some linguists still bemoan the official breakup of the formerly joint language, while others maintain that the separate languages always existed and have legitimate and rich histories. The nature of the Bosnian and Montenegrin standards remains unclear, and the final linguistic divorce between Serbian and Montenegrin has not yet occurred. Committees in Croatia and Serbia continue to push for new norms for Croatian and Serbian, while foreign scholars work to treat Bosnian/Croatian/Serbian as a single language course in University curricula and as a single "linguistic system" that can still be subsumed under "Central South Slavic." Perhaps matters would become clearer in a future edition of this book, but for the meantime, I would have to conclude by saying that these South Slavic standard languages are still in transition and the future status planning issues for Bosnian and Montenegrin may not be resolved for many years to come.

Many colleagues have made excellent suggestions regarding areas that this book did not address. I have no doubt that much new fieldwork is necessary with the aim of analyzing the impact of the new languages on the first generation of speakers in the newly independent countries. To what extent have Croatian neologisms been accepted within Croatia, and to what degree have Serbs avoided grammatical forms that might be perceived as Croatian, such as the use of the infinitive? Are Bosniacs more likely to use *h* or Turkish/Arabic borrowings, and will Montenegrins, depending on whether they are nationalists or not, adopt some of Nikčević's proposed Montenegrin features? Does the average citizen find all these efforts of creating new language differences to be a viable affirmation of their identity, or a political hogwash, and that after a few drinks they will admit that the different languages are still one language?

Another area of future research would consider the platforms of political parties in the successor states, and whether specific parties espouse distinct language platforms. Do individuals belonging to former Communist parties maintain a Yugoslav orientation towards language? Is the issue of supporting the new national languages a right-wing vs. left-wing issue or merely a nationalist vs. non-nationalist issue?

Many other areas of research are possible, especially regarding dialectal features in the Central South Slavic speech territory. Are there more Čakavian and Kajkavian elements entering the Croatian language? Is Serbian becoming increasingly a language with more features typical of the Balkan speech area?

Some of my critics have called this book an attack on linguistics, since it accepts the new ethnic/political terms for the languages ignoring the linguistic facts that suggest that a single language still remains. However, in studying the former Yugoslavia, I have learned that the same "fact" is frequently interpreted in an opposite way depending on one's ethnic/national affiliation. Moreover, in the Slavic world it is frequently difficult to determine the precise boundaries among languages, and in the past there have been claims made that some Croatian dialects belong to Slovenian, that Macedonian and Bulgarian are one language, or that Czech and Slovak are a single language. This book demonstrates that sociolinguistic processes frequently do trump the linguistic facts, and we cannot and should not ignore the new situations that result.

Appendix A

Text of the 1850 Literary Agreement

We, the undersigned, aware that *one* people needs to have *one* literature, and in that connection with dismay witnessing how our literature is splintered, not only by alphabets, but still by orthographic rules as well, have convened these past days to discuss how we could agree and unify in our literature as much as is now possible. And so we have:

(1) Unanimously recognized that it is not worthwhile through the mixing of dialects to construct a new idiom, which does not exist among the people; rather it is better to choose one of the vernacular dialects for the literary language. All this is (a) because it is impossible to write whereby everyone would be able to read in their own dialect; (b) because any such a mixing [of dialects], as a creation of man, would be worse than any of the popular dialects at all, which are God's work; and (c) because other peoples, such as the Germans and Italians, have also not constructed a new idiom out of their own dialects; rather, they chose one of their popular dialects, and use it for the writing of books.

(2) We have unanimously recognized that it is most proper and best to designate the southern dialect as literary, and this is (a) because most of the people speak that way; (b) because it is the closest to the old Slavic language, and therefore to all other Slavic languages; (c) since nearly all the folk poems are created in this dialect; (d) since all the old Dubrovnik literature is written in this dialect; (e) since most of the literary figures of both the Eastern and Western faiths already write in this way (although not all mind all the rules). Therefore, we have agreed that in those places where in this dialect there are two syllables *ije* will be written, while where there is one syllable, then *je* or *e* or *i* will be written, each where necessary, for example *bijelo, bjelina, mreža, donio*. And in order for everyone to be able to know more easily where there are two and where there is one syllable in this dialect, and where it is necessary to write *je*, where *e*, and where *i*, all the rest of us have asked Mr. Vuk Stef. Karadžić to write the primary rules for this, which are appended below.

If there is anyone who for whatever reason prefers not to write in this dialect, we think that it would be most practical for the people and literary unity, that such persons write using one of the other two popular dialects of their choice, so long as they do not mix them or create a language which is not found among the people.

(3) We have found it good and necessary for literary figures of the Eastern faith to write *x*, everywhere that it belongs etymologically, just as the adherents to the Western faith write *h*, and as our people of both faiths speak in many places in our southern regions.

(4) We have all recognized that it is not necessary to write a final *h* for nouns in the genitive plural, since in this case the *h* is neither etymological, nor is it found in either the mainstream popular speech, or the old Slavic language, nor does it have a place in the other contemporary Slavic languages. We have noted that there will be writers, who will say that precisely for these reasons it would be worthwhile to write this *h* in order to distinguish this case from the other cases, or even that it would be worthwhile to show these differences with some other means rather than *h*. But since, on the one hand, with many words the forms of this case are [already] distinctive (e.g., *zemalja, otaca, lakata, trgovaca*, etc.), and since, on the other hand, we have other cases with identical forms, which we do not in any way distinguish in writing, and such things are widely known among other peoples as well—we have all concluded that neither *h*, nor any other symbol is to be written in the above-mentioned place, except when it would not be possible to understand from the context that a word is in the genitive plural, in which case the accents will be marked (something that will be necessary for us to do in other similar instances).

(5) We have all unanimously concluded that before *r*, functioning on its own as a syllable, neither *a* nor *e* should be written; rather, *r* should stand by itself (e.g., *prst*). And this is (a) because the people speak this way; (b) because writers of the Eastern faith all write this way (except for one or two); (c) because the Czechs also write this way; (d) since many Slavic books using glagolitic letters are written this way; and (e) since it has now been proven that also in the old Slavic language it was not necessary to write the jers [(reduced vowels)], with either *r* or *l*, since both these letters in these positions represented vowels, just as in Sanskrit.

This is what we have thus far completed. If God grants that these thoughts of ours are accepted by the people, we are convinced that great obstacles will be removed from the path of our literature, and that we will advance significantly towards a true unity. Therefore, we ask all writers who genuinely wish their own people happiness and advancement to adhere to our thoughts herein, and to write their works accordingly.

Vienna, 28 March 1850
Ivan Kukuljević
Dr. Dimitrije Demeter
I. Mažuranić
Vuk Stef. Karadžić

Vinko Pacel
Franjo Miklošić
Stjepan Pejaković
Gj. Daničić[1]

Dolje potpisani znajući da *jedan* narod treba *jednu* književnost da ima, i po tom sa žalosti gledajući, kako nam je književnost raskomadana, ne samo po bukvici, nego još i po pravopisu, sastajali smo se ovijeh dana, da se razgovorimo, kako bismo se što se za sad što više može u književnosti složili i ujedinili. I tako smo:

(1) Jednoglasice priznali, da ne valja miješajući narječja graditi novo, kojega u narodu nema, nego da je bolje od narodnijeh narječja izabrati jedno, da bude književni jezik; a to sve a) zato, što nije moguće pisati tako, da bi svak mogao čitati po svojeme narječju, b) zato, što bi svaka ovakova mješavina, kaono ti ljudsko djelo, bila gora od kojega mu drago narodnoga narječja, koja su djela božija, a c) i zato, što ni ostali narodi, kao n.p. Nijemci i Talijani, nijesu od svojijeh narječja gradili novijeh, nego su jedno od narodnijeh izabrali, te njim knjige pišu.

(2) Jednoglasice smo priznali, da je najpravije i najbolje primiti južno narječje, da bude književno, i to a) zato, što najviše naroda tako govori, b) što je ono najbliže staromu slavenskom jeziku, a po tome i svijema ostalijem jezicima slavenskijem, c) što su gotovo sve narodne pjesme u njemu spjevane, d) što je sva stara dubrovačka književnost u njemu spisana, e) što najviše književnika i istočnoga i zapadnoga vjerozakona već tako piše (samo što svi ne paze na sva pravila). Po tom smo se složili, da se na onijem mjestima, gdje su po ovome narječju dva sloga (syllaba), piše *ije*, a gdje je jedan slog, ondje da se piše *je* ili *e* ili *i*, kako gdje treba, n.p. *bijelo, bjelina, mreža, donio.* A da bi svaki lakše mogao saznati, gdje su po ovome narječju dva sloga, gdje li je jedan i gdje treba pisati *je*, gdje li *e* gdje li *i*, zamolili smo svi ostali g. Vuka Stef. Karadžića, da bi napisao o tome glavna pravila, koja su dolje priložena.

Ako li kogod iz kojega mu drago uzroka ne bi htio pisati ovijem narječjem, mi mislimo, da bi za narod i za književno jedinstvo najprobitačnije bilo, da piše jednijem od ostala dva narodna narječja, kojijem mu je volja, ali samo da ih ne miješa i ne gradi jezika, kojega u narodu nema.

(3) Našli smo za dobro i za potrebno, da bi i književnici istočnoga vjerozakona pisali *x* svuda, gdje mu je po etimol[o]giji mjesto, kao što oni vjerozakona zapadnoga pišu *h*, i kao što narod naš obadva vjerozakona na mnogo mjesta po južnijem krajevima govori.

(4) Svi smo priznali, da *h* u samostavnijeh imena na kraju u r[o]d mn. ne treba pisati, jer mu ondje ni po etimologiji, ni po općenome narodnom govoru, ni po starome slavenskom jeziku, ni po ostalijem današnijem jezicima slavenskijem nije mjesto. Mi smo se opominjali, da će se naći književnika, koji će

---

[1] This translation is my own. The original text was reprinted in Simić 1991: 346–8.

reći, da bi ovo *h* samo zato valjalo pisati, da se ovaj padež razlikuje od ostalijeh, ili najposlije, da bi ove razlike radi mjesto *h* valjalo pisati kakav drugi znak. Ali jedno zato, što se u mnogijeh riječi ovaj padež po sebi razlikuje (n.p. *zemalja, otaca, lakata, trgovaca* itd.), a drugo, što u nas ima i drugijeh padeža jednakijeh, pa ih u pisanju nikako ne raz[l]ikujemo, i što ovakovijeh stvari ima mnogo i u drugijeh naroda—mi smo svi pristali na to, da se ni *h* niti ikakav drugi znak na pomenutome mjestu ne piše, osim samo kad se iz smisla ne bi moglo razumjeti, da riječ stoji u rod. mn., da se naznače akcenti (koje će nam valjati činiti i u ostalijem ovakvijem događajima).

(5) Svi smo jednoglasice pristali, da se pred *r*, gdje ono samo sobom slog čini, ne piše ni *a* ni *e*, već samo r neka stoji (n.p. *prst*) i to a) zato, [što] narod tako govori, b) što književnici istočnoga vjerozakona svi tako pišu (osim jednoga, dvojice), c) što i Česi tako pišu, d) što su i mnoge slavenske knjige glagoljskijem slovima tako pisane, e) što se sad dokazuje, da ni u starome slavenskom jeziku na ovakijem mjestima nije trebalo pisati jerova ni kod *r* ni kod *l*, jer su oba ova slova na ovakijem mjestima bila samoglasna, kao i u Sanskritu.

Ovo smo dakle za sad svršili. Ako da Bog, te se ove misli naše u narodu prime, mi smo uvjereni, da će se velike smetnje književnosti našoj s puta ukloniti, da ćemo se k pravome jedinstvu mnogo približiti. Zato molimo sve književnike, koji upravo žele sreću i napredak narodu svojemu, da bi na ove misli naše pristali, i po njima djela svoja pisali.

U Beču, 28. ožujka p.n. 1850
Ivan Kukuljević
Dr. Dimitrije Demeter
I. Mažuranić
Vuk Stef. Karadžić
Vinko Pacel
Franjo Miklošić
Stjepan Pejaković
Gj. Daničić

Appendix B

Text of the 1954 Novi Sad Agreement

The undersigned participants of the meeting, convened by the editorial board of the *Letopis Matice srpske* at the completion of its survey about the Serbo-Croatian language and orthography, following a multilateral discussion held on December 8, 9, and 10, 1954, in Novi Sad, reached the following conclusions:

(1) The popular language of Serbs, Croats, and Montenegrins is one language. Therefore, the literary language, which has developed on its basis around two main centers, Belgrade and Zagreb, is also a single language, with two pronunciations—ijekavian and ekavian.

(2) In naming the language, it is necessary in official use always to state both of its constituent parts.

(3) Both scripts, Latin and Cyrillic, are equally legitimate; therefore, it is necessary to ensure that both Serbs and Croats learn in the same manner the two scripts, a goal to be reached especially by means of school instruction.

(4) Both pronunciations, ekavian and ijekavian, are also equally legitimate in all respects.

(5) In order to exploit the entire lexical wealth of our language and of its correct and full development, the required work on a reference dictionary of the contemporary Serbo-Croatian literary language is essential. For this reason, the initiative of the Matica srpska, which together with the Matica hrvatska has taken on this task, should be welcomed.

(6) The issue of developing joint terminology is also a problem requiring urgent resolution. It is necessary to develop terminology for all areas of economic, scientific, and, broadly speaking, cultural life.

(7) The common language should also have a common Orthographic manual. The development of this manual is today a most urgent cultural and social necessity. A mutually agreed-upon Commission of Serb and Croat experts will develop a draft of the Orthographic manual. Before its final acceptance, the draft will be made available for discussion among the societies of writers, journalists, educators, and other members of the public.

(8) It is necessary to stand up decisively against the placing of artificial barriers to the natural and normal development of the Croato-Serbian literary language. It is necessary to curb the harmful phenomenon of arbitrary "translating" of texts, and to respect the original texts of the writers.

(9) The Commissions for the Orthographic manual and terminology will be determined by our three universities (in Belgrade, Zagreb, and Sarajevo), two academies (in Zagreb and Belgrade), and Matica srpska in Novi Sad, and Matica hrvatska in Zagreb. For the development of terminology it is necessary to initiate cooperation with the federal institutions responsible for legislation and standardization, and with other groups of specialists.

(10) Matica srpska will make these conclusions available to the Federal Executive Council, and the Executive Councils of the People's Republic of Serbia, the People's Republic of Croatia, the People's Republic of Bosnia and Herzegovina, and the People's Republic of Montenegro, as well as to the universities in Belgrade, Zagreb, and Sarajevo, to the academies in Zagreb and Belgrade, and to Matica hrvatska in Zagreb; and will also publish them in daily papers and journals.

Novi Sad, 10 December 1954[1]

Potpisani učesnici sastanka koji je sazvala Redakcija *Letopisa Matice srpske* na završetku ankete o srpskohrvatskom jeziku i pravopisu posle svestrane diskusije održane 8., 9. i 10. decembra 1954. godine u Novom Sadu doneli su ove

Zaključke

(1) Narodni jezik Srba, Hrvata i Crnogoraca jedan je jezik. Stoga je i književni jezik koji se razvio na njegovoj osnovi oko dva glavna središta, Beograda i Zagreba, jedinstven, s dva izgovora, ijekavskim i ekavskim.

(2) U nazivu jezika nužno je uvek u službenoj upotrebi istaći oba njegova sastavna dela.

(3) Oba pisma, latinica i ćirilica, ravnopravna su; zato treba nastojati da i Srbi i Hrvati podjednako nauče oba pisma, što će se postići u prvom redu školskom nastavom.

(4) Oba izgovora, ekavski i ijekavski, takodje su u svemu ravnopravna.

(5) Radi iskorišćavanja celokupnog rečničkog blaga našeg jezika i njegovog pravilnog i punog razvitka neophodno je potrebna izrada priručnog rečnika

---

[1] The translation is my own. The text was published as the opening pages of the Matica srpska/Matica hrvatska joint orthographic manual (*Pravopis* 1960).

savremenog srpskohrvatskog književnog jezika. Stoga treba pozdraviti inicijativu Matice srpske koja je u zajednici sa Maticom hrvatskom pristupila njegovoj izradi.

(6) Pitanje izrade zajedničke terminologije takodje je problem koji zahteva neodložno rešenje. Potrebno je izraditi terminologiju za sve oblasti ekonomskog, naučnog i uopšte kulturnog života.

(7) Zajednički jezik treba da ima i zajednički pravopis. Izrada toga pravopisa danas je najhitnija kulturna i društvena potreba. Nacrt pravopisa izradiće sporazumno komisija srpskih i hrvatskih stručnjaka. Pre konačnog prihvatanja nacrt će biti podnet na diskusiju udruženjima književnika, novinara, prosvetnih i drugih javnih radnika.

(8) Treba odlučno stati na put postavljanju veštačkih prepreka prirodnom i normalnom razvitku hrvatskosrpskog književnog jezika. Treba sprečiti štetnu pojavu samovoljnog "prevodjenja" tekstova i poštovati originalne tekstove pisaca.

(9) Komisije za izradu pravopisa i terminologije odrediće naša tri univerziteta (u Beogradu, Zagrebu i Sarajevu), dve akademije (u Zagrebu i Beogradu) i Matica srpska u Novom Sadu i Matica hrvatska u Zagrebu. Za izradu terminologije potrebno je stupiti u saradnju sa saveznim ustanovama za zakonodavstvo i standardizaciju, kao i sa stručnim ustanovama u društvima.

(10) Ove zaključke Matica srpska će dostaviti Saveznom izvršnom veću i izvršnim većima: NR Srbije, NR Hrvatske, NR Bosne i Hercegovine i NR Crne Gore, univerzitetima u Beogradu, Zagrebu i Sarajevu, akademijama u Zagrebu i Beogradu, u Matici hrvatskoj u Zagrebu, te će ih objaviti u dnevnim listovima i časopisima.

U Novom Sadu, 10. decembra 1954.

Works cited

ALBIN, ALEXANDER. 1970. "The Creation of the Slaveno-Serbski Literary Language." *The Slavonic and East European Review* 48/113: 483–91.

ALEXANDER, RONELLE. 1993. "Remarks on the Evolution of South Slavic Prosodic Systems." *American Contributions to the Eleventh International congress of Slavists* 1: 181–201.

—— 2006. *Bosnian Croatian Serbian: A Grammar with Sociolinguistic Commentary*. Madison: University of Wisconsin Press.

—— Ellen Elia-Bursac. 2006. *Bosnian Croatian Serbian: A Textbook with Exercises and Basic Grammar*. Madison: University of Wisconsin Press.

ANDERSON, BENEDICT. 1983. *Imagined Communities*. London: Verso.

ANIĆ, VLADAMIR. 1991. *Rječnik hrvatskoga jezika*. Zagreb: Novi Liber.

ANIĆ, VLADIMIR and JOSIP SILIĆ. 1986. *Pravopisni priručnik hrvatskoga ili srpskoga jezika*. Zagreb: Novi Liber.

——. 2001. *Pravopis hrvatskoga jezika*. Zagreb: Školska knjiga and Novi Liber.

AUTY, ROBERT. 1958. "The Linguistic Revival among the Slavs of the Austrian Empire, 1780–1850: The Role of Individuals in the Codification and Acceptance of New Literary Languages." *Modern Language Review* 53: 392–404.

——. 1973. "The Role of Purism in the Development of the Slavonic Literary Languages." *Slavonic and East European Review* 51: 335–43.

BABIĆ, STJEPAN. 1995. "Neka objašnjenja pravila i postupaka u *Hrvatskome pravopisu*." *Jezik* 43/2: 57–72.

——. 1996. "Znanstvena podloga hrvatskih vukovaca." *Jezik* 43/5: 167–74.

——. 1997. "Hrvatski književni jezik u Bosni i Hercegovini." *Jezik* 45/1: 29–34.

——. 2002. "O danima hrvatskoga i njemačkoga jezika." *Jezik* 49/1: 39–40.

——. (ed.). 1991. *Tisućljetni jezik naš hrvatski*. Zagreb: Tiskara "Spiridion Grušina."

——, BOŽIDAR FINKA, and MILAN MOGUŠ. 1971 [2004]. *Hrvatski pravopis* (sixth edition). Zagreb: Školska knjiga.

BANAC, IVO. 1984. "Main Trends in the Croat Language Question." *Aspects of the Slavic Language Question* (eds Harvey Goldblatt and Riccardo Picchio) 1: 189–260. New Haven: Yale University Press.

BAOTIĆ, JOSIP. 1999. "Standardni jezici štokavskog narječja." *Simpozij o bosanskom jeziku (zbornik radova)*, 89–95.

BARIĆ, EUGENIJA, MIJO LONČARIĆ, DRAGICA MALIĆ, SLAVKO PAVEŠIĆ, MIRKO PETI, VESNA ZEČEVIĆ, and MARIJA ZNIKA. 1995. *Hrvatska gramatika*. Zagreb: Školska knjiga.

——, LANA HUDEČEK, NEBOJŠA KOHAROVIĆ, MIJO LONČARIĆ, MARKO LUKENDA, MILE MAMIĆ, MILICA MIHALJEVIĆ, LJILJANA ŠARIĆ, VANJA SVAĆKO, LUKA VUKOJEVIĆ, VESNA ZEČEVIĆ, and MATEO ŽAGAR. 1999. *Hrvatski jezični savjetnik*. Zagreb: Školse novine.

BARJAKTAREVIĆ, DANILO. 1966. "Novopazarsko-sjenički govori." *Srpski dijalektološki zbornik* 16: 1–177.

BAŠIĆ, NATAŠA. 2001a. "Hrvatski jezik i njegov pravopis." *Jezik* 48/2: 42–55.

——. 2001*b*. "Politička pozadina osporavanja Hrvatskoga pravopisa." *Jezik* 48/3: 87–95.
BELAMARIĆ, BILJANA. 2003. "Resolving Ethnic Conflict: The Constitution of the Republic of Macedonia." *South-East European Politics Online* 4/1: 25–40. Available at www.seep. ceu.hu.
BELIĆ, ALEKSANDAR. 1930. *Pravopis srpskohrvatskog književnog jezika: Prema propisima ministarstva prosvete.* Belgrade: Izdavačka knjižarnica Gece Kona.
——. 1935. "O čakavskoj osnovnoj akcentuaciji." *Glas Srpske akademije nauka i umetnosti* 168: 1–39.
——. 1949. *Borba oko našeg književnog jezika i pravopisa.* Belgrade: Kolarčev narodni univerzitet.
——. 1958. "Periodizacija srpskohrvatskog jezika." *Južnoslovenski filolog* 23: 1–15.
BIRNBAUM, HENRIK. 1980. "Language, Ethnicity and Nationalism: The Linguistic foundation of a Unified Yugoslavia." *The Creation of Yugoslavia, 1914–1918*, 157–82. Santa Barbara: Clio Books.
BORANIĆ, DRAGUTIN. 1940. *Pravopis hrvatskoga ili srpskog jezika* (fourth edition). Zagreb: Školska knjiga.
BRBORIĆ, BRANISLAV. 1996. "Predistorija i sociolingvistički aspekti." *Srpski jezik na kraju veka* (ed. Milorad Radovanović), 17–36.
——. 2001. *S jezika na jezik* (=*Sociolingvistički ogledi* 2). Belgrade: Centar za primenjenu lingvistiku.
BRODNJAK, VLADIMIR. 1993. *Razlikovni rječnik srpskog i hrvatskog jezika.* Zagreb: Hrvatska sveučilišna naklada.
BROZ, IVAN. 1892. *Hrvatski pravopis.* Zagreb: Naklada kr. -slav.-dalm. Zemaljske vlade.
—— and F. IVEKOVIĆ. 1901. *Rječnik hrvatskoga jezika.* Zagreb: Štamparija K. Albrechta.
BROZOVIĆ, DALIBOR. 1970. *Standardni jezik.* Zagreb: Matica hrvatska.
——. 1971. See Spalatin (1975).
——. 1995. "Stanje i zadatci jezikoslovne kroatistike." *Jezik* 43/1: 23–34.
——. 1997. "Tri desetljeća poslije." *Jezik* 44/3: 85–89.
——. 1999. "Odnos hrvatskoga i bosanskoga odnosno bošnjačkoga jezika." *Jezik* 47: 13–16.
BUDMANI, PIETRO. 1867. *Grammatica della lingua serbo-croatian (illirica).* Vienna: the author.
BUGARSKI, RANKO. 1995. *Jezik od mira do rata.* Belgrade: Slovograf.
——. 1997. *Jezik u društvenoj krizi.* Belgrade: Cigoja.
——. 2000. "Serbo-Croatian: How Many Languages?" *Die Sprachen Südosteuropas heute* (ed. B. Kunzmann-Mueller). Frankfurt: Peter Lang, 192–9.
BUJAS, ŽELJKO. 1999 [2001]. *Veliki hrvatski-engleski rječnik* (second edition). Zagreb: Globus.
BULIĆ, REFIK. 2001. *Bosanski jezik: jezičko-pravopisni priručnik za učenike osnovnih i srednjih škola.* Tuzla: Bosanska riječ.
BUTLER, THOMAS. 1970. "The Origins of the War for a Serbian Language and Orthography." *Harvard Slavic Studies* 5:1–80.
ĆEDIĆ, IBRAHIM. 1999*a*. "Predgovor." *Simpozij o bosanskom jeziku (zbornik radova)*, 7–8.
——. 1999*b*. "Jedna karakteristična crta bosanskog jezika." *Simpozij o bosanskom jeziku (zbornik radova)*, 117–21.
CIPRA, FRANJO and A. V. KLAIĆ. 1944 [1992]. *Hrvatski korijenski pravopis.* Zagreb: Hrvatska sveučilišna naklada.
ĆIRILOV, JOVAN. 1989. *Srpsko-hrvatski rečnik varijanti* (=*Hrvatsko-srpski rječnik inačica*). Belgrade: Stilos.

CLYNE, MICHAEL (ed.). 1992. *Pluricentric Languages: Differing Norms in Different Nations.* Berlin, New York: Mouton de Gruyter.

ĆORIĆ, BOŽO. 1994. "Ijekavsko-ekavsko dvojstvo srpskog književnog jezika." *Vaspitanje i obrazovanje* 3: 59–61.

——. 1995. "Neka aktuelna pitanja nauke o srpskom jeziku," *Znamen* 1/2: 7–13.

DANIČIĆ, DJURA. 1847 [1997]. *Rat za srpski jezik i pravopis.* Belgrade: Narodna biblioteka Srbije.

——. 1864 [1983]. *Oblici srpskoga jezika.* Biograd: Državna štamparija.

DEŠIĆ, MILORAD. 1976. "Zapadnobosanski ijekavski govori." *Srpski dijalektološki zbornik* 21: 1–316.

——. 1994. "Nepodobna ijekavica," *Vaspitanje i obrazovanje* 3: 48–50.

——. 1995. *Pravopis srpskog jezika: priručnik za škole.* Belgrade: Unireks.

DESPALATOVIĆ, ELINOR. 1975. "The Illyrian Solution to the Problem of Modern National Identity for the Croats." *Balkanistica* 1: 75–94.

DJUKANOVIĆ, PETAR. 1996. "Oktroisana ekavica," *Riječ* 2/1–2: 86–9.

DJUROVIĆ, RADOSAV. 1995. "Jatove varijacije i standardni jezik," *Znamen* 1–2: 71–6.

EDWARDS, JOHN. 1985. *Language, Society, and Identity.* Oxford: Blackwell.

FINKA, BOŽIDAR (ed.). 1986–1995. *Rječnik hrvatskoga kajkavskoga književnoga jezika* 1–3. Zagreb: JAZU/HAZU.

FISHMAN, JOSHUA. 1972. *Language and Nationalism.* Rowley: New Berry House Publishers.

——. 1989. "Language, Ethnicity, and Racism." *Language and Ethnicity in Minority Sociolinguistic Perspective.* Clevedon: Multilingual Matters, Ltd., 9–22.

——. (ed.). 1993. *The Earliest Stage of Language Planning: the "First Congress" Phenomenon.* Berlin, New York: Mouton de Gruyter.

FORD, CURTIS. 2001. "The (Re-)Birth of Bosnian: Comparative Perspectives on Language Planning in Bosnia-Herzegovina." Ph.D. Dissertation, University of North Carolina at Chapel Hill.

——. 2002. "Language Planning in Bosnia-Herzegovina: The 1998 Bihać Symposium." *Slavic and East European Journal* 46/2: 349–61.

FRIEDMAN, VICTOR A. 1998. "The Implementation of Standard Macedonian: Problems and Results." *International Journal of the Sociology of Language* 131: 31–57.

——. 1999. *Linguistic Emblems and Emblematic Languages: On Language as Flag in the Balkans.* Columbus: Department of Slavic and East European Languages and Literatures at the Ohio State University.

GLENNY, MISHA. 1996. *The Fall of Yugoslavia.* New York: Penguin Books.

GREENBERG, ROBERT. 1994. "Southwest Balkan Linguistic Contacts: Evidence from Appellative Language." *Journal of Slavic Linguistics* 2/2: 275–83.

——. 1996. "The Politics of Dialects Among Serbs, Croats, and Muslims in the Former Yugoslavia." *East European Politics and Societies* 10/3: 393–415.

——. 1998. "Dialects and Ethnicity in the Former Yugoslavia: The Case of Southern Baranja (Croatia)." *Slavic and East European Journal* 42/4: 710–22.

——. 1999. "In the Aftermath of Yugoslavia's Collapse: The Politics of Language Death and Language Birth." *International Politics* 36/2: 141–58.

——. 2000. "Language Politics in the Federal Republic of Yugoslavia: The Crisis over the Future of Serbian." *Slavic Review* 59/3: 625–40.

——. 2001a. "Language, Nationalism and the Yugoslav Successor States." *Language, Ethnicity, and the State: Eastern Europe after 1989* (ed. C. O'Reilly). London: Palgrave, 17–42.

GREENBERG, ROBERT. 2001*b*. "The Dialects of Macedonia and Montenegro: Random Linguistic Developments or Evidence of a *Sprachbund*." *Južnoslovenski filolog* 56/1–2: 295–300.

——. 2001*c*. "Balkan Dialects, Migrations, and Ethnic Violence: The Case of the Bosnian Serbs," Paper presented at conference "Voice or Exit: Comparative Perspectives on Ethnic Minorities in Twentieth Century Europe," Humboldt University, Berlin, 14–16 June 2001.

GUBERINA, PETAR. 1940 [1997]. "Zašto možemo govoriti o posebnom hrvatskom književnom jeziku." *Jezik* 44/5: 162–91.

HALILOVIĆ, SENAHID. 1990. "Govor Muslimana Tuholja (okoline Kladnja)". *Bosansko-hercegovački dijalektološki zbornik* 6. Sarajevo: Institut za jezik i književnost.

——. 1991. *Bosanski jezik.* Sarajevo: Bosanski krug-biblioteka Ključanin.

——. 1996. *Pravopis bosanskoga jezika.* Sarajevo: Preporod.

——. 1999*a*. "O standardizaciji bosanskoga jezika." *Simpozij o bosanskom jeziku (zbornik radova)*, 97–103.

——. 1999*b*. *Pravopis bosanskoga jezika: priručnik za škole.* Zenica: Dom štampe.

——, DŽEVAD JAHIĆ, and ISMAIL PALIĆ. 2000. *Gramatika bosanskoga jezika.* Zenica: Dom štampe.

HAMMEL, EUGENE. 1993. "The Yugoslav Labyrinth." *Crisis in the Balkans* (H. Kreisler, ed.). Berkeley: University of California, Institute of International Studies, 1–33.

——. 2000. "Lessons from the Yugoslav Labyrinth." *Neighbors at War: Anthropological Perspectives on Yugoslav Ethnicity, Culture, and History.* (D. Kideckel and J. Halpern, eds.). University Park: Pennsylvania State University Press, 19–38.

HAUGEN, EINAR. 1982. *Scandinavian Language Structures: A Comparative Historical Survey.* Minneapolis: University of Minnesota Press.

HAWKESWORTH, CELIA, and RANKO BUGARSKI (eds). 1992. *Language Planning in Yugoslavia.* Columbus: Slavica.

—— 2004. *Language in the Former Yugoslav Lands.* Bloomington: Slavica.

HAYDEN, ROBERT. 1992. "Constitutional Nationalism in the Formerly Yugoslav Republics." *Slavic Review* 51/4: 654–73.

——. 1999. *Blueprints for a House Divided: Constitutional Nationalism.* Ann Arbor: University of Michigan Press.

HEKMAN, JELENA (ed.). 1997. *Deklaracija o nazivu i položaju hrvatskog književnog jezika—gradja za povijest Deklaracije 1967–1997.* Zagreb: Matica hrvatska.

ISAKOVIĆ, ALIJA. 1995. *Rječnik bosanskoga jezika.* Sarajevo: Bosanska knjiga.

IVIĆ, PAVLE. 1957. *O govoru galipoljskih Srba (=Srpski dijalektološki zbornik 12).* Belgrade: Serbian Academy of Sciences and Arts.

——. 1958. *Die Serbokroatischen Dialekten: Ihre Struktur und Entwicklung.* The Hague: Mouton and Co.

——. 1961. "Basic Problems in Current Research in Yugoslav Dialectology." *Slavic and East European Journal* 5: 103–10.

——. 1971 [1986]. *Srpski narod i njegov jezik.* Belgrade: Srpska književna zadruga.

—— et al. 1989. *Prilozi pravopisu.* Novi Sad: Matica srpska.

JAHIĆ, DŽEVAD. 1990. *Jezik, nacija, nacionalizam.* Sarajevo: Oslobodjenje.

——. 1991. *Jezik bosanskih Muslimana.* Sarajevo: Biblioteka Ključanin.

——. 1999*a*. "Lingvistički i kulturno-historijski izvori bosanskog jezika: glavna problemska pitanja." *Simpozij o bosanskom jeziku (zbornik radova)*, 25–30.

JAHIĆ, DŽEVAD. 1999b. *Školski rječnik bosanskoga jezika.* Sarajevo: Ljiljan.

JONKE, LJUDEVIT. 1969. "Osnovni pojmovi o jeziku Hrvata i Srba." *Hrvatski književni jezik i pitanje varijanata* (ed. V. Pavletić). Zagreb: Časopis "Kritika," 236–40.

KAČIĆ, MIRO. 1997. *Croatian and Serbian: Delusions and Distortions.* Zagreb: Novi most.

KARADŽA, MEVLIDA. 1999. "Sociolingvistički aspekti jezičke situacije u Bosni i Hercegovini." *Simpozij o bosanskom jeziku (zbornik radova)*, 31–9.

KARADŽIĆ, VUK S. 1818 [1966]. *Srpski rječnik.* Belgrade: Prosveta.

KAŠUNOVIĆ, AHMED. 1998. "Bibliography of Sources on the Language of Bosnia-Herzegovina." *Balkanistica* 11: 19–29.

KATIČIĆ, RADOSLAV. 1984. "The Making of Standard Serbo-Croat." *Aspects of the Slavic Language Question* (eds Harvey Goldblatt and Riccardo Picchio) 1: 262–95. New Haven: Yale University Press.

——. 1995. "Hrvatski jezik u svijetu." *Jezik* 43/1: 15–22, 226 from 7 April 1997.

——. 1997. "Undoing a 'Unified Language': Bosnian, Croatian, Serbian." *Undoing and Redoing Corpus Planning* (M. Clyne, ed.). Berlin: Mouton de Gruyter, 269–89.

——. 1999. "Normiranje književnoga jezika kao lingvistički zadatak." *Norme i normiranje hrvatskoga standardnoga jezika* (ed. Marko Samardžija). Zagreb: Matica hrvatska, 114–27.

KLOSS, HEINZ. 1978. *Die Entwicklung neuer Germanischer Kultursprachen seit 1800* (second edition). Düsseldorf: Schwann.

——. 1984. "Umriß eines Forschungsprogrammes zum Thema 'Sprachentod.'" *International Journal of the Sociology of Language* 45: 65–76.

KOVAČEVIĆ, MILOŠ. 1997. *U odbranu jezika srpskoga.* Belgrade: Trebnik.

KRLEŽA, MIROSLAV (ed.). 1955. *Enciklopedija Jugoslavije.* Zagreb: Leksikografski zavod FNRJ.

KULJIŠ, TOMISLAV. 1994. *Jezik naš hrvatski ovdje i sada.* Dubrovnik: Matica hrvatska.

LANGSTON, KEITH. 1999. "Linguistic Cleansing: Language Purism in Croatia after the Yugoslav Break-Up." *International Politics* 36/2: 179–201.

LOERSCH, ANDRÉ. 1999. "Conflict in the Balkans: The Language of Ethnicity," available at **www.mondediplo.com/1999/06/09loersh.**

MAGNER, THOMAS. 1966. *A Zagreb Kajkavian Dialect.* University Park: Pennsylvania State University Press.

——. 1967. "Language and Nationalism in Yugoslavia." *Canadian Slavic Studies* 1/3: 333–47.

——. 1988. "Language and Nationality in the Balkans: The Case of Yugoslavia." *Geolinguistics* 14: 108–24.

——, and MILENA MARIĆ. 2002. "Bosnian: The Crafting of a Language." *Geolinguistics* 28: 55–65.

MAR-MOLINERO, CLARE. 2000. "The Iberian Peninsula: Conflicting Linguistic Nationalisms." *Language and Nationalism in Europe* (eds. Stephan Barbour and Cathie Carmichael). Oxford: Oxford University Press, 83–104.

MARETIĆ, TOMISLAV. 1899 [1963]. *Gramatika i stilistika hrvatskoga ili srpskoga književnog jezika.* Zagreb: Štampa i naklada Knjižare L. Hartmana.

MAROJEVIĆ, RADMILO. 1995. "Lingvistička razmatranja iz fonologije i ortografije." *Riječ* 1/2: 77–98.

——et al. 1998. *Slovo o srpskom jeziku.* Belgrade: Foundation for Truth.

MIHAILOVICH, VASA. 2000. "Introduction." *The Mountain Wreath by Petar II Petrović Njegoš* (trans. Vasa Mihailovich). Belgrade: Project Rastko—Digital library of Serbian Culture, at www.rastko.org.yu/knjizevnost/umetnicka/njegos/mountain_wreath.html.

MOGUŠ, MILAN. 1995. *Povijest hrvatskoga književnoga jezika.* Zagreb: Globus.

MOSKOVLJEVIĆ, MILOŠ. 1966. *Rečnik savremenog srpskohrvatskog književnog jezika s jezičkim savetnikom.* Belgrade: Tehnička knjiga and Nolit.

NAYLOR, KENNETH. 1978. "The Eastern Variant of Serbocroatian as the *lingua communis* of Yugoslavia." *Sociolinguistic Problems in Czechoslovakia, Hungary, Romania and Yugoslavia* (eds William Schmalstieg and Thomas Magner). Columbus: Slavica, 456–68.

——. 1980. "Serbo-Croatian." *The Slavic Literary Languages* (eds Alexander Schenker and Edward Stankiewicz). New Haven: Yale University Press, 65–83.

——. 1992. "The Sociolinguistic Situation in Yugoslavia with Special Emphasis on Serbo-Croatian." *Language Planning in Yugoslavia* (eds. Ranko Bugarski and Celia Hawkesworth). Columbus: Slavica, 82–90.

NIKČEVIĆ, VOJISLAV. 1993. *Piši kao što zboriš.* Podgorica: Crnogorsko društvo nezavisnih književnika.

——. 1997a. *Crnogorski jezik: geneza, tipologija, razvoj, strukturne osobine, funkcija.* Cetinje: Matica crnogorska.

——. 1997b. *Pravopis crnogorskog jezika.* Cetinje: Crnogorski PEN centar.

OKUKA, MILOŠ. 1998. *Eine Sprache viele Erben: Sprachpolitik als Nazionalisierungsinstrument in Ex-Jugoslawien.* Klagenfurt: Wieser Verlag.

OSTOJIĆ, BRANISLAV. 1989. *Vuk i književni jezik u Crnoj Gori.* Nikšić: Univerzitetska riječ.

——. 1994. "O krizi srpskoga književnog jezika." *Vaspitanje i obrazovanje* 3: 5–17.

PANTIĆ, MIROSLAV (ed.). 1995. *Memorandum of the Serbian Academy of Sciences and Arts: Answers to Criticisms* (trans. Margot and Boško Milosavljević). Belgrade: Kultura.

PAŠALIĆ-KRESO, ADILA. 1999. "Education in Bosnia and Herzegovina: Minority Inclusion and Majority Rules." *Current Issues in Comparative Education* 1/2: 1–8. Available at www.tc.columbia.edu/cice/articles/apk121.pdf.

PAVLETIĆ, VLATKO (ed.). 1969. *Hrvatski književni jezik i pitanje varijanata.* Zagreb: Časopis "Kritika."

PAVUNA, STANKA. 1993. *Govorimo li ispravno hrvatski?: mali razlikovni rječnik.* Zagreb: Integra.

PECO, ASIM. 1964. "Govor istočne Hercegovine." *Srpski dijalektološki zbornik* 14: 1–200.

——. 1975. "Ikavskošćakavski govori zapadne Bosne I." *Bosanskohercegovački dijalektološki zbornik* 1: 1–266.

PELEŠIĆ-MUMINOVIĆ, FATIMA. 1997. *Bosanski jezik/Bosnian language.* Zenica: Bemust.

PEŠIKAN, MITAR. 1994. "Prilog raspravi i aktuelnim pravopisnim pitanjima." *SPONE* 26/5–6: 68–76.

——, JOVAN JERKOVIĆ, and MATO PIŽURICA. 1994. *Pravopis srpskoga jezika.* Novi Sad: Matica srpska.

——, ——, ——. 1995. *Pravopis srpskoga jezika, školsko izdanje.* Novi Sad: Matica srpska; and Belgrade: Zavod za udžbenike i nastavna sredstva.

POLJANEC, FRANJO. 1940. *Istorija srpskohrvatskog i slovenačkog književnog jezika.* Belgrade: Izdanje kreditne i pripomoćne zadruge profesorskog društva.

Pravopis srpskohrvatskog književnog jezika. 1960. Zagreb and Novi Sad: Matica hrvatska and Matica srpska.

RADIĆ, PRVOSLAV. 2002. "Balkan Features in Standard and Colloquial Serbian." Paper given at the Thirteenth Biennial Conference on Balkan and South Slavic Linguistics, Literature, and Folklore, University of North Carolina at Chapel Hill, 17–20 April.

RADOVANOVIĆ, MILORAD. 1996. "Predgovor." *Srpski jezik na kraju veka* (ed. Milorad Radovanović). Belgrade: Institut za srpski jezik pri SANU, 1–16.

RAMET, SABRINA. 1997. *Whose Democracy? Nationalism, Religion, and the Doctrine of Collective Rights.* Lanham: Roman and Littlefield Publishers.

REMETIĆ, SLOBODAN. 1970. "Fonetske i morfološke karakteristike govora Srba u Kladnju i okolini." *Prilozi proučavanju jezika* 6: 105–33.

Rječnik hrvatskoga ili srpskoga jezika 1–23. 1880–1975. Zagreb: Jugoslavenska akademija znanosti i umjetnosti.

SALIHOVIĆ, RAMIZ. 1999. "Gramatika stara stotinu i osam godina." *Simpozij o bosanskom jeziku (zbornik radova)*, 161–4.

SAMARDŽIĆ, MIROSLAV. 1995. *Tajne Vukove reforme.* Kragujevac: Pogledi.

ŠATOR, MUHAMED. 1999. "Principi standardizacije bosanskoga jezika." *Simpozij o bosanskom jeziku (zbornik radova)*, 105–15.

SEKEREŠ, STJEPAN. 1977. "Govor Hrvata u južnoj Baranji." *Hrvatski dijalektološki zbornik* 4: 323–484.

SIMIĆ, RADOJE. 1994. "Lažna zabrinutost nad lažnim problemima: Zaključci naučnog skupa." *SPONE* 26/5–6: 77–86.

———. 1991. *O našem književnom jeziku.* Nikšić: Univerzitetska riječ.

———, Božo ĆORIĆ, MILOŠ KOVAČEVIĆ, BRANISLAV OSTOJIĆ, and ŽIVOJIN STANOJČIĆ. 1993. *Pravopis srpskoga jezika sa rječnikom.* Belgrade and Nikšić: Unireks.

SITO-SUČIĆ, DARIA. 1996. "The Fragmentation of Serbo-Croatian into Three New Languages." *Transition* 2/24 (29 November 1996). Available at **www.cla.wayne.edu/POLISCI/krause/Easteurope/sources/sucic.htm**.

ŠKALJIĆ, ABDULAH. 1973. *Turcizmi u srpskohrvatskom jeziku.* Sarajevo: Svjetlost.

SKOK, PETAR. 1971–1974. *Etimologijski rječnik hrvatskoga ili srpskoga jezika* 1–4. Zagreb: Jugoslavenska akademija znanosti i umjetnosti.

SPALATIN, CHRISTOPHER. 1961. "The First Common Orthography for Croatians, Serbs, and Montenegrins." *Journal of Croatian Studies* 2: 3–20.

———. 1975. "The Rise of the Croatian Standard Language." *Journal of Croatian Studies* 16: 8–18.

ŠTAMBUK, ZDENKO (ed.). 1972. *Srpskohrvatski jezik: Enciklopedijski leksikon.* Belgrade: Interpres.

STANIĆ, MILIJA. 1974. "Uskočki govor." *Srpski dijalektološki zbornik* 20: 1–259.

STEVANOVIĆ, MIHAILO (ed.). 1969–1976. *Rečnik srpskohrvatskog književnog jezika* 3–6. Novi Sad: Matica srpska.

———, and LJUDEVIT JONKE (eds.). 1967. *Rečnik srpskohrvatskoj književnog jezika* 1–2. Novi Sad and Zagreb: Matica srpska and Matica hrvatska.

TANOCKI, FRANJO. 1994. *Hrvatska riječ.* Osijek: Matica hrvatska.

TATALOVICH, RAYMOND. 1995. *Nativism Reborn: The Official English Language Movement in the United States.* Lexington: University Press of Kentucky.

TEŽAK, STJEPKO and STJEPAN BABIĆ. 1973. *Pregled gramatike hrvatskoga književnog jezika* (sixth edition). Zagreb: Školska knjiga.

———. 1996. *Gramatika hrvatskoga jezika.* Zagreb: Školska knjiga.

THOMAS, GEORGE. 1988. *The Impact of the Illyrian Movement on the Croatian Lexicon.* Munich: Otto Sagner.

——. 1991. *Linguistic Purism.* London: Longman.

THOMAS, GEORGE. 1992. "Lexical Purism in Language Cultivation." *Language Planning in Yugoslavia* (eds. Ranko Bugarski and Celia Hawkesworth). Columbus: Slavica, 176–88.

VAZDAR, ZDENKO. 1993. *Razlikovni rječnik hrvatskoga i srpskoga graditeljskoga nazivlja.* Zagreb: Anteum.

VUJIČIĆ, DRAGOMIR. 1984. "Dijalekatska baza i standardnojezički izraz u odnosu na nacionalnu strukturu u Bosni i Hercegovini." *Sveske* 5–6: 383–92.

——. 1994. "Izmedju dva nova pravopisa." *SPONE* 26/5–6: 13–17.

VUJOVIĆ, LUKA. 1969. "Mrkovićki dijalekat." *Srpski dijalektološki zbornik* 18: 73–400.

VUKOVIĆ, JOVAN. 1938–1939. "Govor Pive i Drobnjaka." *Južnoslovenski filolog* 17: 1–114.

VULETIĆ, FRANE. 1890 [1994]. *Gramatika bosanskoga jezika za srednje škole.* Wuppertal: Bosanska riječ.

VUŠOVIĆ, DANILO. 1927. "Dijalekat istočne Hercegovine." *Srpski dijalektološki zbornik* 3: 1–70.

WILSON, DUNCAN. 1986. *The Life and Times of Vuk Stefanović Karadžić 1787–1864.* Ann Arbor: Michigan Slavic Publications.

Index